KT-171-411

Eve's War

The Diaries of a Military Wife during the Second World War

EVELYN SHILLINGTON

Edited by Barbara Fox

sphere

SPHERE

First published in Great Britain in 2017 by Sphere

Copyright in the diaries © Jane-Claire Wall 2017, under license to Shaun Sewell
Footnotes and historical background text and selection © Barbara Fox, 2017
Edited by Barbara Fox

1 3 5 7 9 10 8 6 4 2

The right of Evelyn Shillington to be identified as the author of this
work has been asserted by Jane-Claire Wall in accordance
with the Copyright, Designs and Patents Act 1988

All rights reserved.
No part of this publication may be reproduced, stored in a
retrieval system, or transmitted, in any form or by any means, without
the prior permission in writing of the publisher, nor be otherwise circulated
in any form of binding or cover other than that in which it is published
and without a similar condition including this condition
being imposed on the subsequent purchaser.

Photograph on page 141 © Ken Fisher – by kind permission

A CIP catalogue record for this book
is available from the British Library.

ISBN 978-0-7515-6702-1

Typeset in Bembo by M Rules
Printed and bound in Great Britain by
Clays Ltd, St Ives plc

Papers used by Sphere are from well-managed forests
and other responsible sources.

Sphere
An imprint of
Little, Brown Book Group
Carmelite House
50 Victoria Embankment
London EC4Y 0DZ

An Hachette UK Company
www.hachette.co.uk

www.littlebrown.co.uk

To Elizabeth Clifford Davies,
who saved the diaries in the first place

And in memory of Evelyn Shillington.
We have so enjoyed getting to know you.

J, S and B

RENFREWSHIRE COUNCIL	
242618921	
Bertrams	26/07/2017
941.083	£8.99
LIN	

Contents

Preface

Evelyn Shillington, the writer of these diaries, was my mother's cousin. I first remember meeting her when we went to visit her in Bournemouth in the mid-1960s. She would have been in her seventies then, twenty years older than my mother, Elizabeth, and I was just a girl. She had recently been widowed, but in spite of her grief she was a lively presence. I recall her piercing blue eyes and how she talked incessantly and engagingly about all sorts of things. She owned a beach hut – what a joy for a twelve-year-old! – and if I close my eyes I am back in that real-life Wendy house, which was kitted out with a kettle and comfortable beach furniture, amusing myself while my mother and Cousin Eve (as Mum used to call her) had their grown-up conversations.

I didn't see her again until the summer of 1976. Evelyn had moved to Cornwall to live with my uncle Tony in his hotel in Penzance and I had gone to work there for a few weeks. Now in her eighties, she was frailer but as animated as ever. What did we talk about when we were together? Did the war ever crop up in any of our conversations? Sadly, I don't think we ever spoke about the past. Nor did I ask the questions I would have asked her today. On the contrary, Evelyn was more interested in hearing about the months I had spent living in an artists' colony in Italy, an experience that had inspired me to give up my career in PR and saw me, at the age of twenty-four, about to embark on a degree in textiles.

Looking back, I can see that she was lonely in Cornwall, and not long after that summer Evelyn moved to a care home back in Bournemouth. My mother continued to visit her until her death in 1981 but I never saw her again. When she died she left part of her estate, including a trunk of papers, to my mother, and when my mother died in 1997 they passed to me.

Little did I know that nearly forty years after our last meeting I would get to know Evelyn as I never knew her in life; nor that the precious record she kept of some of her most interesting life and times would slip through my fingers and be rescued by a stranger.

I knew a bit about Evelyn's background from my mother, for it was an unusual one. She was born Evelyn Beatrice Clifford in Hampshire in 1893, the only child of Harold Mills Clifford, a captain in the Scottish Rifles, and his wife Emlie (née Bennet), and spent part of her childhood at Chatham Barracks, though by the time of the 1901 census the family were living in Kensington, London. Emlie was a playwright who wrote under a variant of her husband's name, Clifford Mills, perhaps believing she would be taken more seriously if people thought she were a man. Her plays *Where the Rainbow Ends* and *The Luck of the Navy* were West End hits and both were made into films in the 1920s and 1930s. The former was as famous as *Peter Pan* in its day and was performed every Christmas for fifty years. (A twelve-year-old Noël Coward was in the original 1911 production at London's Savoy Theatre.)

Sometime between 1903 and 1905, Evelyn's father left his wife and child and moved in with another woman with whom he started a new family. Despite Emlie's career in the liberal theatrical world, this unconventional situation must surely have caused embarrassment to both mother and daughter, and, in fact, I know from my mother that it was considered something of a family scandal. It is probably not surprising that Evelyn's relationship with her father was an awkward one, and when in 1925 she married Captain Rex Shillington it was a family friend and not Harold who gave her away.

I first spotted Evelyn's diaries the day I went hunting for some information about Roger Quilter, the composer whose music for *Where the Rainbow Ends* had been hugely popular. I had been contacted out of the blue by musician and teacher Dr Valerie Langfield, who was writing a biography of Quilter and had discovered that I was a relative of Emlie/Clifford Mills. And so I found myself rummaging for the first time through the trunk my mother had left me. Most of its contents related to Emlie and her works, but the diaries were there, too, marked as such in my mother's writing and wrapped in brown paper and string. Perhaps if I hadn't been looking for something else at the time I would have stopped to open them. Perhaps if my mother had mentioned them as being worth looking at I would have removed them from the trunk and put them aside to study later. But, being somewhat preoccupied with my quest, and having no recollection of ever hearing about them, I simply carried on with what I was doing.

Two years later my life was turned upside down when my first husband died. Leaving the large mill we had been renovating together for somewhere far smaller, I sought advice about where the best home for Emlie's archive might be – I even wrote to the V&A and the British Library, offering to donate it to them, but neither responded. When I moved again and found myself hauling the trunk up into yet another attic, I asked myself what I was still doing with it. An auction seemed to be the solution and its contents were duly catalogued – the focus of the sale being very much on Emlie and her work as Clifford Mills. I still didn't look at the diaries.

So Evelyn's life passed from my hands, and that might have been the end of the story if it wasn't for a man called Shaun Sewell. Shaun has a reputation for being a 'diary detective', and is seemingly blessed with a talent for unearthing old journals that bring the past to life. Something about the lot caught his eye, and after placing the winning bid he undertook some clever detective work to track me down.

What a glorious find it has been for both of us.

In this book, I want to sit down and introduce you to Cousin Eve as I meet her all over again – and get to know her better than I ever did in life. For when Rex was posted to the Far East in 1931, as well as writing long letters home to her mother she began to keep a journal of the exotic travels they made while they were there. When they returned to the UK just over three years later, she began a more formal diary, writing it throughout countless moves around Britain in the years leading up to and during the Second World War, and continuing to do so during a spell in Italy when the war was over. In these extraordinary accounts, we are granted a privileged view of life on the inside as an Army wife – with its fierce loyalties and friendships, its petty jealousies, its constant comings and goings – witnessed during one of the most momentous times in world history. It is also a great love story – that of Evelyn and Rex.

Evelyn is clearly recognisable as the woman I got to know all too briefly: sociable, compassionate, strong-willed and with a great sense of humour. I ought not to have been surprised that the daughter of a playwright should be an accomplished writer herself, but I don't think I could ever have hoped for something so vivid, so fresh, so entertaining.

I wondered why she didn't tell me some of these stories herself when we were together in Cornwall. Maybe, having set them down, she felt that was all that could be said. Maybe reliving her time with Rex was too painful, reminding her of her loneliness when I knew her. But even if it was not her intention at the time of writing, there is evidence that she went back to edit some of the entries later and that she therefore hoped they would be read by others one day.

When she writes her last entry in April 1947 as they sail home from Italy – with Rex's retirement not far off and a new life out of the Army awaiting them – she appears to be putting an end to her diary-writing years but it is hard to imagine that she stopped writing altogether.

Evelyn ended up alone, with no children and few relatives. I have no children myself and I am the last of that line. Now that Shaun has rescued them, I want to pass her stories on to you. They are Evelyn's stories, but they are also part of the story of a very special generation and, as my own experience shows, something we can all too easily lose.

Jacy Wall

Note from the editor

Evelyn was a natural storyteller; the changes I have made to her original text are minimal and consist mainly of grammatical corrections and improvements I felt were required to present her writing to the large readership she deserves. I have added explanatory text in square brackets within the diary entries when this could be done briefly and without interrupting the flow of the narrative. Longer passages of background information are in italicised paragraphs between the entries.

As it is her diary and not a history book, I have not resorted to changing any minor inconsistencies that may occur.

The pre-war and wartime diaries are published almost in their entirety, but the Italian post-war diary – which amounted to almost as many words as all the other diaries put together – had to be shortened. For this I have concentrated on sharing the most entertaining and illuminating parts of Evelyn's extraordinary experience of living in a conquered country in the immediate aftermath of war.

Barbara Fox, 2017

Evelyn's people

Relatives

Uncle Alec (Alexander) Clifford 1875–1950. Her father's brother. Father of journalist Alexander Clifford and Jacy Wall's mother Elizabeth and their brother Henry (known as Tony).

Alexander Clifford 1909–52. Her cousin. Eldest child of Alec and Marian. War correspondent for *Daily Mail* 1940–46. Awarded OBE in 1946. His archive of diaries and letters are with the Imperial War Museum.

Aunt Alice Clifford 1871–1950. Her father's sister.

Elizabeth Clifford (later Davies) 1915–97. Her cousin. Daughter of Alec and Marian Clifford; mother of Jacy Wall.

Aunt Elsie Clifford 1877–1961. Her father's sister.

Emlie Clifford (née Bennet) 1861–1933. Her mother. Playwright who wrote under the name Mrs Clifford Mills. Her most famous works are *Where the Rainbow Ends* and *The Luck of the Navy*.

Eva Buckingham 1882–1956. Her stepmother. Harold's second wife; mother of Peggy and Hugh.

Harold Clifford 1867–1946. Her father.

Uncle Harry (Henry) Clifford 1861–1947. Her father's brother.

Hugh Clifford 1916–1993. Her half-brother. Son of Harold and Eva Buckingham.

Aunt Marian Clifford 1880–1966. Wife of Uncle Alec; mother of journalist Alexander Clifford and Jacy Wall's mother Elizabeth and their brother Henry (known as Tony).

Aunt Mary (Mrs Ward Poole) 1854/5–1946 Not a relative. Lives with Aunt Elsie.

Peggy (Margaret) Clifford 1905–76. Her half-sister. Daughter of Harold and Eva Buckingham.

Rex (Herbert Reginald) Shillington (1892–1963) Her husband. A career soldier in the British Army who reached the rank of brigadier on his retirement in 1949.

Friends and acquaintances

General Body At the War Office.

Signor and Signora Cenzato Owners of the villa in Naples where Rex and Evelyn live from July to October 1946.

Mr and Mrs Chotzner Fellow residents at the school Maiden Erlegh, Evelyn's home from March to December 1941.

Italia Conti Actress who founded the theatre school that bears her name. Most closely associated with *Where the Rainbow Ends*, she sets up the charity the Rainbow League in 1932.

Brigadier (Joe) and Ida Coyle Rex's brigadier in Edinburgh.

Betty Craig Fellow paying guest in Lady Place. Her husband is a brother officer of John Sinclair, son of the owner.

Colonel and Mollie Earp Neighbours at Hilsea Barracks in the 1920s when Evelyn and Rex are newly married; later together at Bramley and Burscough Ordnance Depots.

Colonel (Michael) and Ina Egan Originally friends of her parents, their son, Frank, was Evelyn's first love before his death in the First World War.

Colonel Ferguson With the Ordnance Depot in Graz, Austria.

Audrey and Guy Fossick Audrey is Nella Hutchison's sister.

Captain Fox Runs the school Maiden Erlegh near Reading, Evelyn's home from March to December 1941.

Louis and Ruby Freedman Neighbours of Mrs Sinclair; Evelyn forms a strong friendship with them.

Peggy and Douglas Gluckstein Douglas is at Luton Hoo with Rex and is the grandson of the founder of Lyons' Corner Houses.

Billy and Hilda Grellier Army friends who later sail to India.

Jane Hadden Evelyn's closest friend; the pair met in Hong Kong.

Pat Hadden Jane's (estranged) husband.

Colonel (Jem) Hamilton Evelyn and Rex met Jem on the ship coming home from Hong Kong.

Sam Harris Manager of the Glen Eagle Hotel, Harpenden, Evelyn's home from December 1943 to September 1945.

Nigel Headington Bursar at Maiden Erlegh.

Brigadier (Jack) and Mary Heywood Jack works for the Royal Army Service Corps and is based in Italy with Rex.

Nella Hutchison Wife of Percy; an actress.

Percy Hutchison Actor-manager/director/producer. Originally a friend of Evelyn's mother, Emlie.

Major and Nan Impey Of the Lincolnshire Regiment, they first met in Hong Kong and are re-acquainted in Edinburgh.

Major Lee-Wood With the Ordnance Depot in Naples.

David Lyle Jane Hadden's former lover.

Colonel and Mrs Mapleson He becomes Rex's Commanding Officer in Bramley on the departure of Colonel Earp.

Mrs Mead One of the Army wives at Bramley Depot.

Mr and Mrs Petersen Owners of the holiday cottage in Guernsey that is a favourite destination for Evelyn and Rex.

Mrs Sinclair Owner of Lady Place, Sutton Courtenay, Evelyn's home from December 1941 to May 1942.

(Edward) D'Arcy and Lita Staunton Senior chaplain to the Forces in Italy.

Nan Temple-Morris Army wife and friend in Bramley Depot. They may also have known each other in the Far East.

Captain (Tom) and May Rook Friends in Bramley Depot, they later sail to Egypt.

Marjorie Smith A resident of the Clifton Hotel in Southport, Evelyn's home from January to December 1938.

Colonel and Mrs Tanner Predecessors of the Earps in Bramley Depot.

Maggie Webster Owner of the house in Sutton Courtenay where Evelyn lives from May 1942 to May 1943.

Evelyn as a young woman

PART ONE

A home of our own at last!

January 1935–January 1936

Evelyn and her husband, Rex, are returning to the UK from Hong Kong, where Rex, a major in the Royal Ordnance Depot of the British Army, has been on a three-year tour of duty. She is forty-two, Rex slightly older. They have no children. In 1933, halfway through the tour, Evelyn's mother, Emlie, died. The two were devoted to each other; the letters between them while Evelyn was abroad show how difficult they both found their separation – particularly Emlie, who was lonely and missing her daughter terribly. Evelyn is dreading returning to an England without her mother and has been grateful that life on board ship – with new and old friends and endless activities to fill her time – has helped to keep dark thoughts at bay.

As the passengers wrote light-hearted verse on each other's menu cards on their last night together, everyone singled out Evelyn's sense of fun, causing her to write in her journal later, 'If only they knew how heavy my heart has often been.'

Friday, 11 January 1935

The troopship *Somersetshire* docked at Southampton this morning. It was a dull, cheerless January day with a piercing north-east wind blowing and the prospect as we stepped down the gangway was as bleak as my heart. To return to England like this is hard indeed!

All was bustle and confusion as the Gordon Highlanders disembarked for Edinburgh and farewells were said. Our good friend Colonel (Jem) Hamilton will go with them but will be returning to London for leave and we have planned to meet again. We hear from our pals in the regiment that his wife, older than he, is an alcoholic. How terribly sad!

Boris and Nan Bacon are on the quayside to meet us. Nan and Boris knew and loved my mother and I can sense their loving sympathy as we all go to have lunch at the Polygon before we catch the 3.30 train to Waterloo. We have booked a room at the Palace Hotel, Piccadilly, for our stay in London.

As I sit in the train I remember how I have longed to see my beloved London again during these three years of exile. The broad Thames! The Houses of Parliament! The flower girls selling snowdrops and violets round the statue of Eros in Piccadilly! The parks where my mother and I used to walk! How terribly empty it all seems to me now. After unpacking and having dinner we go to bed. Feeling utterly miserable.

Saturday, 12 January 1935
Wake with raging neuralgia, due to reaction, I suppose. Rang Batchelor and made an appointment to see him on Monday. There is a lot of business to attend to – all my mother's affairs – which I must get down to.

Monday, 14 January 1935
Yesterday Rex and I went to Woolwich to have tea and supper with Jane and Pat Hadden. They have a quarter in the barracks there. It

was wonderful to see Jane again, my dearest and closest friend in Hong Kong, and they gave us a warm welcome.

Today we saw Mr Batchelor. There is so much to see and to do. My mother's furniture is stored at William Whiteley's and will have to remain there until Rex knows where he is to be posted.

Evelyn met Jane Hadden in 1932 while she and Rex were on their Far East posting. Evelyn commented in her diary at the time that Jane was '. . . fascinating. Not pretty but with lovely grey eyes and she is so amusing!' They hit it off immediately.

Evelyn and Rex on their wedding day, 1925

Tuesday, 22 January 1935

Spent a very happy weekend with Colonel and Mrs Egan in Windsor. Ina and Michael are very dear friends of ours of many years. They loved my mother and came to every first night of her plays in London, and are great *Rainbow* fans. It was like coming home to be with them.

When we arrived back at the Regent Palace Hotel we found Jem Hamilton waiting for us. He took us to dine at Grosvenor House. A delicious dinner, and we danced afterwards to a splendid band. On the floor were the Duke of Kent and his lovely bride, Princess Marina – a beautiful girl – both obviously very much in love.

Michael and Ina Egan were friends of Evelyn's parents. Their son, Frank, who was killed in the Battle of Jutland in 1916, was Evelyn's first love. When Evelyn married Rex in 1925 it was Michael Egan and not her father who gave her away, suggesting that the delicate situation between Harold and Emlie made Harold's presence at the wedding too awkward.

Thursday, 24 January 1935

In bed with a sore throat and cough. Rex got the doctor and I have laryngitis. What a bore! Feeling awful, with a temperature. Hope to be well enough to go to Storrington to stay with Aunt Alice on Saturday week.

Rex has been to the War Office and he is to be posted to Bramley, a large depot near Basingstoke, and we are to have a quarter! This will be our first real home since we were married nine years ago.

Monday, 4 February 1935

Just back from a very happy visit to Aunt Alice in Storrington. Such a warm and loving welcome from her and dear Uncle Harry;

and dear Aunt Elsie and Aunt Mary came over to have lunch with us at Harry's house. So lovely to see them all again! Uncle Harry was very interested in our time in China; he has visited Japan and has some beautiful Chinese and Japanese treasures in his house and studio.

Alice, Elsie and Harry (Henry) are siblings of Evelyn's father, and they will pop up regularly throughout the diaries as Evelyn is a devoted niece. Neither Alice nor Elsie married and Harry is a widower. Aunt Mary (Mary Ward Poole), a widow, is not a relative but lives with Aunt Elsie.

Thursday, 7 February 1935

Caught the 1.45 train to Nottingham where Rex's brother, Arthur, and youngest sister, Gladys, met us. His mother and eldest sister, Maud, all so glad to see us and so kind and understanding.

Sunday, 10 February 1935

Left Nottingham as Rex has to report for duty on Monday. We have been thoroughly spoilt and were taken for a lovely drive in Sherwood Forest and to a football match on Saturday (Nottingham Forest 2 – Notts County 3).

A slow (and very cold) train journey; luckily we had sandwiches and coffee with us. Glad to get back to the Regent Palace Hotel.

Monday, 11 February 1935

Up early and caught the train to Basingstoke. We shall have to find a hotel to live in until our quarter is vacated and decorated. Hated Basingstoke on sight! A more mouldy spot one couldn't imagine, and the hotel – in which we were shown a double bedroom with a gas-fire with its 'teeth' missing – just about finished us; but Colonel Powell came over from Bramley and drove us over to the Great

Western Hotel in Reading where we had a super lunch and saw a lovely big double bedroom on the first floor. The proprietor, Mr Mermoud – who is Swiss – and his French wife were both so nice. Rex's leave ends tomorrow. So thankful to be settled in this comfy hotel!

Tuesday, 12 February 1935
Rex off to Bramley on duty. Explored Reading and certainly like it; good shops and one can get onto the towpath along the Thames. Rex back for a late tea. He likes the new job and says the major's quarter is rather charming. The Knox-Wilsons are in it at present and have invited me over to lunch with Rex on Thursday.

Thursday, 14 February 1935
Perfectly lovely day! How beautiful England is in the spring! Went by train to Bramley, where the entrance to the depot is through a police gate. The depot contains large sheds which house all the necessary equipment for a British Expeditionary Army in case of war, and no one can enter it without a permit. Here one boards a marvellous contraption – a trolley which traverses the enormous depot (which is extremely pretty and has a trout stream running through it). This takes us up a hill to another gate near the officers' mess and the officers' quarters, which are in a row, all set in delightful gardens and of different sizes. The one the Knox-Wilsons have, and which will be ours, is a large bungalow with a lovely garden and I fell in love with it at once.

It has a large hall and sitting room (which has French windows onto a nice veranda), a large dining room, a double bedroom and two single bedrooms and a small study – all facing south over the garden. There are very good kitchen quarters including a maid's bedroom, a very pleasant kitchen and various pantries; a separate 'loo' and bathroom, large airing cupboard and a huge boiler, which is serviced by the gardener, Knott.

He is a marvellous gardener and the large lawn, borders and rose garden are all beautifully kept, and – oh, joy! – there is a very fine vegetable garden!

We have lunch with the Knox-Wilsons and afterwards go to have tea with Colonel and Mrs Tanner in their quarter next door. Colonel Tanner is retiring soon and the good news is that he is to be replaced by Colonel Earp, currently in Burscough, Lancashire, who with Molly, his wife, are very good friends of ours from Hilsea days [Rex and Evelyn's barracks when they were newly married]. Molly will make a splendid CO's wife!

Mrs Tanner tells me that when they leave I shall have to take over the Ladies' Guild, which consists of the officers' wives, the sergeants' wives and, here in Bramley, the wives of the large police force which guards the depot. She explains that as the police force is more permanent than the Army, there exists always a certain amount of tension between the wives of the police and the sergeants, which I feel won't make my task easy. There will also be a lot going on due to it being the silver jubilee year of the King and Queen. I seem fated to have to take over the jobs of colonels' wives, and Rex, of course, will have more to do till Colonel Earp arrives, but he will be coming before Molly, who will have to see to the packing-up, etc. (they have three daughters of school age).

Saturday, 16 February 1935

Letter from Percy Hutchison to say that my mother's play, *The Luck of the Navy*, is playing in Bournemouth tonight and could Rex and I go. Rex couldn't make it but I caught the train to Bournemouth where Percy met me. The play went wonderfully well and it was lovely to see it, but – oh! – how I missed my beloved mother! Met the company afterwards and we all went to a club run by a Mrs Jordan Muir, where Percy, Nella and I stayed the night.

Percy Hutchison (1875–1945), an actor-manager, director and producer, was born into a theatrical family. His first stage appearance was as a boy in Blackpool as a member of his mother's company, and he would join forces with Miss Emma Hutchison, as his mother was known, to mount productions all over the country, often directing and starring in them himself. Emma was the sister of Sir Charles Wyndham, for whom Percy worked as stage manager, later managing Wyndham's Theatre in London after his uncle's death, as well as some provincial theatres. Evelyn almost certainly got to know Percy through her mother, for he was one of the original stars of Emlie's The Luck of the Navy, *a play he successfully took to North America in 1919. He married Nella, a member of his touring companies, after the death of his first wife, actress Lilias Earle. Her friendship with Percy is very important to Evelyn and one of the many ways she is able to preserve her mother's memory.*

Sunday, 17 February 1935
A lovely morning, Bournemouth looking very beautiful. Percy, Nella and I went for a walk to Alum Chine and met Miss (Italia) Conti, and in the afternoon had a drive to Corfe Castle and back to Miss Conti's house on the East Cliff. So nice to hear all about *Rainbow* and to see her St George's flag flying over the house! Caught train back to Reading – very tired but so glad I went.

Italia Conti, known today for the theatre school that bears her name, started her career as an actress. When the producer Charles Hawtrey asked her to train the children for the first production of Where the Rainbow Ends *at the Savoy Theatre in 1911, she realised her talent as a teacher and virtually gave up acting, founding her school in a basement studio in London's Great Portland Street. In the early 1920s she took over control of the annual Rainbow productions and in 1932 she formed the charity the Rainbow League to support children's causes throughout the British Empire. It also financed 'Rainbow beds' for children in hospital.*

Saturday, 23 February 1935

Had a strenuous week! Up to town to stay with the Hutchisons, met Jane and did some shopping. London looking very lovely, the parks with early spring flowers and everyone getting excited over the jubilee celebrations. Returned today, very tired, but so glad to be with Rex.

Sunday, 24 February 1935

Rex and I had a lovely walk along the towpath to Caversham. We can't move into our quarter till 29 April as it has to be redecorated after the Knox-Wilsons move out. Then my mother's furniture will have to be moved out of storage. How can I endure seeing all her things again? How I dread this ordeal!

Friday, 8 March 1935

Mrs Tanner came to tea today to say goodbye. She said there was a problem regarding the Ladies' Guild that she wanted to explain to me. It is always the wife of the senior sergeant-major who takes over the duties of secretary of the guild, but in this case, Mrs Tanner says, the sergeant-major's wife is Italian and very temperamental indeed, and with the situation as it is between Army and police wives, this has caused some trouble. So Mrs Tanner has seen fit to 'demob' Mrs Knell and has delegated the next sergeant's wife to be secretary over her. This is quite unprecedented and Rex thinks, as I do, that it will lead to trouble. He thinks that as CO's

wife, Mrs Tanner should have dealt differently with the problem
as one can imagine what an atmosphere this has created. I feel she
is leaving me with a pretty kettle of fish and a very nasty situation.
Thank goodness when Molly Earp comes it will be her job, as colonel's wife, to sort it out.

Thursday, 28 March 1935

Today I had to take over the Ladies' Guild in place of Mrs
Tanner, who has left. Had to address about forty women and
could feel the atmosphere was very strained. Had a committee
meeting afterwards: quite an ordeal and very sticky! Mrs Tanner
has certainly left me with a problem to keep things going till
Molly Earp takes over. There is obviously a 'Mrs Knell faction',
who feel she has been outrageously treated, and those behind
Mrs Mead, the new secretary. However, I managed to persuade
them to continue as at present until our new colonel's wife comes
to take over and I think they appreciate what a difficult position
I am in.

Mrs Knell, a large, full-bosomed liquid-eyed Italian, mother
of five children, sits and broods, darting venomous glances at Mrs
Mead who is surrounded by her supporters who cast equally venomous glances at Mrs Mead's faction. Not a happy afternoon!

Saturday, 6 April 1935

Have been to Bramley several times to choose wallpaper for the
quarters, which the sappers are redecorating. Have chosen an
attractive pale grey matt-finish for the sitting room and plain for
the other rooms, and shall have chintz curtains in the dining room.
I have fallen for some lovely seagulls – my favourite birds! – flying
across the sea in the bathroom. We are getting the extra furniture,
carpets, etc from Newbery's in Reading on hire purchase.

Today my dear Jane came to spend the day and we took her over to see the quarter. She is enchanted with it and the garden. There is a pale pink cherry blossom just outside one of the sitting-room windows in the rose gardens.

Friday, 12 April 1935

The ladies' whist drive and dance today – I gave away prizes. Thank heaven all went off well! I am getting to know the other officers and their wives. They are a very cheery and friendly lot. The Rooks, May and Tom, have a captain's quarter next to the mess and two very lively red-headed sons. There are the Bransburys, a charming couple, and Colonel and Mrs Harper, and there seems to be lots going on here. There is tennis in the summer and an open-air swimming pool, and badminton in the winter. Shopping is done from the NAAFI or in Basingstoke. The depot is huge, full of bunnies and pheasants, and Rex hopes to fish in the trout stream. Senior officers come down from the War Office in the appropriate season for a shoot on Saturdays.

There is a small garrison church at which the vicar of Bramley Parish Church comes to preach sometimes.

Rex has arranged that the furniture and my mother's personal belongings be brought to the depot from Whiteley's and that they are stored in one of the Army huts so that I can go through them before we move into our quarter. I dread this task . . .

Palm Sunday, 14 April 1935

To Bramley for church and church parade; lunch in the mess. Colonel Earp here and on Rex's advice I told him of the Ladies' Guild dilemma and asked his advice as Molly will not be coming for a little while yet.

He is horrified at Mrs Tanner's tactless and high-handed action in 'demoting' the regimental sergeant-major's wife, but says the damage is done and the best thing to do now is call a ballot and let the ladies decide who they want to be secretary. This is of course the democratic way, but I do wonder if it will solve the problem. I sincerely hope it does! I am glad to have an authoritative ruling on the matter. The ballot will have to wait now till next month.

Wednesday, 17 April 1935

The last two days I have been over to Bramley to tackle the heart-breaking job of sorting out my beloved mother's personal belongings, which were packed by Whiteley's. Smashed china and glass; clothes riddled with moths and her fox fur the same; a sugar basin still full of sugar ... Was there no one who cared enough to do this last service for you, oh my darling, and I was all those thousands of miles away.

Everything reminded me so vividly of her and days gone by. Her fur, her trinkets, all tore at my heart as I realised that in spite of all I suffered in Hong Kong and since, I have never <u>really</u> faced up to the fact that never in this life shall I see her again.

Rex, who understands so well what an ordeal this is to me, came to fetch me to lunch in the mess and it is an indication of his love and deep understanding that he never remarked on my tear-stained face – just a loving pressure of his arm about me as he shows me where to go for repairs to the damage in my appearance, and that loving look which tells me there is nothing he would not do to spare me this ordeal. After lunch I go back to the sad task, with Knott to help me get rid of the smashed crockery, and I returned to finish it today. May Rook's eldest son, eight years old, accompanied me, and his presence and artless chatter was a great comfort and helped to dispel the dark cloud of misery which threatened to engulf me.

Tuesday, 30 April 1935

We moved into the quarter yesterday. The furniture arrived from Reading and we had the carpets down and curtains up and it certainly looks very nice. We have chosen a dove-grey carpet, green velvet curtains and a grey-green suite for the sitting room, which set off our Chinese 'comprador' table and our Chinese lamps, vases and ornaments.

We have chintz curtains in the dining room and in the bedrooms. We shall use the large veranda for meals and have furnished it with a rustic table and chairs, and it has green bamboo 'chicks' [rollable blinds to keep out direct sunlight] for hot weather.

We are lucky to have been able to engage the Knox-Wilsons' maid, Kathleen, until she gets married. She is an excellent cook and will train her younger sister, Charlotte, to take her place when she leaves. They are daughters of a gamekeeper.

We also have a very nice woman, a Mrs Ham, who comes to clean (and also sells eggs, most appropriately!), and if we entertain we can have the mess head waiter to wait at table.

Thursday, 2 May 1935

Motored with the Rooks up to London. It looks like a fairy city, one mass of bunting and stands all ready for the jubilee celebrations next Monday.

Monday, 6 May 1935

Perfect day for the jubilee celebrations. The Rooks and ourselves listened in to the royal procession to St Paul's Cathedral and heard the wonderful reception given to Their Majesties.

General Body came down from the War Office and the Egans came to lunch with us before going to Sherfield [village adjoining Bramley depot] to take part in the jubilee celebrations. The depot has co-operated in supplying tents, etc. as well as personnel for the village. They put on a splendid show, with a Maypole dance and sports, and I presented the prizes.

Thursday, 9 May 1935

Had a private meeting with Mrs Knell and Mrs Mead, and Colonel Earp explained that he had decided that a ballot should be held this afternoon to decide who should be secretary of the Ladies' Guild. It was a bit fraught, with Mrs Knell getting very temperamental and repeatedly swearing 'on the heads of her children' in broken English, but we managed to calm her down with cups of coffee and it was at last decided that they would both abide by the ballot decision.

Later:

Thank God all went well! Supported by the officers' wives we arranged the ballot between the sergeant and police wives and by a large majority they chose Mrs Mead to be secretary. Although the small Knell faction was of course disappointed, we feel that all may now be peace.

Sunday, 12 May 1935

All this week we have been hearing over the radio eyewitness reports of the marvellous scenes outside Buckingham Palace as huge crowds call for the King and Queen to appear on the famous balcony, and last night, whilst listening with the Rooks, we suddenly decided we had to be there too and piled into the car and set out for London, arriving at about 10.15 p.m. After parking the car at the Piccadilly car park we made our way through dense crowds all along The Mall to the palace, where we arrived in time to join the immense crowd calling for the King and Queen, with all eyes on the balcony. And as we all shouted, 'We want the King!' and

'We want the Queen!', out they came (for the umpteenth time) to a deafening roar each time and to the singing of 'God save the King' and the cheers which must surely touch their hearts. A most thrilling experience!

Home in the small hours of the morning.

To church this morning, still feeling very tired after last night's expedition – but so well worth it!

Monday, 27 May 1935

Met Jane at Reading. She had her cat with her. Alas, she and Pat have decided to part and Jane is going to live in a hotel in Shortlands, Kent, where she can't have the cat, and so we have offered to give her a home. She is a lovely half-Persian who rejoices in the name of Garbo (smoke-coloured with blue eyes) and is very conscious of her beauty, though a little fraught after the journey. However a saucer of milk and some delicious fish prepared by Kathleen soon restored her, as Jane introduced her to her new home. It is so lovely to see Jane!

Jane and Pat have had a rocky relationship from the start. Jane had been married young, to a captain in the Royal Army Medical Corps (RAMC), but was widowed only a few months later when the Germans bombed the hospital in Boulogne during the First World War. Heartbroken, she joined the ATS (Auxiliary Territorial Service) and went to France where she met Pat, a friend of her late husband. They married when the war was over, only to discover they had little in common. While stationed with her husband in India, Jane met and fell in love with David Lyle, a young captain in the Welsh Regiment. They wanted to marry but Pat refused to give her a divorce and she reluctantly broke up with David, promising Pat that she would have no further contact with him. David went on to marry and have a daughter but is now divorced.

Thursday, 30 May 1935

A lovely day. Jane and I down in the depot to watch the operation of re-stocking the stream. Rex and Captain Crawford have been the prime movers in this scheme (being keen fishermen) and watch with great satisfaction as the new trout are introduced into the water.

Saturday, 22 June 1935

Teddy, Rex's brother, to stay the weekend. He is a barrister and rather tall like Rex and very nice.

Great news! Molly Earp has come and they have moved into their quarter next to ours. Apart from the fact we have always been such good pals, it is marvellous to have the CO's wife here to take over her duties, especially someone as tactful and competent as dear Molly.

Thursday, 27 June 1935

The Earps to dine. All of us wives under Molly are working very hard to make the fête on 12 July a big success.

Saturday, 29 June 1935

Kathleen leaves today to be married, and her sister, Charlotte, whom she has been training, takes over, assisted by Mrs Ham who comes to do the washing-up when we entertain. Charlotte is an excellent little cook, her pastries and pies a dream, and she has learnt to wait at table, looking very attractive in a dark green dress and coffee-coloured organdie collar, apron and cap. She is blonde.

When the Hutchisons came down to stay last time they brought their two dogs with them, a rather aged dachshund called Greta and a very fine little Aberdeen Terrier, very young. As they are now living in a flat in London they asked us to keep the two dogs, which we did, but they took Greta back with them as she fretted. However, they asked if they might give the Scotch Terrier to us as he wants a lot of exercise, and of course we were delighted to have him. He is very well bred and has a pedigree, but alas, the Hutchisons have no idea how to train a puppy, as we found out when they stayed with us. He is only six months old and housetrained, but has no idea of walking to heel or coming when called – and no wonder! The Hutchisons, after yelling themselves hoarse, proceed to give him a beating and call him, 'Bad dog!' when they do get him to return (a difficult task in a depot full of bunnies), which of course completely confuses the poor little chap. We shall have to see what we can do.

He seems to have taken to Rex and adores 'walkies' in the depot with its bunnies and lovely smells. His idea of chasing them is to go full tilt, giving tongue at the top of his range, which of course scares them stiff and quite obviates any chance of him ever catching one. We have named him Chaser!

Tuesday, 2 July 1935

To London with Rex to Highgate Cemetery to put flowers on my mother's grave. She is buried with her father, James Bennet, and we had some difficulty in finding the grave. Highgate is a very old cemetery and many of the graves are sadly neglected. I am arranging for hers to be attended to and shall have a special marble scroll made. As I stood there I had a strong feeling that her spirit was very near me. Oh my darling, how I miss you!

Friday, 12 July 1935

A glorious day for the fête. Very hot. The Egans came over from Windsor and the Eagles from Aldershot to lunch and stayed to supper. A great success.

Our lovely cat, Garbo, is proving a real vamp, as her name implies. Already the male cats from 'the Lines' – where the other ranks have their quarters – are constantly around our bungalow and serenade her at night. Garbo, reclining on a cushion in delicious languor, flexes her paws and stretches sinuously with half-closed eyes while gently purring to herself. With so many ardent amorous males courting her, we fear the worst!

Kathleen, who was our maid, got married on 6 July. Her husband works in the NAAFI.

Wednesday, 21 August 1935

The inevitable happened and our beautiful Garbo was pregnant! In spite of all attempts to provide her with a comfortable and suitable place for her accouchement, what does she do but select for the birthplace of her offspring Rex's dressing-room cupboard, on the top of his shoes! (Most uncomfortable, I should think!)

Now Rex has a 'thing' about his shoes, which must always be immaculate and highly polished. He spends hours of loving care to get the best results and Garbo could not have chosen a more fatal place for the birth of her family, over the discovery of which it is best to draw a veil.

Poor Garbo's stock is very, very low indeed as Rex surveys her and her kittens with a jaundiced eye, muttering darkly, 'She will have to go.'

We have now transferred Garbo and family into one of the pantries we had reserved for her, with all mod cons.

The last weeks have passed quickly with tennis, entertaining, etc. Rex's leave commences on 5 September.

Thursday, 22 August 1935

Margaret Scudamore and her daughter Peggy to lunch. Margaret, who acted in my mother's play, *The Man from Hong Kong*, has a son (by her first husband) who is an actor, Michael Redgrave, who she says is doing very well on the stage. Margaret's second husband, known as Andy, is a businessman and they have a charming house in Chapel Street. Margaret was one of my mother's dear friends. Peggy is married to a dentist.

Garbo and family have disappeared! No sign of them, although we have searched. Where can they be?

Three days later Knott hears a faint mewing and discovers Garbo and company shut into a disused shed in the vegetable garden. Garbo is very thin and wan-eyed, but all alive, thank goodness! We are keeping one male kitten, a black quarter-Persian with green eyes, and giving the rest to the families in the Lines, where their progenitor doubtless lives. Jane has found a home for Garbo with a former 'Miss Mop' of hers, who loves her. Better for this charmer to live where there are not so many amorous pussies nearby!

Tuesday, 8 October 1935

Rex and I to Southampton to stay with Eva and Peggy for her wedding to John Murray. He is very nice and is on the staff of the Limmer Trinidad Company [the Limmer & Trinidad Lake Asphalt Company, road-builders]. John will be going to Trinidad to live in a quarter near the amazing Pitch Lake, the source of the company's wealth.

Peggy looked very sweet in pale gold to match her hair, holding a golden bouquet of autumn flowers. Afterwards, a grand reception at the hotel, where Daddy introduced me to his somewhat startled friends as 'my daughter by my first marriage' as I don't think that they knew there had been one 'with issue', as the lawyers say! However, he was superb and has such aplomb and charm that between us we carried the whole thing off splendidly.

He and Eva have a great number of friends here and Pegs has some lovely wedding presents. Hugh is very tall, like Eva, and is much addicted to jazz music, which he performs with gusto in his room, having formidable equipment for producing the same.

Aunt Alice, Marian and Elizabeth were also at the wedding.

I had rushed up to town to buy a wedding garment and found a long green velvet dress with full sleeves at John Lewis and a green velvet beret to match, and was glad I felt my best to meet all those guests. I hope I did Daddy proud! Rex did, of course. Came home on Sunday.

Peggy and Hugh are Evelyn's half-sister and half-brother from her father's relationship with Eva Buckingham, whom he married after the death of Emlie in 1933. Evelyn's relationship with her father is not always an easy one – and we know that he was not present at her own marriage – but perhaps, with the passing of Emlie, both are attempting to heal wounds, and indeed, on this occasion, all seems to have gone smoothly. The guests Marian and Elizabeth she mentions are Evelyn's aunt and cousin, the grandmother and mother of Jacy Wall, author of the preface.

Friday, 29 November 1935

Rex and I to stay with Daddy and Eva for the Rotary dance, a very grand affair with a magnificent dinner and gifts for the lady guests. Daddy dances beautifully and as light as a feather. I do wish Eva would sometimes allow me a word with him alone! I hardly ever see him alone and he seems afraid to speak to me, alas!

He came up to me and slipped a pound note into the pocket of my cardigan, muttering, 'Get yourself a pair of stockings, Evelyn,' and I fear we shall never get any closer to one another. How sad! I would love to feel I really had a father.

He and Eva have a large and pleasant house just off the Common, which Eva runs with great efficiency and a rod of iron. Everyone except Hugh – who for some reason is exempt – has to be down for breakfast (dressing-gowns are allowed) however late one has been up the previous night.

Every morning Daddy's car, complete with chauffeur, having deposited him at his office, comes back to pick up Eva, elegantly attired with every hair in place plus long red fingernails, to take her to Bonhams, where a table is specially reserved for her and she holds court to her friends. She and Daddy entertain a lot, and very well.

Eva's sister, Babs, who is tall and elegant like her and whom we like very much, lives with them. She has a husband somewhere in Australia, a son in his teens, and helps a lot in the house. Daddy, who is general manager for this part of the Limmer Trinidad Company, is also quite something in the Rotary world and, according to Rex (who has been with him), a totally different person in the club, where he is the life and soul of the party and full of Clifford charm!

Wednesday, 18 December 1935

To London to see *Where the Rainbow Ends* matinee, Michael and Ina with us. The theatre was packed with enchanted children and their elders of all ages who are great *Rainbow* fans and have been coming to see the play since they were children themselves.

As I sat in the theatre and saw this lovely work of my mother's for the first time without her, I realised more than ever how deeply I miss her and always shall. Thank God part of her lives on in her beautiful play and those ideals in which she so passionately believed.

*

Where the Rainbow Ends was inspired by Evelyn herself, who as a child wrote a poem lamenting the fact that while St Andrew and St Patrick were duly celebrated on their feast days, no fuss was made for St George. Emlie is supposed to have told the patriotic fairy-story adventure – in which four children are helped by England's patron saint as they set off on a quest to find their parents, facing various dangers on the way – to a young Evelyn when she was suffering from measles, and later turned it into a play. By now it had been performed every Christmas for twenty-five years.

Christmas 1935

The Hutchisons came to stay with us for Christmas. Church and church parade and cocktails with the Earps, and the Rooks came in after dinner when Percy showed us his slides of the tour of *The Luck of the Navy*, my mother's play, in Canada. A terribly wet day, but mild.

I was thankful to have guests with us, and there was a dance on New Year's Eve. And so ends 1935, a year of much sadness of heart but also of deep thankfulness to God that at last Rex and I have a home of our own, and for my Rex, who has been such a dear comfort and support to me through all the trials of the past twelve months.

Wednesday, 1 January 1936

The year opens very wet and cold and with bad news: Colonel Earp has applied to return to Burscough and his request has been granted. He is due for retirement soon and his daughters are at school in Liverpool, so one can understand why he and Molly, who is in Lancashire, want to remain up north; but it is sad news for us, especially for me to lose Molly, such a good friend.

We hear that Colonel Mapleson will be taking over as CO, and from the Egans, who know him and his wife, that Mrs Mapleson

is always in 'delicate health'. They are now living in the Langham
Hotel in London and we hear that Mrs Mapleson will not be well
enough to take up her duties as wife of the CO here, at any rate not
for some time, so it seems it will devolve to me again.

*During a weekend visit to friends Billy and Hilda Grellier in Netley
Barracks, the party hear on the news that King George V is seriously ill
with cardiac trouble. By the time Evelyn and Rex are home, his condition
has worsened.*

Monday, 20 January 1936
Tonight this message came over the radio: 'The King's life is drawing peacefully to its close.' Wept bitterly.

Tuesday, 21 January 1936
King George V passed away at 11.55 a.m. We feel we have lost not
only a beloved monarch but a friend. Edward VIII is our new King.

PART TWO

A short and inglorious reign

January–December 1936

Monday, 27 January 1936

During the last days huge crowds have been forming to file past the coffin of our late beloved King, lying in state in Westminster Hall, and today Rex and I went to pay our last respects.

We joined a long, long queue stretching from Westminster Hall all along the Embankment, past the Houses of Parliament, and had a long wait before at last we entered this beautiful and imposing hall, and with the silent crowd filed past the dais on which the coffin stood, draped in velvet and with the Crown of England reposing upon it. It was guarded by the motionless figures of four tall Gentlemen-at-Arms and guards with reversed rifles, their heads bent in their full busbies between the tall candlesticks, and not a sound was heard except the occasional stifled sob as his people bade a last farewell to a much-loved monarch.

The funeral is to be tomorrow, 28 January, and the Hutchisons have booked seats for us all on the roof of a house in Edgware Road so that we can see the funeral procession. We shall stay the night in town.

Tuesday, 28 January 1936

Up early and joined the Hutchisons on Edgware Road at 5 a.m. as all roads are blocked to traffic while the vast crowds assemble all along the route of the procession.

The house on whose roof we have seats is derelict, but we shall have a fine view from up here as it is not very high. Seats have been provided and we are well wrapped up and have brought rugs. The hours pass quickly, enlivened by the ever-growing crowds below us, incidents in the packed throng and the soldiers lining the street.

We are served coffee downstairs and afterwards I find I have to pay a visit to the loo before returning to our seats on the roof. On enquiring I am told the only loo is in the deserted house next door and I am shown how to get there.

Having climbed up three floors I find the lavatory, and having accomplished my purpose I go to leave the small (and not very savoury) closet when to my horror the rickety handle of the door falls off on the outside and I find myself trapped!

What to do? Shouting is no use, and as I slipped away unnoticed no one knows where I am. The hour of the procession passing is fast approaching. Rex and the Hutchisons will be on the roof of the house next door and it is just possible that in the excitement of the moment I shall not be missed. My only hope is that someone may have the same urge as myself. After an agonised interlude I hear voices and steps ascending the stairs, and after calling out, the handle is retrieved and I am released by the mother of a small son, very irate because her offspring has had the urge to retire just as the procession is entering the far end of Edgware Road. He is an unprepossessing little urchin, but oh, I could have embraced him!

I rush back to the roof just as the solemn strains of the 'Dead March' can be heard, and give a reassuring smile to Rex, who

having noticed my absence was getting anxious. Then, drawn by
Bluejackets walking in perfect unison, the coffin approaches and
passes beneath us, followed by our new King, Edward, flanked by
his brothers, Gloucester and Kent.

   He looked ghastly!

Closed carriages followed, carrying the widowed Queen Mary
and other members of the Royal Family and the many foreign roy-
alties and visitors. Passing between the silent mourning crowds the
cortege moved slowly towards Paddington Station where the Royal
Train waited to bear our late monarch to his last resting place at
Frogmore. A sad, solemn and most moving occasion.

   Later we hear that the Star of India, one of the great diamonds,
fell out of the Imperial Crown as they were passing across the
Palace Yard. Some say this is a bad omen . . .

Thursday, 6 February 1936

Our new CO, Colonel Mapleson, came to lunch today. He is a tall
man with a somewhat ineffectual manner. He apologised profusely
for the absence of Mrs Mapleson, who is still unwell. They will not
be taking up their new quarter on the other side of the depot for
some time and she will be living at the Langham Hotel.

   As we hear from the Egans that she is a chronic invalid, it
doesn't seem as if we shall have much joy with her as 'Colonel's
Lady', but in the meantime the guild is going well and everyone
will rally around to help it remain so. Colonel Mapleson thanks me
for taking on Mrs Mapleson's duties.

Saturday, 8 February 1936

Party in the mess to say farewell to the Earps, who are off to
Burscough. They will be sadly missed.

Sunday, 23 February 1936

Michael brought Ina over to stay with us. They have a grace and favour apartment in Windsor Castle and are full of stories about our new King Edward.

I happened to remark something about the King, whereupon Ina – who is so loyal she always stands up for 'God save the King', even if heard in the distance – said to our amazement, 'Your king – not mine!'

It seems that the behaviour of our new monarch has shocked and disgusted the citizens of Royal Windsor. The way he had all the clocks his father kept fast altered almost before the breath was out of his body; the rowdy parties in the Jerusalem Chamber; the presence at his side (and even seen at the window of St James's Palace on the occasion of the proclamation of his accession) of an American woman, a Mrs Wallis Simpson, the once-divorced wife of Ernest Simpson, an Englishman.

We all know the predilection of Edward, as Prince of Wales, for married women. Mrs Dudley Ward has been his constant companion for years and there have been many others – Lady Furness, another American, amongst them – but they have always been in the background of his life. Now it seems things are very different and since the summer of 1935 this Wallis Simpson has been a dominant figure in his life and is assuming an importance, the Egans say, that is causing consternation to all around him – the King now surrounding himself only with those who are her friends.

His staff are complaining of his unpunctuality and utter lack of consideration, and although the general public, so far, have no inkling of what is going on, the Egans are at the hub of things at Windsor and know what they are talking about.

Wednesday, 18 March 1936

Beautiful day. Went with Rex to Aldershot for him to pay his official call on the Duke and Duchess of Gloucester (to sign the visitors' book) and afterwards had tea at the Officers' Club. This brought memories of my mother, who used to love to come here with us when she stayed with us in Farnborough. If only she was here now!

The news that Captain and Mrs Hughes of the South Wales Borderers – who were with us in Hong Kong – are coming to Bramley is very welcome. They will have a quarter near ours, and the Temple-Morrises [also newly returned from the Far East] will be in what used to be the colonel's quarter next door.

Tuesday, 24 March 1936

Heard on the radio that the *Queen Mary* was launched today.

Sunday, 24 May 1936

My birthday! Had cards and presents from the family and friends. Church and a birthday party, and in the evening Daddy showed us his slides of Peggy's wedding.

The Egans came to lunch. More rumours about the King and Mrs Simpson. The Egans say she is official hostess now at Fort Belvedere [Edward's home – a country house in Windsor Great Park – since 1929], where Edward spends much of his time.

Monday, 15 June 1936

Aunts Elsie and Alice coming to stay tomorrow. Rex and I are turning out of our bedroom and he will sleep at the mess and I in our single spare room. Daddy and Eva are coming on Wednesday and we are all going to the Aldershot Tattoo.

Aunt Alice in her later years

Wednesday, 17 June 1936

A glorious day! The garden at its best. Daddy and Eva came over
to lunch, which was a little strained as Eva, for some reason, would
voice her strong feelings against the Army as a career, asserting in
a piercing voice that nothing would induce her to allow Hugh to
enter the Army. As she was being entertained by an Army officer,

Aunt Elsie when she was active in the Girl Guides

this was rather tactless, to say the least, and I wondered – as Daddy's great love had been the Army and he fought in the Boer War – what <u>his</u> feelings must be; but as usual he said nothing. Even Eva's final dictum, 'I am always right!' brought no visible reaction, though it was too much for dear Elsie, and her spontaneous ejaculation of, 'How awful!' was, I am sure, echoed in all our hearts!

Thank goodness the break-up of the party after lunch broke the tension. After tea Daddy took snaps of us in the garden, then supper and over to the tattoo.

This was marvellous, performed in a beautiful natural setting with the woods as background, in the light of the setting sun. The South Wales Borderers depicted the action against the Zulus at Rourke's Drift with great realism, and as the searchlight went on, the pipers came out of the darkening wood and into the arena with their kilts swaying to the music. A lovely end to a most thrilling evening.

Thursday, 18 June 1936

Another glorious June day. Uncle Alec came over to lunch and took Alice home to Storrington. She has so enjoyed her visit. Elsie is staying on. Alas, it seems from what dear Elsie says that the idea of putting my two dear aunts together in one bedroom was not such a good one. Elsie says Alice's snores are terrific and kept her awake. However, we are moving back now and she has the spare room, so all is well.

Tuesday, 23 June 1936

Dear Elsie left today. Took her into Reading. The weather has broken with violent thunderstorms.

Sunday, 28 June 1936

The Hutchisons to lunch and Hilda [Grellier] to stay. The weather has improved. Tennis is in full swing, swimming in the pool and fishing picnics as well as preparations for the fête on 9 July, a big affair which involves the combined efforts of everyone in the camp. Jane is coming to stay with us for it.

It is a real joy to have a home to entertain one's friends and family in, the first time in our married lives. The lovely garden, now at its best, the amenities of tennis, etc. and the fact that we all combine to entertain one another's friends and that everyone likes ours so much make life very pleasant. And I do thank God that I am able to see something of my own family at last.

Rex and I have decided to spend his leave in Guernsey. The Farquharson-Roberts have given us an address to write to in Icart. La Pastorelle is run by a Mr and Mrs Petersen. He is a Dane who was valet to an old gentleman who left the house to them; she is an excellent cook. And the bathing in Saints Bay below is, they say, marvellous. We are much looking forward to our first visit to the Channel Islands.

Thursday, 2 July 1936

Went to Highgate Cemetery to my mother's grave and took her flowers. The new marble scroll looks very nice and the grave is well kept, but – oh! – the miss in my heart for her is just as great and always will be. Met Jane for lunch and went to see *Lady Precious Stream*.

Lady Precious Stream *was a popular Chinese story adapted and written in English by Hsiung Shih-I (1902–1991), who with it became the first Chinese person to write and direct a West End play. It had such a successful run in London that it later transferred to Broadway, and was adapted for television in 1950.*

Thursday, 9 July 1936

A fine day, thank God, for the garden fête! Jane came to stay yesterday and we all helped with the various stalls and entertainments. As usual, Rex's skill at the coconut shy and the shooting gallery resulted in our having plenty of coconuts and prizes! The vicar of Bramley Church, having offered to judge the most beautiful baby, found himself the most unpopular male in the district as the mothers of the losers registered their anger with such dark glances that the poor man retired early from the scene!

However, everyone said it was a great success and a good sum made for charity.

Mrs Mapleson made her first appearance as the CO's lady and gave the prizes away. She is a short, rather plump little woman with an affected air, and kept on apologising to everyone for her inability – through delicate health – at not being able to take up her duties, and was fulsome in her thanks to me.

The wives to whom she spoke tell me that they assured her not to worry as, 'Mrs Shillington is running the Ladies' Guild wonderfully.' I am not sure this was a good thing to say!

Tuesday, 14 July 1936

Up to town and did some shopping at Simpson's in Piccadilly to find the shop assistants fuming at the conduct of Mrs Simpson, the inamorata of our King. She had been shopping in the store and they told me how she delights in flaunting her dominion over him, and that he waits outside in the car while she takes her time over her purchases, which she does in a very high-handed way. As one of them said to me, 'She's just a cheap American – and he is <u>our King</u>!' He seems to be losing all sense of decorum and the obligations of his position as our monarch.

The Egans tell of the deep resentment at this behaviour at one of the royal garden parties at Buckingham Palace this season, which have taken the place of the 'drawing rooms' at which debutantes were presented in former days. His attitude to these duties was one of complete boredom, and when a shower of rain interrupted the proceedings as the debutantes were passing before him, he immediately gave the order that the next lot of presentations were to be taken as 'made' and disappeared into the palace, and although the shower soon passed, the King was not seen again. Unfortunately, during the presentations a photographer caught the utter boredom on the royal countenance as the curtseying debs passed before him, and so a picture of his discourtesy was broadcast to the world.

Thursday, 23 July 1936

Lunch at Roehampton with the Egans and Brigadier and Mrs Hoare for corps tennis week, always a very happy event for seeing a lot of pals. It was dull and rain threatening but the tennis went on.

More tales of Edward and Mrs Simpson. She has now a town house in Mayfair at which Edward is a constant visitor, his car and chauffeur standing outside. The Egans tell us that one of Queen Mary's favourite parts of the gardens at Windsor Castle in the spring is a lovely walk which is then a mass of white cherry blossom and daffodils. Mrs Simpson also has a penchant for blossom with which to fill her rooms, and when the blossom was at its best at Windsor, King Edward ordered that it should all be cut and sent to decorate Mrs Simpson's flat – this in spite of the fact he knows his mother loves it so well. Such rude and unbecoming behaviour to a beloved and revered royal lady has naturally infuriated the staff and the inhabitants of Windsor, the Egans included. And it shows the influence this woman has over him.

After a few days with Aunt Alice in Storrington, Evelyn, Rex and Chaser spend a blissful holiday at the guest house they have been recommended in Guernsey. La Pastorelle in Icart lives up to its reputation and they enjoy walking, sightseeing and swimming before returning to Bramley in mid-September.

Thursday, 24 September 1936

Opening of the Ladies' Guild. Mrs Mapleson is still in London so I am carrying on in her place. After the success of our social evening and the charades, we have decided to present one of Mabel Constanduros's plays. It is ideal for our purpose, very funny and with wonderful parts for all the sergeant and police wives, who are most enthusiastic to do it. They have asked me to produce it and I have accepted. It should be fun!

Mabel Constanduros was an actress, screenwriter and writer of novels and short stories, known primarily for her comedy radio creation The Buggins Family, *of which 250 episodes were broadcast by the BBC between 1928 and 1948.*

Tuesday, 13 October 1936

My mother's birthday. Went up to Highgate Cemetery with Percy Hutchison to her grave. He brought a lovely sheaf of chrysanthemums and it was a comfort to have someone who was so fond of my mother with me as Rex was unable to come. A golden day, as golden as my memories of her, my darling!

Thursday, 15 October 1936

The Egans over to lunch, full of stories of Edward and Mrs Simpson. Although nothing appears in our press, he is now completely cut off from his friends and advisors and the rift grows deeper every day. He spends much of his time at Fort Belvedere, where she is now the acknowledged hostess. There she receives the guests and apologises to his friends of long standing for his not being present to welcome them, making no pretence that she is not completely in control of the King of England. Ernest Simpson has dropped completely out of the picture and there are rumours of a divorce being arranged.

Friday, 16 October 1936

Went to stay with Jane at Shortlands in Kent. A very hot day, like summer. It is lovely to be with Jane in this very nice hotel, and we have so much to talk about.

Evelyn's mother, Emlie Clifford, top,
and above, a young Evelyn with her father, Harold

She and Pat have now parted definitely. She told me how she has met David Lyle again, and how sad she was to find from friends that he is now in a home for inebriates and the divorced. Jane says he is sadly changed from the handsome young man she knew, his marriage had broken up because of his drinking, but he told Jane he still loved her and that she was the only woman he had ever really cared for and that if they had been able to marry his life would have been completely different.

Jane feels that by coming into his life as she did and falling in love with him, she, as a married woman, was wrong, and that she is in a way responsible for the ruin he has made of his life. She told me that she feels she should do all she can to help him. He assures her that with her help he could overcome his alcoholism. How will it all end!

Wednesday, 4 November 1936

Had lunch with Jem Hamilton and his mother at her hotel. Jem is full of King Edward's behaviour while at Balmoral this year.

It is the custom for the two youngest officers of whichever regiment mounts guard at the castle – the Gordon Highlanders this year – to be received by the monarch, who entertains them to drinks. Two young captains (one of them Hunter-Blair, whom we know) arrived at the appointed time, only to be kept waiting until a very embarrassed equerry came to inform them that their host, Edward the King, was not able to see them. They were given a sherry and dismissed.

This unprecedented and appalling behaviour on the part of the monarch was because Wallis Simpson was arriving to stay at Balmoral, and worse still, he abandoned an engagement to open the Aberdeen Infirmary and openly appeared waiting on the platform to welcome her – an insult for which Scotland will never forgive him!

Monday, 23 November 1936

We dined with Mrs Cole, a very charming person and an aunt of
Neville Chamberlain, who has a beautiful house near the Duke of
Wellington. She had as guests two couples from the Diplomatic
Corps. After dinner the talk turned to the present situation
between the King and Mrs Simpson and they told us that he is
determined to marry her. Her divorce from Ernest Simpson will be
completed by the end of April next year and his intention is that she
should be beside him at the coronation and be crowned as Queen
of England! <u>We can't believe it!</u> She, a twice divorced woman with
two husbands living and who has proved herself so utterly unsuit-
able for the high office of royal consort! They say that if he can't
get his own way in the matter he threatens to abdicate. All this has
been kept out of our press so far, but they say the American papers
are full of it.

Thursday, 3 December 1936

At last the news has broken that the King intends to marry Mrs
Simpson!

The nation is stunned. He must be mad to think we would
accept this woman as our queen! Pictures in the illustrated papers
show Edward and Wallis Simpson on the holiday they took on the
yacht chartered from Lady Cunard, in which it is apparent he made
no attempt to hide the fact they were lovers from the press pho-
tographers, who followed the trip with great interest. It is reported
that the King says, 'No marriage – no coronation!' and it is fixed
for 1 May.

Saturday, 5 December 1936

Mrs Simpson has left England. There were hostile demonstrations
outside her house in Mayfair, and windows broken. All hell is

let loose, with the Commonwealth, Canada, Australia and New Zealand making it very plain that <u>they</u> will never accept Mrs Simpson as queen; and the news is published that the King intends to abdicate rather than give her up! Feeling in the country seems to be that if he cares more for her than for his subjects and his country – <u>let him go!</u>

Thursday, 10 December 1936

Rehearsal of the Ladies' Guild play. Things are going very well. The casting was quite easy and everyone is happy with their parts. We can only have one rehearsal a week, but if everyone turns up we should be ready by 26 February. We have been promised complete co-operation from the depot workshops for any scenery etc. we will want (Tom Rook in command), and the wives who are playing men's parts are borrowing their husbands' trousers!

Friday, 11 December 1936

King Edward signed the Instrument of Abdication and left England for the continent from Portsmouth in a destroyer tonight. So ends the short and inglorious reign of this uncrowned monarch, and the Duke of York becomes our King, with his Duchess, Elizabeth Bowes-Lyon, daughter of the Scottish earl, as Queen. Their daughter Elizabeth is the heir to the throne. God save the King!

Tuesday, 22 December 1936

Miss Conti has raised through the Rainbow League and a matinee performance, money to endow a bed in the children's ward of St George's Hospital, and I went up for the dedication of the bed by the Bishop of London in memory of my mother.

'St George' from *Where the Rainbow Ends* – which is playing at the Victoria Palace – was there; also Miss Conti and the Egans and

Percy Hutchison. It was a very lovely and moving occasion and I know my mother would have been pleased that a child will be able to receive nursing care in a bed in her name.

Thursday, 24 December 1936
The Hutchisons came to spend Christmas with us. How I wish my mother could have been with us! Decorating the church and a cocktail party with the Rooks.

Thursday, 31 December 1936
New Year's Eve dance. And so ends the year 1936. We have so much to be thankful for, and a new King. May his reign bring us happiness!

PART THREE

A jealous woman's enmity

January–December 1937

Rex spends most of January, February and March on a senior officers' refresher course at Sheerness – which he is soon calling 'Sheer Hell' – returning only at weekends. Both he and Evelyn have been suffering from flu.

Wednesday, 27 January 1937

Up, but feeling very shaky and missing Rex very much. Chaser our Scotty and Luck our cat seem to sense this, and when after my solitary dinner I am sitting before the fire listening to the radio they come in and sit with me, Chaser by my feet on the hearth rug and Luck on my lap. I find their company a great comfort, bless them!

Luck has grown into a lovely black cat with traces of Persian and jade-green eyes. Having been brought up from a kitten with Chaser, he thinks he is a dog and always accompanies master when Rex goes to the office after breakfast, trotting along beside him.

Chaser, who is 'death on cats', does not seem to relate Luck to the feline tribe, which he looks upon as his pleasure and privilege to chase, and has adopted a very protective attitude towards Luck, whom he looks upon as his property. Woe betide any dog who dares to bark at or harass Luck! Chaser sees them off in grand style.

Tuesday, 16 February 1937

Rex and I are going to spend the weekend with Uncle Alec and
Aunt Marian at Haywards Heath. Went to look out things to pack
and discovered that my diamond engagement ring of three diamonds is missing. I always keep it in my chest of drawers and I last
wore it for the Temple-Morris cocktail party. Searched everywhere
for it. I am terribly upset.

Wednesday, 24 February 1937

The last few weeks, while Colonel Mapleson has been living in the
mess, he has taken to calling on the officers' quarters at odd times.
He always apologises profusely for his wife's absence and is loud
in his praise at the way I am undertaking her duties. He harps on
about her delicate health and how grateful she is. He usually blows
in after dinner and always requests a glass of milk. (We shall have
to step up our milk order!)

It doesn't seem – with the fatigue of moving from the Langham
Hotel to the new quarter – that Mrs Mapleson will be strong
enough for some time to take over her duties as colonel's wife.

Friday, 26 February 1937

Terrible storm, gales and snowstorms. Rex back from Sheerness. Guild
play performed – a great success. The acting first class, and the direction, though I say it myself, quite professional! Everyone concerned to
be congratulated. I sat next to Mrs Mapleson and she said she was very
thankful that the difficulties left by Mrs Tanner have been smoothed
out and that we are now a very happy and united company.

*After failing to find her diamond ring and deciding that it has almost cer-
tainly been stolen, Evelyn notices that a garnet necklace and an antique ring
have also gone missing.*

Tuesday, 30 March 1937

The police have been called in by the insurance company and have questioned everyone who has access to our bungalow. This means Charlotte, our maid; nice Mrs Ham, who cleans for us; Knott, our gardener who services the boiler; and the window cleaners. All very distressing.

The police tell us that there have been thefts at the NAAFI, and that Charlotte's brother-in-law, Kathleen's husband, is the suspect. Charlotte, in floods of tears, refuses to answer any questions and her behaviour gives rise to the suspicion she may be involved.

The jewellers in the district have all been notified and given a description of it, and oh, how I pray I may recover it!

Thursday, 1 April 1937

Nella came to stay. At last a warm spring day and we went primrosing in the depot.

Thursday, 15 April 1937

A notice has been circulated to all in the camp that, owing to the wild cats in the depot, poison has been put down. As most of us have pet dogs we exercise there and cats 'walk on their wild own' this has naturally caused great consternation; but when Colonel Mapleson was approached and told how horrified everyone was, he just said, 'Yes, you must be, but there is nothing I can do about it!' (As CO he must have been responsible for the order!) Feeling very worried.

Monday, 19 April 1937

Letter from the insurance company regarding my ring to say police enquiries have satisfied them that it was theft and so sent off claim. I have hoped to the last that it would be found – no money could ever compensate for its loss.

Wednesday, 21 April 1937

Our beloved black cat, Luck, is missing. He never stays out at night but always joins Rex, Chaser and me after dinner. Please God he has not fallen victim to the poison in the depot!

Saturday, 24 April 1937

Still searching frantically for Luck. So unhappy about him. Every night we go out and call his name, but no reply.

Wednesday, 12 May 1937

Coronation of King George VI. A lovely day. We listened in to the coronation ceremony with the Rooks and attended local celebrations. Mrs Mapleson being still in London, I gave away the prizes. Dance in the evening.

Thursday, 27 May 1937

Lovely day. Corps golf tournament at Fleet. Our hearts are still heavy for Luck, and we both still call to him at night. We can't bear to think what he may have suffered.

Sunday, 6 June 1937

Glorious weather. Tennis in full swing. The Maplesons have now moved officially into their quarter and Mrs Mapleson will take over the guild in September, glory be!

Friday, 25 June 1937

The Maplesons' cocktail party.

The Colonel recruited the officers' wives to help as Mrs Mapleson is so frail and it's all too much for her. They have a lot of antique furniture, due – say the Egans, who knew them well – to Mrs Mapleson's father having an antiques shop in Dover. She is very well off and Colonel Mapleson dances attendance on her.

They have given a series of dinner parties, to which all of us have been invited in turn, and we are convulsed to discover that the same patter is handed out each time.

It goes like this:

Colonel to Mrs Mapleson: 'Darling, have you done as I said and insured your mink coat?'

Mrs Mapleson: 'Oh, yes!'

Colonel: 'And the Persian lamb?'

Mrs Mapleson: 'Oh yes, dear, all my furs. (To audience) They are very valuable, you know!'

Then, as their visitors leave, escorted by Colonel Mapleson, he catches sight of a bottle of port (very cobwebby) on the hall table and exclaims, 'How careless of me! I quite forgot to take the port (stating very special vintage) into the dining room when I brought it up from the cellar.'

Naturally, we are immensely amused at this extraordinary performance, so obviously intended to impress us, but what folly to repeat it so closely! Surely they must know that in a camp like Bramley we are bound to compare notes.

Saturday, 17 July 1937

Atmosphere in the depot is very strained. Colonel Mapleson behaving in a very odd way, snooping round and muttering darkly about 'scandal talked at officers' wives' coffee parties' and even hinting of action of libel to be taken by his solicitors, Lewis and Lewis. All this is a storm in a teacup and if they behave in such a ridiculous manner, only to be expected. Mrs Mapleson is not at all popular with the sergeants' wives (except Mrs Mead, who has become her shadow) or the police wives, and May Rook and I are doing our best to smooth things over.

Wednesday, 21 July 1937

The atmosphere is now so tense we don't like to meet for coffee as we know our most innocent gatherings are considered centres for deepest scandal. But although one may laugh, this has cast a cloud over what was once such a happy community, and the prospects for the guild, when we reassemble in the autumn, are hardly rosy.

Rex and I will be glad to get away from it all when his leave commences and we sail to Guernsey. I pray things may have settled by the time we return.

Friday, 13 August 1937

We have had two weeks of perfect weather here in Guernsey and find it even lovelier than ever. The beautiful bays, the lovely cliffs and walks, the bathing in Saints Bay and all our old haunts are our idea of a perfect holiday.

The amazing thing is that it is never overcrowded. Even on August Bank Holiday we are able to have a day in Joannet Bay with the whole beautiful cove all to ourselves. The Petersens say it is because so many people can't face the sea crossing, which can be very bad. We came via Weymouth and it was very choppy. Luckily we (and Chaser) are good sailors, and we had booked a cabin, but anyone who suffers from seasickness could be daunted.

Chaser, who detests sea-bathing, has been induced to sail on a lilo. At first he was very suspicious and I had to be with him, but gradually his confidence increased till now he floats happily by himself, looking with scorn at lesser dogs with wet paws and coats, who bark insults at him as a cissy!

Thursday, 2 September 1937

Nice to be home again, the garden looking lovely, ablaze with autumn flowers. But I return to disturbing news. Far from the trouble blowing over, Nan (Temple-Morris) and May tell me that Mrs Mead, secretary of the Ladies' Guild, has been busy in my absence running me down to Mrs Mapleson. It appears they are now thick as thieves and Nan and May warn me to expect trouble.

Luckily I have had the support of the guild and we have had much happiness and success in all our ventures. But the very success we have had seems to have roused the jealousy of Mrs Mapleson (although she was not prepared to fulfil her job as CO's wife) and now that it has devolved upon her she seems determined to make things difficult for me. If only they knew how <u>thankful</u> I am to hand over the presidency to Mrs Mapleson! To have to play the part of CO's wife when only a major's wife is no easy task, and I had enough of that in Hong Kong.

I can see May and Nan are worried at the way things are going and feel we may expect <u>squalls</u>.

Thursday, 7 October 1937

None of us have had any notification from Mrs Mapleson of the opening of the Ladies' Guild, which should be this month, so I rang her up. She was extremely cool and informed me, to my amazement, that she is consulting Mrs Body, General Body's wife at Aldershot, as to how the guild should be run! Also that Colonel Mapleson is 'drawing up new rules'. This is, of course, a direct snub to me, and the idea of consulting Mrs Body will be to give her the impression I have made a mess of running the guild in Mrs Mapleson's absence.

Wednesday, 13 October 1937

My darling mother's birthday. Rex and I went to Highgate Cemetery to put flowers on her grave. <u>How</u> I miss her still!

No news whatever about the guild. Everyone amazed at the

extraordinary decision to reorganise it. The Egans rang up to ask if they can come to lunch next Thursday and as I am plainly not to be consulted about the opening of the guild we have said we shall be delighted to see them.

Tuesday, 19 October 1937

A notice sent round to say that the opening meeting of the guild will be on Thursday. Rang Mrs Mapleson to tell her that as the Egans were coming to lunch I might be a little later than 2.30 p.m. She was <u>very</u> chilly!

Thursday, 21 October 1937

Michael rang to say Ina had a cold and that they would not be able to come, so I was able to go to the guild on time after all.

To my utter surprise Mrs Mapleson seized the occasion to launch a bitter attack on me before the whole guild, accusing me of having done nothing to help her and refusing to allow me to say a word in my defence. The guild sat in stunned silence while she made this terrible scene – she seemed quite demented – and having in vain tried to speak for myself, I just got up and said, 'I think I had better leave,' and <u>very quietly</u> left the room, terribly shaken.

I felt quite sick at the venomous animosity of her attack, but felt I must try and speak to her alone, so waited till she came out – but all in vain. I tried to appeal to her, reminding her it was she who had kept me in the dark about the guild and told me she was making new rules with Mrs Body's help, but it was quite hopeless. She had worked herself into such a state of fury that even my appeal – pointing out to her the very serious consequences of a quarrel between the two senior ladies in the camp – was to no avail and she swept away leaving me terribly shaken, utterly unable to think what I had done to deserve such a terrible ordeal. Nan,

May and my other friends came to sympathise and to tell me of the reaction of the other wives, who were all stunned by this attack on me – they all know I have done all I could for the guild.

Sunday, 24 October 1937

The Egans asked us to lunch at Windsor. They are appalled at Mrs Mapleson's behaviour and say it all stems from jealousy. Ina rang up Mrs Body, who is a great pal of hers, and was amazed to hear that Mrs Mapleson had never approached her about the Ladies' Guild. What a liar Mrs Mapleson is! So that was just to upset me. She is a BITCH!

Monday, 25 October 1937

Feeling awful. I am getting a lot of sympathy from the wives and my friends, but, consoling as this is, the effect in the camp is very bad and shouldn't be allowed to go on. Rex is trying to see Colonel Mapleson to ask him to arrange that Mrs Mapleson and myself should meet and discuss this in a calm manner to try and bring an end to this unfortunate episode which could have such disastrous consequences, not just for the running of the guild but for the whole atmosphere in the camp. I hear the wives are in a turmoil, split into two sections: those who support me and the few behind Mrs Mapleson – headed of course by Mrs Mead – who think they see which way their bread is buttered.

To be the bone of contention is the last thing I want and I am willing to overlook Mrs Mapleson's rudeness to me in the interest of peace.

Wednesday, 27 October 1937

Rex managed to get a word with Colonel Mapleson and he says he will speak to Mrs Mapleson and see Rex tomorrow.

Thursday, 28 October 1937

Colonel Mapleson saw Rex to tell him Mrs Mapleson refuses to see me unless I apologise to her. This is outrageous! After all, she insulted me before the entire guild and refused to hear me say one word in my defence. Anything she had to say to me should have been said in private and, as Rex says, I cannot apologise for an offence I did not commit. He has asked again that Mrs Mapleson should see me. Colonel left the office early to avoid speaking to Rex.

Friday, 29 October 1937

Colonel too ill to come to office today. Think he is afraid to face Rex and also afraid of Mrs Mapleson! The Egans say he is completely under her thumb – she holds the purse strings.

Tuesday, 2 November 1937

Colonel Mapleson still away from the office, to the amazement of his officers. He is not popular. An indecisive, nervy man, preoccupied with his health, does not make a good CO. He is obviously avoiding Rex.

Friday, 5 November 1937

Guy Fawkes Day. Fireworks and a sherry party in the mess afterwards. The Maplesons not there. The Colonel had a collapse last night and is going to see a specialist.

Saturday, 6 November 1937

Colonel Mapleson made a remarkable recovery and was able to play host at the mess to General Hill, our DOS (Director Ordnance Services) and his wife and other senior visiting officers down for the shoot at the depot. Mrs Hawker was able to see Mrs Hill (who hasn't seen Rex and me since we were at Aldershot before we went to Hong Kong) and was able to tell her about the trouble over the Ladies' Guild.

Sunday, 7 November 1937

At church today General and Mrs Hill made a point of talking to me, and all the others rallied round to support me at this very trying and upsetting time. I do thank them from the bottom of my heart.

Monday, 8 November 1937

Colonel ill in quarter again! Rallied on Wednesday when he went to Southsea. He is obviously avoiding Rex, thus creating a really serious situation of what could have been surely settled between Mrs Mapleson and myself. Is it possible that the Maplesons wish to get rid of us? This would be grossly unfair to Rex, who has had no part in this sorry affair and who is doing a good job here.

Thursday, 11 November 1937

Went with the Temple-Morrises to Southampton to say goodbye to the Grelliers and Tom and May Rook, who sail east on the *Lancashire*, the Grelliers to India and the Rooks to Egypt. Lunch on board, and who should I meet but Moncrieff Paul with his wife! He was one of my 'beaux' of the 1914 war days, and used to take me dancing after the war. He was one of the few young men left alive and was a lieutenant in the Middlesex Regiment and in the retreat from Mons. He was a very eligible bachelor and I liked him, but that was all, and I haven't seen him since I married in 1925. He introduced me to his wife, the widow of a naval officer, and he met Rex for the first time. They are off to India.

Sunday, 14 November 1937

Knowing the Maplesons would be there I dreaded the thought of facing them, but Colonel and Mrs Man had come over to have lunch with us and I entered the church with a cohort of supporters, which probably did nothing to increase my popularity with the Maplesons but which was most encouraging to me. The Mans were so very kind and are so indignant over the way I have been treated. They were our colonel and his wife at Hilsea Barracks when we were first married and we are so lucky to have them as our friends.

After lunch Colonel Man and I walked round the garden and he tried to cheer me up. I can stand anything but Rex being drawn into this affair.

Tuesday, 23 November 1937

Colonel Mapleson called Rex into his office and told him he has consulted Brigadier Hoare, who says that the matter must be cleared up at once. Rex again asked that Mrs Mapleson see me, but she refuses to do so unless I apologise to her – for what, I wonder! As Rex refuses to allow this as she is in the wrong, we are at a deadlock. What will be the outcome of all this?

Monday, 29 November 1937

Confirmation in church and to the mess afterwards. Mrs Mapleson cut me dead before everyone! Rex has written to her and asked her to see me so that I can state my case, as a last hope that some way may be found to clear up this awful state of affairs, as Brigadier Hoare has decreed. He, of course, has never heard my side of the case. It looks more and more as if the Maplesons want to force the issue.

Wednesday, 1 December 1937

Over to have lunch with the Egans. They take a very serious view of the way things are going and say that my side must be represented to General Hill, our DOS. Michael rang up and arranged to take me over to see him tomorrow.

Thursday, 2 December 1937

Mrs Hill (who has always been so kind to me) was so sweet and gave me coffee before I went in to see General Hill. He listened to all I had to say and was most sympathetic. He sees it as a serious situation, as it is impossible to have two senior ladies not on speaking terms in a camp like Bramley. Mrs Mapleson's cutting me dead shows her attitude to me, and her dictum that I must apologise to her before she will even speak to me makes any hope of a settlement impossible.

He does not like Mapleson or his way of making expensive presents to senior officers in order to curry favour by putting them in his debt, and I could feel his very real sympathy for me in this dilemma. I shall always remember how kind he and Mrs Hill were to me and it is a great comfort that, through the Egans, I know that the head of the corps knows the true state of affairs.

The Egans, with whom I had lunch, say that it is quite evident that Mrs Mapleson's jealousy of me is at the root of the matter and that the only way to get rid of me is to have Rex removed from Bramley. The camp is in a turmoil and feelings running high, and this, of course, can't be allowed to continue.

Monday, 6 December 1937

Colonel Mapleson informed Rex today that he is to be sent to Burscough, an ordnance depot in Lancashire! He says this is Brigadier Hoare's decision and that Rex will be taking over a fourth class officer's job under Colonel Earp. This is so bitterly unfair, and everyone is furious.

Rex has requested to see Brigadier Hoare. It is so wrong that my side of the matter has never been represented. Colonel Mapleson cannot refuse his request.

Wednesday, 8 December 1937

Brigadier Hoare has granted Rex's request but stipulated that Colonel Mapleson had to be present. Rex saw him and he was very sympathetic, but he says in a case like this it is the <u>junior officer who must go</u> – there is no alternative.

So we are to lose our much-loved home, the first one we have ever had, and to be turned out because of a jealous woman's enmity! We both feel very bitter over this as neither of us has done anything to deserve it.

Thursday, 9 December 1937

Mrs Mapleson lost no time in venting her spite. Today I was informed that a Mrs Mansfield would be coming to see our quarter as Major Mansfield will be taking over Rex's job in January.

It nearly broke my heart to have to show her round this home where we have been so happy. Mrs Mansfield was very distant and treated me as if I had done something disgraceful – she has obviously been primed by Mrs Mapleson and wants to be on the right side of the Colonel's wife. Feeling utterly miserable.

Sunday, 12 December 1937

Colonel and Mrs Man came to lunch. They are so very kind and sympathetic and don't think Brigadier Hoare handled the matter as well as he might have done. They could see how terribly upset I am as I feel, though it was no fault of mine, that I am the reason Rex is being moved to Burscough. It is ironic that of all the ordnance depots I have always hoped he would not be sent to, it is Burscough that should be our fate. Set in miles of flat cabbage fields outside Southport, it is isolated and hideous and I know from Molly Earp that the quarter which – when Colonel Earp retires – will eventually be ours is huge, ugly and riddled with cockroaches. Ugh!

Dear Colonel Man, who has always been very fond of me and Rex, took me for a walk round the garden and I poured out my heart to him. He said how deeply he felt for us both in this very sad and unjust situation, but that the bitterness would fade in time. I answered with some heat that I didn't feel I would ever get over it, and he listened with patience and deep understanding; then he said to me something, which, although I rejected it then, has profoundly influenced all my life. 'Of course you are feeling bitter, dear Eve, but always remember that it isn't what happens to you that matters, but what you let it do to you.'

Thank God for these wonderful true and loving friends!

Evelyn's comment that Colonel Man's advice continued to influence her has clearly been added to the diary at a later date.

Tuesday, 21 December 1937

Today a most unexpected and exciting thing happened!

My mother's play *Where the Rainbow Ends* is being performed in the West End, and this morning Miss Italia Conti, who produces it, rang up to tell us that 'a most important person' is coming to see it. As it is a private visit, Miss Conti could tell us no more, but if Rex and I could get to the matinee, 'Do come!'

Well, Rex couldn't get away but I took the eldest son of the Temple-Morrises with me and arrived at the Holborn Empire to find everyone in a state of great excitement. Queen Elizabeth was bringing Princess Elizabeth to see the play (Princess Margaret had a cold)!

I was introduced to Lady Asquith (not Margot, the wife of the politician), who was to receive the Queen, and she told me how it is the custom when royalty visit a theatre for them to enquire if the author is in the house, and if so, he or she will be presented. In this case, as my mother is no longer alive, she said it might well be that the Queen could ask to see me.

This put me in a whirl. As I listened she told me the correct proceedings for such an occasion – to keep my gloves on, to curtsey, and to call the Queen 'Your Majesty' the first time and 'Ma'am' afterwards – and I went down to my seat in the stalls before the royal party arrived feeling very excited – and scared!

I watched the royal box as the play unfolded to the packed house of excited children and grown-ups, and saw how thrilled Princess Elizabeth was as the adventures of the children took them through the perils of the Dragon's Wood, to their imprisonment in the Dragon's Castle, until at last they meet their parents again in the Land Where the Rainbow Ends and where all lost loved ones are found.

Before the last act a note was handed to me. On it was scribbled that I was to be in the front of the foyer to meet the Queen! With trembling knees I made my way there. Everything had been cleared for the royal party. With the royal car drawn up outside, a considerable crowd had gathered.

As I stood in the long passage the Queen and Princess Elizabeth approached, and there was Queen Elizabeth before me! Then Lady Asquith made the presentation and the Queen held out her hand to me with that smile which has captured all our hearts. No one who meets our beloved Queen could feel shy in her presence! I executed a tolerable curtsey and she said how very much she had enjoyed the beautiful play, and turning to her daughter added, 'And you did too, didn't you, Elizabeth?' Elizabeth, who was dressed in a green velvet coat and hat, said, 'Oh yes! It was thrilling!' Then Her Majesty asked me about my mother, and I told her how the play was written for me when I was about the same age as Her Royal Highness the Princess Elizabeth is now. The Queen, after saying how lovely Roger Quilter's music was and giving me that gracious farewell smile of dismissal, then passed on out to the royal car to the cheers of her loving subjects.

It was truly a wonderful and never to-be-forgotten experience and my one regret was that Rex was not there to share it with me; but nothing in this world could have come at a more appropriate time to dispel the misery of these last weeks and raise my diminished morale.

Thursday, 23 December 1937

We are at Windsor spending Christmas with Ina and Michael Egan. They are so delighted at my presentation to the Queen, and Michael has sent off a notice of it to be put in the corps gazette – as they say, 'It will make the Maplesons furious!'

Saturday, 25 December 1937

Christmas Day! Service in St George's Chapel. How good God is to let us be here to spend this sad Christmas with these dear, true and tried friends of ours.

PART FOUR

An uneasy peace

January 1938–August 1939

Saturday, 1 January 1938

What will this year bring us, starting as it does with a terrible sense of injustice at Rex being moved from Bramley and the loss of our much-loved home? We leave on 12 January.

Wednesday, 5 January 1938

The feeling in the camp is explosive! Colonel, very tight-lipped, avoiding Rex in a shame-faced manner. What a feeble, spiritless creature he is! The officers are making no effort to hide the contempt they feel for the way he has let us be sacrificed to his wife's jealousy and wrecked the peace of the whole camp.

I have been left in no doubt of the feelings of all those with whom I worked so happily; but as the last thing I wish is to bring more misery to the camp, I am avoiding the Army and police wives as I don't want anyone to be victimised for my sake.

Nan tells me that the Ladies' Guild is now quite dead and only Mrs Mapleson, Mrs Mead and her supporters now attend.

Saturday, 8 January 1938

We are having a lot of loving support from our pals here, and a succession of farewell parties to try and soften the bitterness of our departure. We are deeply touched and it has helped a lot. The Maplesons are virtually sent to Coventry and we both feel – for the sake of all at Bramley – the sooner the Shillingtons are away the better!

Monday, 10 January 1938

This morning I received a letter and a charming present from the police wives of the camp. The letter says:

> *Dear Mrs Shillington,*
>
> *We are very sorry indeed to hear you are about to leave Bramley, and wish to express our gratitude for all you have done for us. May we, as a token of remembrance, send this small gift with our sincerest thanks for your many kindnesses, at the same time hoping you will be happy in your new station.*
>
> *Always yours very sincerely,*
>
> *Mrs Dodd, Brown, Dwyer, Evans, Hall, Handley, Lowe and Samphire*

I am deeply touched by this kind gesture on their part, which I feel is one on behalf of all the wives of the Ladies' Guild. The police wives do not come under the Army, but even so, it is courageous of them to send me this token of appreciation as they know what happens to those who fall foul of the Maplesons!

I answer, thanking them warmly for their present – a charming, green zip writing pad, writing paper and envelopes, which I shall always treasure – and their good wishes.

Tuesday, 11 January 1938

Newbery's came today to move our furniture into storage. Heaven knows when we shall have a home of our own again, and when the Earps go I don't look forward to taking over that large, beetle-ridden quarter in Burscough.

We are spending the night with the Temple-Morrises and leave Bramley tomorrow morning.

The one bright spot is that dear Molly is at Burscough and we know we will get a warm welcome from them both. They have booked a room in a hotel for us in Southport.

We say goodbye to Knott, our gardener, who remains with the quarter. He is very glum indeed and has taken a dislike to Mrs Mansfield who has been so hostile in her attitude to me and has ordered him to root up all the lovely beds of wallflowers he and I had planted in graduated colours, because she 'hates' wallflowers. The heaps of wilting bodies are the last thing I see as we leave our dearly loved home.

Wednesday, 12 January 1938

We left Bramley this morning on the 11.15 train. The departure we had so dreaded was turned into a triumphal one by all our friends. No one turned up at the office: instead we had a 'guard of honour' of cars which took us in procession from the mess to the station to see us off. Hear Mapleson is livid!

We arrived at Southport in the evening. The Earps had booked us into the Gordon Hotel and I don't like it at all. I know I'm not in the mood to like anything at the moment, but it smells of cabbage, has an awful brass double bed in the depressing bedroom and a notice on the sitting-room door saying, 'Talk cheerfully!'

Thursday, 13 January 1938

Rise determined to get out of this dump as soon as possible. Awfully stuffy and full of old ladies who certainly don't 'talk cheerfully'! Rex goes off in an official car to Burscough and I set forth with Chaser on my quest. Remembering what my mother always told me: 'Start at the top – you can always come down!' I make for the promenade where the best hotels are. Southport is very attractive. Lovely gardens line the front, with ornamental pools and tennis courts. The sea is so far out one can scarcely see it. I pick out a very fine hotel, the Clifton, and boldly ask to see the manageress. She is charming and shows me a delightful large room on the second floor overlooking the front and I settle for it for 'service terms' (providing Rex approves) which will cost no more than the dreadful Gordon. Rex comes to see it after lunch and is delighted. We move in tomorrow.

Friday, 14 January 1938

Our move to the Clifton is completed after Rex gets back in the evening. As there is a dance at Burscough at which we are to be introduced to the officers and their wives we have no time to unpack properly and have a rush to dress before we make our first appearance to the hotel inmates with Rex in full glory of mess kit and me in pale blue taffeta evening gown! The food is excellent and a band plays during dinner. Colonel Earp calls for us and we spend a very cheery evening at the dance. Feeling less depressed!

Friday, 21 January 1938

We like this hotel and Southport very much. Lord Street has excellent shops and is bordered by charming gardens where a band plays and one can have coffee sitting out in the open (not at this time of year, of course) giving it a continental atmosphere. Have had some lovely walks with Chaser along the magnificent sands whose dunes he has explored in hopes of Bramley bunnies, while I have made some acquaintances in the hotel. One, a Miss Marjorie Smith, I like very much. There are a lot of wealthy widows here as residents; there is a bridge hostess and a beautiful Palm Court where one can dance to an excellent band, and the food is first class.

Evelyn and Chaser on Lord Street in Southport

I have been with Molly Earp to the Ladies' Guild. It is grand to be with Molly again. She is good fun and an excellent colonel's lady, and I like the officers' wives I have met.

Burscough lives up to its reputation – utterly hideous, set in miles of flat country, mostly cabbage fields. The Earps' quarter, which we would have to occupy when Colonel Earp retires, is appalling! It is huge, depressing and devastated with beetles. Ugh! I had enough of those in Hong Kong. Molly assures me that Colonel Earp is doing all he can to get the sappers to condemn it. It is a disgrace as a quarter and not worth the cost of redecorating. Please God he is successful!

Over to Blackpool to see Percy Hutchison in a farce called *Is Your Honeymoon Really Necessary?* Very funny. Percy tells me that Nella is going to have a baby. He is delighted, bless him! He is giving us an introduction to Mr Colman, cousin of Ronald Colman [1891–1958, British leading man of the 30s and 40s who would win an Oscar for the 1947 film *A Double Life*], who is manager of the Theatre Royal here, and he very kindly gave us two complimentary seats for the 'special Friday nights'. They get plays from London and if Rex doesn't want to come I shall invite Miss Smith, with whom I am becoming very good friends. She had polio when she was in her teens and is lame, but is very attractive, very slight, and has dark hair and green eyes and a great sense of humour.

Very sad news of Michael from Ina – he has cancer of the throat. I feel terribly upset. They are my oldest friends since I was a child down at Chatham Barracks when Daddy was there with his regiment, the Scottish Rifles, and Michael gave me away at my wedding. They have taken a flat in Worthing.

Thursday, 28 April 1938

Have developed a sore throat and an earache after taking Chaser out on the dunes in a tearing wind. I was in agony for over a week and my excellent doctor feared a mastoid. He managed to lance the abscess and I spent two days dancing round the room having to put peroxide in the ear. Marjorie Smith was an angel, getting me books from the library and taking Chaser for 'walkies'. At last the doctor gave me the OK when he found I could hear his watch ticking, but he says that my tonsils are infected and is sending me to Millbank Military Hospital to see a specialist. Don't fancy the thought of an operation!

Wednesday, 1 June 1938

Had an appointment with Sir John Hare at Millbank. Colonel Earp had to go to the hospital himself so I went with him and Molly. I liked Sir John very much, but he strongly advises an operation. I had my tonsils 'guillotined' – as then was the fashion – when I was quite small, and Sir John says they grow again and give trouble. He wants to arrange for me to go into his private nursing home in Victoria as soon as possible. Feeling distinctly blue I rejoin the Earps, and as we sit waiting for the lift to take us down we hear the most ghastly noise, like someone being murdered. Along comes a wheeled stretcher – accompanied by a nurse – on which is lying a young man who is yelling, 'My God! My God!' I ask in trembling voice what the matter is, to which the orderly replies, 'Oh, he's just had a tonsil operation.' My legs feel like jelly and I collapse on the bench. Molly roars with laughter. 'If you could only see your face!' she tells me later. I don't see the joke.

Back to Southport and Rex. He has filled our room with flowers.

We have decided if the dates fix, and as Rex gets leave from 9 July, we will go to our beloved Guernsey where we can book a room at La Pastorelle. This gives me something to look forward to. I need some support, as when they hear that I am contemplating a tonsil operation all the old girls gather round with frightful tales of the dreadful consequences of friends of theirs who ventured to have their tonsils removed at my age. The lurid accounts are regaled with sadistic detail. Rex is furious, calling them names which I will not put in this diary!

Saturday, 25 June 1938

I went into Sir John's very nice nursing home and had the operation at 5.30 p.m. They were awfully kind and gave me one shot in the arm to stop the bleeding (the worst bugbear of the operation until recently) and then another one when I was on the trolley by my bed. I knew no more till I came round back in bed, with Rex by my side. Couldn't talk as throat too sore, but had a special night nurse who gave me dissolved aspirin which helped.

Sunday, 3 July 1938

Have had a very good time here. Able to go out latterly and see my friends. Everyone is astonished how quickly I have got over the operation. Mrs Hamilton, the Mans, the Harkers, Percy Hutchison and dear Ina come to visit me. She is very anxious about poor Michael. They have seen General and Mrs Watts who she says are both furious at the way the Maplesons have treated us. Rex rings up every day and we are counting the hours till we meet.

Saturday, 9 July 1938

We caught the boat train for Weymouth and arrived in Guernsey to a great welcome from the Petersens. The next three weeks and four days spent enjoying a typical relaxing Guernsey holiday – swimming in the cove, walking round the wonderful coastal roads, lying on the rocks in the evening sunshine, picnics in lovely Joannet Bay where we have the sands all to ourselves, visits to the market and St Peter Port. The only fly in the ointment being that it's the hayfever season and poor old Rex, as usual, gets it badly, though he never makes much of it, bless him.

Thursday, 4 August 1938

Returned from Guernsey – Daddy met us – and on to Storrington to stay with Aunt Alice and to see Elsie and Harry. Then Rex had to return to Burscough and I stayed with Jane at Shortlands. A joy to be with her again. Jane is very fond of David Lyle, who has come into her life again, and I fear that the fact his (Swiss) wife has divorced him and that his daughter and family have deserted him because of his drinking (he is in a home) will touch Jane's soft heart, and that the romance of their long-ago love affair in Srinagar – when Jane said goodbye to him because of Pat – still lingers. I just wonder what it will all lead to . . .

I go on to stay with Nan Temple-Morris back at Bramley and hear all the gossip! It seems that Bramley is not a happy place these days. That unhappy time has left an aftermath and a breach between the Maplesons and the rest of the camp that nothing will heal. The Ladies' Guild – now run by Mrs Mapleson and Mrs Mead – is dead. What a tragedy it is. We were all so happy once!

I saw Knott (it was pathetic to see his pleasure in meeting me again) and he is very gloomy. He hates the Mansfields, and our once-lovely garden looks a wreck. Although it was marvellous to see our pals again, and they gave me a great welcome, I was not sorry to leave Bramley – too many bad memories.

Tuesday, 30 August 1938

Returned to Southport. Wonderful to see Rex again! The situation in Europe is giving cause for anxiety. Whenever one turns on the radio one hears Hitler's high hysterical voice ranting and raving . . . What will be the outcome of it all? If war came it would mean Rex leaving immediately with the BEF. I just dare not think of it.

This is the first time Evelyn mentions the prospect of war. She knows the price of being married to an Army man, and along with most people of her generation has lost loved ones in the First World War – in which Rex himself participated as a young soldier. Though a most capable woman, she dislikes being apart from her husband at the best of times and the prospect of a long-term separation in the future is beginning to make her anxious.

She has good reason to fear: in March, Germany had annexed Austria, meeting little opposition from other European powers. Encouraged by this, Hitler began to press claims on the Sudetenland, a region of Czechoslovakia with a large German population. Evelyn's entries for the rest of 1938 are dominated by the political situation.

Wednesday, 7 September 1938

Rex is promoted to Lt-Colonel (acting colonel) and takes over from Colonel Earp on his retirement. The Earps have taken a flat in Liverpool, so not too far away. Congratulations from many friends and the family, and a celebration dinner.

Monday, 12 September 1938

Trouble in Czechoslovakia. Hitler demands full government for the Sudeten Germans; war might break out at any moment. Terribly anxious and unhappy. Rex away all day.

Wednesday, 14 September 1938

Chamberlain has flown out to see Hitler to try and preserve peace. Glorious day, but I am so anxious and miserable. Took Chaser out on the sand dunes as couldn't stand the hotel. Most of the residents (except Marjorie) seem to shut their minds to the possible outcome should Chamberlain fail in his mission; they just sit smugly drinking coffee or playing bridge and don't even trouble to switch on to hear the news.

On the sands I met a friend of Mr Colman. He takes people up for 'flips' in a rather obsolete aeroplane and asks me if I would care to go up. I say yes – anything would be a relief today! – and although I have never flown in my life and in my full senses nothing would have induced me to trust myself to that antique plane, before I know it Chaser and I (Chaser somewhat reluctantly) have climbed into the interior and we are off over Southport! Certainly one gets a fine view of the place – the swimming pool looks like a large blue plate. We land safely and I thank him, though Chaser is glad to be on terra firma again. Not his kind of place – no trees!

Thursday, 15 September 1938

Chamberlain back from Germany with a 'peace plan' – hope this is true and the horrors of war averted. Tension eased in Europe. Rex not so sure about it all.

Saturday, 17 September 1938

Rumours that Chamberlain has agreed with Hitler that Czechoslovakia should accept partition are causing great concern.

Wednesday, 21 September 1938

News that Czechoslovakia has been forced to accept the 'peace plan', under irresistible pressure. The Labour Party and many Conservatives are opposed to 'appeasement' and the selling of Czechoslovakia to Hitler's demands. Will this mean the end of them? Rex away till late, looking very grim.

Saturday, 1 October 1938

Chamberlain goes to Hitler again. He returns from Munich with a signed paper declaring he has brought 'peace with honour'. Many

people think not. I just don't know what to think. All I know is
that for the time being Rex will not have to go to war. It doesn't
bear thinking about. Hitler has a huge, well-equipped army and
we have disarmed to nothing! Duff Cooper has resigned his post as
First Lord of the Admiralty in protest at this policy of appeasement,
and many others believe that now Hitler will only demand more
and more – Churchill is one of them.

*On 29 and 30 September, representatives of France, Italy, Britain and
Germany met in Munich to discuss the Sudetenland issue. Neither the
Czechs nor their allies the Russians were consulted. Chamberlain accepted
Hitler's offer of peace in Europe in return for the Sudetenland. Like Evelyn,
much of the British public was torn between relief that war had been averted
and fear that Hitler's aggressive behaviour would only continue.*

*In October German troops occupied the Sudetenland and the Czech
government resigned. On the night of 9 November German nationalists
looted and burned Jewish businesses and synagogues across the German
Reich and thousands of Jewish men were arrested and incarcerated in con-
centration camps, which became known as Kristallnacht, or the Night of
Broken Glass. The next day further restrictions were placed on the lives of
Jews living in the Reich.*

Undated, December 1938

I haven't written in my diary for some time. This is a time of
extreme tension. I hardly see Rex as he works all hours round the
clock and I spend a lot of time at the swimming pool and with
Marjorie Smith, trying not to think what will happen if this uneasy
peace is shattered.

Rex has heard officially that the sappers have condemned the
quarter at Burscough and he wants to get our furniture up from
Reading and for us to have a home of our own, however uncertain

the future. We are lucky in finding a charming small house built
by an architect on the site of an old house. It has two double bedrooms, one single, a nice dining room and a sitting room with
French windows opening onto the garden. The architect, who has
built a similar one for himself next door, has been unable to sell
it because of the situation and is glad to rent it to Rex with a service clause (i.e. that the tenancy can be terminated should Rex be
mobilised). And so we move in to 28 Park Avenue in December.
I manage to engage a good maid, an Irish Roman Catholic, who
cooks well.

Sunday, 1 January 1939

The situation in Europe overshadows all else. We love our new
home, and Rex has got a gardener from the Burscough quarter
who has plans to make the garden gay with dahlias, but our hearts
are heavy and we live under the dread of parting.

Preparations are being made in the case of war. Rex's responsibil-
ities as Chief Ordnance Officer (COO), Deputy Assistant Director
of Ordnance Services (DADOS) Lancashire area increase – he
works all hours and I hardly see him. Colonel Earp has been
recalled from retirement to help him. We receive a *First Handbook on
ARP* (air raid precautions) which is distributed to all householders.
Reading it sends a shiver down my back!

Wednesday, 15 March 1939

Hitler makes a triumphant entry into Prague and occupies
Czechoslovakia, thus breaking the Munich Agreement.

Thursday, 16 March 1939

Worldwide horror and disgust, especially USA. Chamberlain con-
demns Hitler for tearing up the peace treaty and warns him that

our patience is exhausted. The non-appeasement group say, 'I told you so!'

Where is it going to stop?

Sunday, 19 March 1939

Hitler back in Berlin to a tremendous welcome. Nothing will stop him now! He is now in control of the enormous Skoda Armament Works. Great Britain guarantees Poland against aggression.

Friday, 7 April 1939

Danzig situation ticklish. The Japs behaving abominably in Tientsin, debagging our officers and cutting the Army families from milk, etc. Life very depressing. Rex working late at night and on Sundays.

I have joined the ARP classes on gas warfare. There seems to be no real defence. We are a strange motley group, including several old ladies very determined to 'do their bit' as they did in the First World War, instructed by a large naval petty officer. When we first assemble the petty officer surveys us with a somewhat jaundiced look and proceeds to instruct us in the horrors that await us if the Germans choose to use gas. Warming to his task, he describes (with what I feel is unnecessary gusto) the awful effects of mustard gas.

'It's 'orrible!' he tells us. 'There's nothing can stop it. If it were to drop on this 'ere 'ouse, it'd eat its way darn through the roof, then darn to the upper floors, and right darn to the cellar!'

He pauses for breath. One of the dear old ladies rises and holds up her hand. 'May I ask you a question, please?' He assents. 'Do you think,' she says in a trembling tone, 'that it would damage my nice dining-room table?' The petty officer, speechless, gives up!

I have made friends with a charming woman, Norah Fitton, who has a delightful house near here. Her husband is a businessman and she has one daughter.

Since then we have progressed to learning to deal with incendiary bombs. This entails equipment of a long-handled shovel and a dustbin lid. Having us all assembled, our mentor proceeds to demonstrate exactly what we should do should one of these bombs fall on the roof. The dear old ladies gather round, listening intently.

'Well,' he says, grasping the shovel, 'this is what you do.' He drops to his knees and seizes the dustbin lid. 'Now you climb onto the roof and proceed on your belly – so! – and you pushes the bomb with your shovel, like this 'ere, and get it on to the dustbin lid which you carries in your left 'and – so!'

The picture of our frail old ladies climbing onto a rooftop, crawling 'on their bellies' and scooping up incendiary bombs is too much for Norah and me and we try to conceal our untimely mirth with a fit of coughing, which gets a <u>very</u> dirty look from our petty officer.

In all the horrors of this time I do thank God I have a companion in Norah Fitton, whose sense of humour matches my own, though as we walk back together to our respective homes we are both sick at heart as we contemplate what it will mean if these instructions ever have to be put into action.

Thursday, 27 April 1939
The King orders conscription!

The Military Training Act required all single British men aged twenty and twenty-one to undertake six months' military training.

Thursday, 20 July 1939
Rex receives a special order from General Sir Henry Jackson [Commander in Chief to Western Command] saying how gratified he has been with the efforts made by the Royal Ordnance Corps

and how particularly impressed with the work of the Ordnance Depot Burscough, and how he fully appreciates the loyalty and spirit in which this work has been carried out.

Thursday, 24 August 1939

Ribbentrop and Molotov have signed a non-aggression pact between Germany and Soviet Russia in Berlin.

Emergency Powers bill passed by the House of Commons. I have now finished my ARP course and obtain a certificate for having passed through a poison gas chamber, equipped with gas mask!

PART FIVE

The bottom has fallen out of my world

September 1939–July 1940

Friday, 1 September 1939

The evacuation of children and mothers with babies commences, and I report for duty. The idea is to get them out of the danger zones in case of bombing. They arrive from Liverpool, and it is our job to see that these poor little bewildered kids, with labels round their necks, are duly delivered to the billets that have been selected for them. We hear that some of the mothers and children are being held at the station as it has been found that it is necessary to delouse them before they can be taken to the house awaiting them! Couldn't have believed people could be in such a terrible state in this day and age! At about 4 o'clock I go outside for a breath of fresh air and see a newsboy with a poster saying, 'The King Orders Mobilisation'.

So the thing I have dreaded has happened . . .

I ask to be let off from further duty and go home and get Rex's uniform trunks out of the garage. At about 6 p.m. Rex walks in with his sergeant. He has to report to Aldershot immediately. He instructs the sergeant to call for him at 6.30 a.m. and we pack till about 1 a.m. then try to snatch a few hours' sleep before the car calls for Rex and he leaves. The bottom has fallen out of my world.

Germany has invaded Poland without a declaration of war. Britain notifies the German government that unless German troops are withdrawn from Poland, Britain and France will fulfil their treaty obligation. This ultimatum to expire at 11 a.m. on 3 September.

Sunday, 3 September 1939

Watching the clock. At 11 a.m. Mr Chamberlain announces that we are at war with Germany.

All alone, I face what this means. May, my Irish maid, has come in to hear the announcement. She now faces me with such a look of hatred as I have never seen before and hisses, 'And I hope to God Hitler comes and conquers the lot of you.' This seems about the last straw in this frightful day!

France declares war on Germany at 5 p.m. Mr Churchill is appointed First Lord of the Admiralty.

Monday, 4 September 1939

Blackout ordered. Spent morning standing in a queue to get black cloth to line curtains. Feel stunned and I am acting like an automaton. Spend afternoon running up curtains – action seems the only thing. Rex rings me up – so wonderful to hear his voice! He sounds very grave and says Aldershot is swarming with troops. He hopes to be able to ring me before he leaves.

Marjorie Smith rings me from Harrogate and asks if I am alone. I say, 'Yes, Rex has gone,' and she says, 'I am taking a taxi and coming to you.' Thank God for this wonderful friend!

Saturday, 9 September 1939

Rex rang me up to say goodbye; he leaves with the BEF tomorrow for an unknown destination. My hearts sinks and I pray for his safety. Marjorie helping me to get the blackout curtains up. The blackout is now in force – not a street lamp is on; England plunged into darkness.

Monday, 11 September 1939

Announcement that the BEF has landed in France. God protect my darling!

Sunday, 17 September 1939

Russia invades Poland!

Monday, 18 September 1939

HMS *Courageous* aircraft carrier torpedoed and sunk.

Wednesday, 27 September 1939

After appalling bombing, Warsaw surrenders to Germany.

Monday, 2 October 1939

Report of a German raider, the *Graf Spee*, in the North Sea.

Saturday, 14 October 1939

The *Royal Oak* sunk at Scapa Flow with considerable loss of life: eight hundred officers and men.

I get spasmodic letters from Rex. He is 'somewhere in France' with GHQ and writes asking for parcels to be sent to him. We rush off to buy his requirements – torch, gumboots, toilet paper, soap, warm underclothes – and Keating's Powder [insect powder, probably for use against fleas]! My poor darling!

Marjorie and I have to pack these items in strong hessian bags, stitch them up and sew the labels on. In the meantime, Mardi Marshall, a friend of Marjorie's, and Norah Fitton organise prayer meetings – a great help. My neighbours Monsieur and Madame Tarbut from Algiers are distracted because their young son is called up. She is very highly strung and very pessimistic at our ever beating Hitler. The news of the sinking of our ships doesn't help.

Friday, 3 November 1939
President Roosevelt signs the American Neutrality bill.

Sending Rex woolly undies (from the family), soap, Horlicks, Lemco [concentrated meat extract], chloride of lime [probably to disinfect drinking water or utensils], Lifebuoy soap – and more Keating's! He is in a very primitive billet!

Wednesday, 8 November 1939
Attempt on Hitler's life – no go, worse luck! The devil looks after his own.

Wednesday, 15 November 1939
Bombs dropped on the Shetlands, first to fall on British soil.

Friday, 17 November 1939
Air raids on Liverpool and Manchester – extensive damage.

Thursday, 23 November 1939
Destroyer *Gipsy* sunk by mine; ten ships sunk yesterday. The Germans are using magnetic mines. Letters from Rex to say he hopes to get leave and be home on 10 January. Oh, to see him! I am half alive these days but now I have something to look forward to. They have had some air-raid warnings near him.

Sunday, 26 November 1939

The *Rawalpindi* sunk in the North Atlantic by the pocket battle-ship *Deutschland*. She went down with her colours flying and with her Captain Kennedy. Feeling very sad as we knew him when we sailed in the *Rawalpindi* from Shanghai. [This would have been in September 1934 when Evelyn accompanied Rex on his tour to other parts of China towards the end of his three-year Far East posting.]

Wednesday, 13 December 1939

The *Graf Spee* engaged in North Atlantic by *Exeter*, *Ajax* and *Achilles*, and chased into the River Plate.

Sunday, 17 December 1939

The *Graf Spee* scuttled outside Montevideo Harbour and her Captain, Hans Langsdorff, shoots himself.

Christmas draws near. I have no heart for it but must make an effort for Marjorie's sake; she has been so good to me. I met Mr Colman in the town and he took me to coffee. He is so like his cousin, Ronald Colman, and very kind and sympathetic. He said to me, 'Only half of you is here, isn't it?' How right he is.

The Knights have asked Marjorie and me to Christmas dinner. Everyone is so very kind to me.

Monday, 25 December 1939

Spent Christmas night with Marjorie and other friends. Felt like the skeleton at the feast but tried hard to be gay. My heart is across the Channel in France. Just living for Rex's leave.

Friday, 12 January 1940

Rex on leave for seven days. Went down to London to meet him at Victoria. Oh, what a wonderful moment that was! Back to Southport where dear Marjorie, with exquisite tact, had moved into a hotel so that we could be alone together for these few precious days.

Rex is not at all happy with the situation in France. The country is riddled with spies. He has seen the vaunted Maginot Line and doesn't think much of it. All very depressing, but not to me – heaven to be together again!

We talk things over and I tell him that I would like to give up the house and move south to be nearer him when he gets leave. It is foolish to have to take two days travelling all this way up north, and this house is no longer home to me with him away. Percy Hutchison and Nella have suggested I might go paying guest with them at Edenbridge in Kent, where they now live with their baby, John. Percy would like me to try to revise my mother's famous First World War play, *The Luck of the Navy*, for the present day. Rex agrees, sees our landlord before he returns to France, and all is arranged. I shall get busy at once.

Everyone thinks I am quite crazy to go to Kent because of the air raids, etc., but to me the main thing is I shall be nearer Rex – nothing else matters.

Move fixed for Wednesday, 28 February. They can't do it sooner and are terribly short of removal men. Weather awful, terribly cold.

Saturday, 3 February 1940

May, the Irish maid, has developed a terrible cough. She is very hostile and I shall be glad to be rid of her. She will insist on going out in this bitter weather. She is raw Irish and says she can't see why we fight Hitler – we'd be just as well off under the Germans!

Monday, 5 February 1940

Doctor Bamford, Marjorie's nice woman doctor, to see May, who is worse. She thinks she may be consumptive and says she may have to send her into hospital, advising Marjorie and me to find a hotel to go to till I leave Southport. This is easier said than done. All the big hotels, including the Clifton, have been commandeered by the Army and the inhabitants turned out at a moment's notice. Those rich pampered residents at the Clifton suddenly found themselves on the pavement, and were lucky that the manager managed to get an empty house somewhere which he hurriedly furnished so that they had a roof over their heads.

Friday, 9 February 1940

May sent to hospital. We have tried to find a hotel that will take us, with no success. Then Mr Colman comes to our rescue – he knows of a small hotel run by a Jewish couple who can give us two rooms. We jump at it!

It is a funny little hotel but they are so kind to us. It is the eve of the Jewish Sabbath and as we pass their living room we see the five-branched candlesticks burning. I have a front room and Marjorie one next to mine, the beds are comfortable and we are given a nice supper and, very tired, retire to bed, thankful to have found this haven.

Saturday, 10 February 1940

Snow and terribly cold. Went to the house to do some sorting and have developed a very sore throat.

Sunday, 11 February 1940

Throat worse. Dr Bamford came and gave me M & B [anti-bacterial drug used widely during the Second World War]. Says I have a germ. How lucky I am in this hotel where they are so kind. We have a little Jewish chambermaid from Germany. She is absolutely terrified of Hitler, who she thinks is invincible – she tells us of the appalling things she saw when the Nazis stirred up the population of her town against the Jews. Friends and neighbours of her family (her father was a doctor) were suddenly transformed into maniacs and stormed into their home with axes and destroyed the furniture, even smashing the grand piano where they had so often brought their instruments to enjoy a musical evening. Her parents had some-how managed to get her out of the country with her sister, but she despairs of ever seeing her family again.

Monday, 12 February 1940
Still in bed, feeling very cheap. Marjorie is wonderful. She takes a taxi to the house (with Chaser, whom she takes for 'walkies') and does some sorting out – there is such a lot to be done, all our per-sonal things to be packed, before the move.

Saturday, 17 February 1940
Temperature down and able to get to the house today. Feeling very wobbly but did some packing. Bitterly cold, snow thick on the ground. I am packing a 'comforts trunk' with cushions, blankets, electric lamp and kettle, saucepan, two vases, etc. as I don't know when I shall see my things again.

Monday, 19 February 1940
Sent off advance luggage to Edenbridge. We are having quite a lot of farewell parties. I am sorry to say goodbye to my good friends here, and most of all to my dear Marjorie. She has got a room in a nice hotel and please God we shall meet again when all this horror is over.

Wednesday, 28 February 1940
Because of the shortage of labour they can only do the move in two halves. Up to the house early. They say that the storage facilities are

all full up and our stuff will be put into a garage. Hope it will not be damp. Have packed all Rex's civilian stuff in newspaper and Flit [insecticide]. They came to cut off the gas and electricity. Our kind neighbours supply us with hot coffee.

Thursday, 29 February 1940

Another bitterly cold session at the house; our neighbours invite us in for coffee to give us the chance of thawing out a bit! Glory be, the move is accomplished before teatime and we get back to the hotel where I write to Rex to say 'mission accomplished'. I am off to Edenbridge tomorrow. Norah's brother is travelling with me on the same train.

Friday, 1 March 1940

Off by early train. Norah and Marjorie saw me off. Travelled first class on my warrant card with Norah's nice brother, who took me back to their flat for tea and drove me to Victoria, where I caught the train for Edenbridge. Due to the blackout we travel in pitch darkness, with only a very small dark blue light and one's fellow travellers like shadows. When we arrive at Edenbridge, I find that my portion of the train is way down at the very bottom of the platform. Chaser and I descend into Stygian darkness and I hear Percy shouting my name and see the light of a 'doused' torch. I have arrived! Deep snow everywhere. Glad to get to the warm house and a welcome from Nella, hot supper and bed.

Saturday, 2 March 1940

Have a very comfortable room and am so thankful to be here. They say we may expect air raids, but nothing for the enemy here except the main railway line bridge. Saw John, the baby. He is the image of Percy! My advance luggage is waiting for me.

Percy Hutchison's house in Edenbridge, Evelyn's home
for a few months in 1940

Monday, 4 March 1940

Letter from Rex: deep snow in France. He slipped and had a fall
and pulled two muscles – very painful. Went to Tunbridge Wells
with Percy.

Friday, 8 March 1940

Another letter from Rex. He is better, thank God. Went to
Haywards Heath and met Jane. Had lunch at a hotel. Jane has a flat
in Hove and wants me to go and stay with her. I would love to.
David is in Brighton and has a job as secretary to a golf club. The
sinking of our ships continues, and terrible air raids on our ports
and industrial centres.

Sunday, 10 March 1940

Went with the Hutchisons to lunch with friends of theirs, the Foghts; he is French, she English. They have a charming bungalow near here. She prides herself on her cooking – very good, I must say – but to me the pleasure is marred by our hostess insisting that we all troop into the kitchen and wash up <u>between</u> each course, so as not to have any dirty dishes at the end!

Monday, 11 March 1940

Letter from Rex: he hopes to get some leave early in April. This is wonderful news! Have started work on *The Luck of the Navy*, making the German spy, Mrs Peel, into a Nazi and revising it to fit this war. So thankful to have something absorbing to do. Out walking with Nella. Still very cold but the catkins are out.

Monday, 8 April 1940

Terrible news – Norway and Denmark invaded! Denmark completely subdued, Norway still fighting – the King in flight to Britain. So Hitler moves again!

Tuesday, 9 April 1940

Down to the village with Nella and Percy. Everyone shocked at this new invasion.

Wednesday, 10 April 1940

Rex's leave has been postponed. Went up to London with Percy. Rumours of a naval battle. Went to the House of Commons; big crowds waiting outside. We saw Churchill, First Lord of the Admiralty, drive in. They say our troops have landed in Norway. Where is Rex, I wonder?

Thursday, 11 April 1940

Huns established in Norway – where next? We are still losing so many ships and men to the magnetic mines. These are dark days. Letter from Rex saying his leave may be resumed, thank God.

Wednesday, 24 April 1940

Telegram from Rex to say meet him at Victoria! We met and had lunch at the hotel, then back to Edenbridge. Heaven to have him back! The next days were bliss; we went to Tunbridge Wells, Penshurst – the lovely fresh green trees and spring flowers were a balm to our souls – and to play tennis at the Foghts' (Rex and I didn't, he has no civilian clothes).

Saturday, 4 May 1940

Rex's last day of leave. Went with him and the Hutchisons to town, had lunch at the Criterion, then Rex and I sat in the park by the Serpentine – so lovely, can't believe he will be gone so soon! When shall we be together again? Rex is very disturbed at the Fifth Column in France and says the country is full of spies – they even plough the fields in a certain direction to give the enemy information about the British troops. They have had air raids on GHQ wherever they move. The Duke of Gloucester is with them. Rex says he's a nice chap.

As Rex leaves at 7 a.m. he persuades me to return to Edenbridge with the Hutchisons. Major Bennett will join him for dinner tonight and they will return to France together. Say goodbye and return with the Hutchisons. God, how miserable I am!

Friday, 10 May 1940

Germans invade Holland and Belgium. So much for another of Hitler's promises! Now what?

Percy, Evelyn, Percy's son Peter and Chaser in Penshurst, Kent, April 1940

Monday, 13 May 1940

No letter from Rex and war news very bad. Germans pushing forward; roads full of refugees. Chamberlain has resigned and Churchill is now prime minister

Tuesday, 14 May 1940

The French defences at Sedan have fallen! I wonder where Rex is. No news from him. Nella is very unsympathetic and as hard as nails. Thank God I go to Jane on Saturday! I have been working madly at making a rock garden these last few days; it helps me to bear this anxiety and tires me out so I hope to sleep.

Mr Churchill gave speech on the radio. He said, 'I have nothing to offer but blood, toil, tears and sweat!' Fierce battle raging on the Meuse. Mr Anthony Eden is Secretary of State for War.

Friday, 17 May 1940

Germans enter Brussels. No news of Rex.

Saturday, 18 May 1940

Sick with anxiety. No news of Rex since he returned to France. He told me he was near Arras. The Dutch royal family have arrived in England. The French army is breaking and the situation in Belgium is desperate.

Off to stay with Jane. She met me at the station. So wonderful to be with her! She has a charming flat. If only I could have news of Rex ...

Sunday, 19 May 1940

Jane and I up on the Downs. Great preparations to defend the coast. Monsieur Reynaud [French prime minister] gives a solemn pledge to Churchill that they will fight on to the end, whether it be 'bitter or glorious'.

Took Chaser to be stripped. As I came back, saw a poster: 'Germans in Arras'. Where can Rex be? Feeling sick with anxiety. Jane very sympathetic. She has joined the ARP and has to go on duty from 8 p.m. and isn't home till after twelve. She makes me promise to go down to the basement for shelter if we get an air raid, 'for Rex's sake'. Spend a wretched evening.

Tuesday, 21 May 1940

Terrible news of our BEF in France retreating to the coast but may be cut off by Germans. God help them! Where can Rex be? Trying hard to be brave but this stress is hard to bear. Can't eat or sleep.

Thursday, 23 May 1940

Went over to Worthing to see Aunt Elsie and Aunt Mary. Elsie opens the door and says, 'Dear child, prepare yourself for a shock!' My heart stands still! She goes on to say that Jane has rung up to say that a wire had come from Rex asking me to meet him at the Hutchisons' tonight! The relief is so enormous I feel quite queer and am reinforced with coffee and much love before I rush off to catch a train back to Brighton where Jane awaits me with my bag packed. I collect Chaser and catch the next train to Edenbridge.

Rex arrives at 8 p.m. So wonderful to see him! Can hardly believe he is safely back. GHQ got to Boulogne hoping to establish a base there, but the place was riddled with spies. Rex attended a conference and, walking back with a brother officer, saw a light flashing in a window and snipers tried to pick them off as an enemy plane flew overhead. A bomb was dropped only twelve feet from them, killing Rex's companion outright. Rex was blown through a doorway and thankfully only damaged his right shoulder. Evacuation was ordered and he only just caught the last boat by doing a sort of Tarzan trick on a rope, with his batman yelling, 'Jump, sir!' as he swung on board. He says it was heart-breaking to see our tanks, guns and equipment abandoned on the quayside.

It is marvellous to have Rex safely back again, but our hearts are heavy as we listen to the news and hear the Germans have reached Calais. What will happen to our BEF now?

Friday, 24 May 1940
My birthday! Can scarcely believe Rex is here with me. The news is terribly grave, the BEF fighting rearguard action. Rex has reported to Tidworth and he has to remain on the end of a phone. Calais is besieged.

Sunday, 26 May 1940
The lovely weather persists; 'Hitler's weather' they call it as it helps his bombers. We can hear the guns firing on the French coast – the enemy is so near now. Planes go over in droves. We wait anxiously for news of our men.

Monday, 27 May 1940
King Leopold of the Belgians has surrendered to the Germans! What would King Albert think of his son? The Belgian government, however, declare that they will fight on with the Allies. Churchill broadcasts that the plight of the BEF is desperate, cut off and fighting for the coast.

Thursday, 30 May 1940
Another lovely day.

It doesn't look as if the BEF can possibly get away now. Rex has to report to Tidworth tomorrow.

Friday, 31 May 1940
Rex off to Tidworth – I shall miss him but thank God he is safely back in England. Thank God, too, for these precious days together.

Sunday, 2 June 1940

More Hitler's weather! The Hutchisons – going over to Brighton
to see their son Peter – took me over to see Jane. We went for a
drive along the cliffs. There was a most curious sort of golden haze
over the sea, which was dotted as far as we could see with small
boats of all sorts and kinds. They surely can't be fishing. Went back
to Edenbridge with the Hutchisons. The news tonight is terrible –
what is going to happen to our men trapped on the beach at a place
called Dunkirk and being bombed all the time?

Nella Hutchison and her son John on Brighton beach

Churchill broadcast tonight, 'The situation of the British and French armies beset on all sides is desperate. We must be prepared for hard and heavy tidings, but our confidence must not be destroyed.' To my horror when I looked round both Percy and Nella were asleep! At this terrible and vital moment when so much is at stake! I never felt so much alone.

Monday, 3 June 1940

No news from Rex. Couldn't sleep last night thinking of our men, then became aware of the noise of trains rushing through the night – the railway line crosses a bridge not far from the house. Wonder what this can be.

Tuesday, 4 June 1940

Glorious news! Our boys are coming back from Dunkirk!

Every small ship and boat, private or otherwise, that could cross the Channel has been mobilised to go and rescue our men stranded on the beaches of Dunkirk. Now we know what those boats we saw were up to! The noise I heard last night was the trains from the coast bringing them back to England. Oh, thank God!

Our little maid came in in great excitement to say that all the village is out watching. I couldn't stay indoors while this was happening. The Hutchisons wouldn't come so Chaser and I went down and found a field not far from the railway bridge where we could watch the trains go by. The first were hospital trains with dark windows, filled with the wounded, then came more filled with the troops just off the beaches of Dunkirk; just as they had been rescued, battered and torn, utterly exhausted after their terrible ordeal, they still had the spirit to stand in the corridors giving the thumbs-up sign! They who had just come through Hell still came up smiling! What a lesson for us all!

I stood knee-deep in buttercups and daisies all day (except for a short break for lunch) crying with pride and joy and waving to them as the trains passed by. There was nothing else I could do as they never stopped, but at least I could stand there and give them a welcome back to the land they love and try to express as they hurtled by how immeasurably glad we are to see them safe again. Where they are going no one knows – it is enough that they are home again.

Later we hear as they crossed the bridge notes were thrown out giving the names of the lads of this district to say they were safely back. There is a most wonderful feeling everywhere. One would think this was a victory instead of a defeat – and so it is! They are back to fight again!

Tonight we have heard on the radio more of the epic story. They came back in little boats manned by civilians, retired navy and mercantile marines, every boat and crew that could be assembled. These were some of the boats Jane and I saw and that queer haze rising a few feet above the water was a sort of protection to hide them while they were assembling. And so, backed by one or two destroyers and RAF and under the ceaseless fire of the enemy, through a sea sewn with mines, they made trip after trip to bring our men safely home again.

Friday, 7 June 1940

Rex came home today. He is to go with General Ironside back to France to establish a base near Brest. He will be leaving Aldershot on 18 June. This is a terrible blow. I feel stunned. To go back now when things are so desperate. He reports at Aldershot tomorrow.

Saturday, 8 June 1940

Nella drove me and Rex over to Aldershot. A perfect June day, but I feel as if I am half alive. Driving there was not easy as every signpost and direction has been removed to make it more difficult for invaders – it certainly did for us! There were road blocks (great masses of concrete), which Rex doesn't think much of – he says the German tanks would just go round them! – and sentries posted near railway bridges. The Germans are just across the Channel now, and Britain, as twice before in her history, is on the alert.

Aldershot presented an amazing sight! Everywhere there were groups of soldiers standing or sitting in the sunshine – some without uniforms, even without shoes – the men of the BEF returned from Dunkirk. And what were they doing? Sitting dejected after the beating they had taken and the ghastly experiences they had endured on the beaches? Not on your life! They were singing – yes, singing to mouth organs or just on their own, singing in the sunshine, old songs and new songs, and the sound of it came from every side. And as we passed they would raise their arms and give the thumbs-up sign, grinning at us. This is no defeated army – not while our men have guts like this.

We had lunch in the mess and then Rex and I said goodbye. When, oh when, will I see him again? I tried to be brave – the memory of those men I had seen helped a lot – but the drive back to Edenbridge was sheer misery. God give me courage that I so badly need.

Monday, 10 June 1940

Rex rang me up to say he will be off soon. I am working like mad on making another rock garden – it really helps me not to think too much and I hope it will tire me out so I get some sleep.

Italy declares war on France and Britain.

Friday, 14 June 1940

Rex arrived unexpectedly. Wonderful to see him! He says everything is in a state of chaos. The men are scattered all over the place and have to be reassembled and re-equipped. All the guns, tanks, ammunition, etc. were abandoned in France and will have to be replaced somehow. Hitler will now try an invasion and we have so little to match the mighty strength of his victorious armies – and he knows it. But thank God for the Navy.

Germany occupies Paris.

Saturday, 15 June 1940

Another lovely day, but my heart is heavy as Rex leaves tomorrow and will cross to France any time now. The idea is to establish a Base Ordnance Depot (BOD) in Brest and to get things going as it is not yet in German hands.

This will be the third time I say goodbye to Rex. I have decided not to stay on here – I can't take Nella's cold, hard attitude and their constant quarrels, though Percy is always kind to me. Rex and I have talked it over and decided that I should go and stay with Jane if she can have me – I would sooner be with her than anyone. I shall send my trunks to Elsie who will store them in her attic.

Sunday, 16 June 1940

Another beautiful day. Has there ever been a more beautiful summer – or such a terrible one! Rex left at 8 a.m. for Aldershot; he may leave tomorrow for France. Trying to be brave but this saying goodbye is tough.

Went to church. Prayers for France. To tea with the Hutchisons to the Foghts'. George Foght, who is French, very despondent. Things are very bad in France, the Germans advancing rapidly, the British Army in disarray. Reynaud has resigned and Marshal Pétain taken over. George electrifies us by announcing that in his opinion the French will ask for a separate peace. All of us, except George, are horrified at such an idea! After dinner Rex rang up – orders to go to France have been cancelled. Thank God!

Monday, 17 June 1940

Under Marshal Pétain France has sued for peace! So George was right. We now stand alone. Hitler's plan is to invade Britain.

Tonight Churchill broadcast to the nation: 'Britain and the British Empire will fight on if necessary for years – if necessary alone – we shall never surrender!'

[It was actually the following day, 18 June, while making his 'Their finest hour' speech, that Churchill reiterated his words from his speech of 4 June, which are paraphrased above by Evelyn.]

In the midst of all this my heart is filled with thankfulness that France's surrender means Rex will not leave England – whatever befalls we shall face it together.

Went down to the village. The feeling there is we are much better on our own! No one seems dismayed. Jane rang to say she would love to have me, and Elsie to say she will store my stuff. Air raid near Edenbridge; bombs dropped. Chaser was terrified (certainly not a gun-dog!).

Rex rang up; still in Aldershot but may be moving any time to 'somewhere in England'. Busy packing up as leaving here tomorrow.

Thursday, 20 June 1940

Sent off heavy baggage to Elsie and left Edenbridge for Jane's. A wonderful welcome and so lovely to be with her again.

Saturday, 22 June 1940

France has surrendered to Germany unconditionally. It is too dreadful to think of those Huns in Paris! Thank God I am not

French. Churchill broadcast: 'Let us therefore brace ourselves to our duties, and so bear ourselves that, should the British Empire and its Commonwealth last for a thousand years, men will still say, "This was their finest hour."' [From the 18 June speech.] These are words to steel the heart!

Just as Jane and I were thinking of going to bed the sirens went off. Jane – who is in the ARP and drives an ambulance – had to leave for her post at once. She insisted on sending me (with Chaser) down to the flat's 'shelter' – really a ground-floor corridor, very dimly lit. Here I sat on the floor, surrounded by other 'shapes' (the other tenants), holding a craven and shivering Chaser, wrapped in a rug, till 4.30 a.m. Bombs dropped nearby. Jane came home worn out. There were casualties to collect and she had a grim time of it.

General de Gaulle raises the standard of Free France in London.

Sunday, 23 June 1940
Air raids as yesterday, casualties and damage. Jane out all night. Chaser and I in shelter. Soldiers posted at all roads leading to the promenade. Hear there is a local defence corps being formed of civilians – only a portion yet armed, drilling with walking sticks – just like the First World War.

Tuesday, 25 June 1940
Rex is at Madingley, Cambridge. I went over to Worthing and had a warm welcome from Elsie and Aunt Mary. They have hoisted a Union Jack at the top of the stairs and are prepared to 'repel invaders'. All my stuff is safely stowed in the attic.

The thought of Evelyn's dear old aunts ready to do their bit and fight off the enemy might seem humorous, but Worthing, like other seaside towns, was

extremely vulnerable to invasion which, after the retreat from Dunkirk, was
now not just feared but fully expected. Its pier had been sectioned in order to
make enemy landing as difficult as possible.

Thursday, 27 June 1940

Took Chaser out to the beach. A lovely morning. Strange to think
the Huns are just across the Channel. The beaches are being cleared
for defence and this afternoon it was pathetic to see the children
leaving the sand for the last time, carrying their little buckets and
spades. The bathing huts are being carried away while barbed wire
is being rolled out along the sands and the front.

As one looks out to sea one imagines the horrors that France is
suffering under the Nazis. Will it be our turn next? Churchill has
said, 'We shall fight on the beaches ... we shall never surrender.'
[4 June speech.]

Sunday, 30 June 1940

Have decided to go to Worthing as Jane has to be on duty most
nights and she finds having me here a bit of a strain; she says she
would never forgive herself or be able to face Rex if anything
happened to me. Also, Rex has written and wants me to go to
Cambridge for a weekend – marvellous!

Back to Worthing where Elsie has booked me a room in a small
hotel opposite her flat.

The Germans have occupied the Channel Islands. Our poor
lovely Guernsey! I wonder if the Petersens have escaped ...
Feeling very sad. Was out in the main street today when a plane
flew over, very low. Looked up and saw there was a swastika
on it! It was a <u>German</u> plane! Luckily for us it did not bomb or
machine gun us, but it did so at Lancing and killed a woman and
baby.

Friday, 5 July 1940

Britain has seized the French fleet at Oran. We were forced to do this to our one-time allies or Germany would have used them against us.

Saturday, 6 July 1940

Chaser and I caught the train to Victoria and taxi to Liverpool Street Station. Most unpleasant as it was pouring with rain and all the glass in the station had been blown out in air raids. Damp but full of joy we caught the train to Cambridge where Rex met us with a most imposing official car with a sort of gas-bag balloon on top. Chaser was delighted to see his master again, but not more so than yours truly.

Rex had to return to Madingley but first saw me installed in a lovely double room at the Bull Hotel, and then came back for dinner and stayed the night. Bliss!

Sunday, 7 July 1940

Heavenly to be here with Rex, but he had to go back on duty after breakfast. Took Chaser for a walk along the Backs, looking so lovely just now. Rex came to dinner and we had another walk along the river before he had to return.

PART SIX

How proud I am to be British!

July–December 1940

Having decided that she should stay in Cambridge in order to be near Rex, and after a fruitless search in the city for cheaper accommodation, Evelyn is offered 'officer's wife' terms at the Bull by its manageress, Mrs MacCloud.

Thursday, 11 July 1940

Went to King's College Chapel this morning. What memories of years ago when my mother and I came down to see Philip Bathurst and Arthur Clapham in their rooms at college! They were great fans of *Where the Rainbow Ends* and always sent my mother red roses on St George's Day. Arthur was killed in the First World War and here we are engaged in another war with Germany. As I watch workmen removing the lovely stained glass from the windows for storing away from bombing, I reflect that here we are after all these years of Christianity still slaughtering one another. I kneel and say some prayers, hearing in memory the glorious singing of the choristers in this chapel all those years ago.

Came home feeling very sad. Rex came in for a short time after dinner. So glad to hear I shall be fixed up at the hotel, he went and thanked Mrs MacCloud. I shall go back to Worthing next week to collect my baggage.

Saturday, 20 July 1940

Arrived in Cambridge about 3.30 p.m. Rex managed to meet me and saw me and Chaser installed in our new room. I shan't see much of him, of course, as he is terribly busy, but I am on the spot and shall try to get a job with the WVS. There must be something I can do!

Talk of invasion everywhere – the Local Defence Volunteers (LDV) are being trained to defend England. The task of assembling our Army and equipping them is of paramount importance with the enemy at the gate. Rex says the armaments are rolling out of the factories, which are working day and night. Rex had to go back after tea. I had a warm welcome from Mr and Mrs Graham [a couple who are living at the hotel]. They are so nice. Had a marvellous dinner and bed early as I am very tired.

Monday, 22 July 1940

Took Chaser for a walk along the towpath. Met a young woman who came up and asked me if I wanted a war job. I said yes, and she told me they are calling for volunteers to help clean rifles that have been sent from the USA for the LDV, as the Army has its hands full. There are no rifles to spare but these have been sent from America by Roosevelt. She told me to be at the Corn Exchange tomorrow morning at 9 a.m. and to bring any rags I can lay my hands on. I went back and told Mrs Graham and she says she will come too, and we asked Mrs MacCloud for some rags, which she gladly supplied.

Tuesday, 23 July 1940

Mrs Graham and I to the Corn Exchange (Chaser came too). We had been warned it would be a filthy job so put on cotton frocks and hoped for the best, carrying our bags stuffed full with rags. The Corn Exchange, a huge building, was packed with people of all sorts and all ages. The floor was littered with long wooden cases (rather like coffins), the lids removed, in which were lying the rifles. The labels read, 'United States Rifles, Model of 1917 Rock Island Arsenal', and they are packed tightly in beeswax.

At a table at the far end of the hall a sergeant sits (the only soldier the Army can spare). He explains to us that the rifles have to be cleaned. What a job! He tells us it is vital that the LDV should get these rifles as soon as possible as they are currently drilling with walking sticks!

'It is up to us to put a rifle into each man's hands for the defence of Britain.'

We listen with some misgiving. Much as we long to do this, none of us has any idea how it should be done, and I doubt if any one of us has ever handled a rifle. The sergeant tells us we are on no account to touch the bore of the rifle, which he will attend to, but that we are to remove <u>every</u> bit of wax and then bring them to him for inspection and to <u>get going as fast as we can</u>!

We are now all raring to go, and lifting the greasy rifles out of the cases we get to work with our rags, sitting on the unopened boxes. But after twenty-three years of storage, the beeswax in which lock, stock and barrel have been liberally coated has hardened to such an extent that all our efforts to wipe it off with our rags meet with little success, and we are soon covered in brown grease, our faces smeared where we have wiped the perspiration from our brows.

Dons' wives, retired dons, schoolboys on holiday, naval cadets and frail old ladies – every one of us, male and female, young and old – are faced with the problem of how to place these desperately needed rifles into the hands of Britain's defenders at the earliest possible moment.

It seems to us that the obvious instrument would be a knife, but we are strictly forbidden to use any sharp instrument (the War Office clearly feeling that to arm ignorant volunteers with such would be to compromise the ultimate purpose of the rifles). We carry on a consultation and come up with an alternative – wood – and someone rushes off and returns with bundles of firewood. With these we try to remove the worst of the grease on the exteriors, but after some abortive efforts it is thought that the answer would be something more like a spatula. We stagger home for lunch in a filthy condition (all except Chaser, who has spent a restful morning on his blanket after being firmly prevented from 'inspecting' the rifle boxes in true doggy fashion).

We ask Mrs MacCloud if she can suggest something to use as a scraper and, obliging as usual, she comes up with some pieces of flat wood. Removing our laddered stockings and with sack cloth for aprons (also provided by Mrs M), we sally forth again. The flat wood is much better for the job and becomes our most treasured implement, and sitting on the rifle boxes we set to with determination. By teatime we are very tired indeed and are glad when the shop girls and those who are employed during the day come to take over. They will work till late at night.

Rex comes to dinner and, hearing of my job, he promises to send down rags and guncotton waste to help with the preliminary cleaning.

Wednesday, 24 July 1940

Off early with Mrs Graham to the Corn Exchange. Rex's sacks of rags and guncotton waste arrive and are handed round and greatly appreciated. Work now goes on at a pace, getting the first layer of grease off the rifles. Our flat pieces of wood are a great success and others have had the same idea. There is no supervision whatever, but with so much enthusiasm and goodwill for the task in hand everything soon sorts itself out, and when Rex comes in for a moment and speaks to our sergeant he is impressed by the way we have got down to it.

Home very tired, but it's grand to have such a worthwhile task.

Friday, 26 July 1940

Off to the Corn Exchange. We now wear our oldest cotton frocks, no stockings, and sandals. We have reached the ticklish job of cleaning the lock and stock of the rifle. Everyone has now thought up some gadget to help with the task before us and one bright soul has thought of pipe-cleaners as the ideal solution (this proves such a brainwave that in a few hours there isn't a pipe-cleaner to be found in the whole of Cambridge!). There is now a sort of pattern emerging in the proceedings: we younger ones lift the heavy rifles out of their beds of beeswax and set to, scraping the grease off the outside. Someone has suggested that the grease should be saved and so jars and tins have been produced into which we scrape the revolting mess. As soon as a rifle is free of this we hand it on to the older members of our gang who, sitting on the packing cases, endeavour as best they can, with rags and pipe-cleaners, to clean the intricate insides. As soon as they are all supplied with rifles we get down to the interior cleaning job too. It is a most difficult task and seems to take an eternity when time is so short and the picture of our brave defenders, drilling with walking sticks as they await these weapons, is always vividly in our minds.

When the rifle seems to be as reasonably clean as possible one has to carry it the whole length of the hall and hand it over to the sergeant. He sits behind a large wooden table with his assistant soldier, and if the rifle passes inspection they attend to the bore and the rifle passes on to its final stage with a red band being painted on it. But if it does not pass inspection the wretched volunteer is handed it back and must make the long return down the hall of the Corn Exchange, head lowered in shame!

I am sharing a packing case with a Mrs Bateman. She is a don's wife and very nice indeed. Chaser comes too and lies on his blanket – chained to a bench, just in case!

I see very little of Rex, but it's grand to know I am near to him, and if he has a chance he runs in to dinner or after for a short time. The pressure on the RAOC is intense, they being responsible for supplying the Army with everything from a button to a gun.

Monday, 29 July 1940

Arrive at the Corn Exchange to hear we are all to be moved to a brewery yard! What has been so amazing about this whole operation is the smoothness with which it has run without any busy 'organisers'. Volunteers have been collected from anywhere, no one has told us how to go about the job (except for the basic rules), and the only supervision is that of the finished rifles by the sergeant. Our new site – lovely smell! – proves no exception. We find all the rifle cases assembled and as the weather is so good we work outside in the sunshine. We soon find that if the boxes are placed in the open, the hot sun does some of our work for us – the grease melts and is much easier to remove. It is also much more likely to transfer itself to one's skin and clothing . . .

By now we are the most extraordinary-looking gang of scallywags! All of us wear our oldest clothing, with sacking aprons tied round our waists with string or tape, no stockings, and our heads tied up with scarves.

The news is more desperate every day but we are far too intent on our job to care about anything else, and we walk through the streets of Cambridge to and from work without a thought of how we look. That is with <u>one</u> exception! This is a young woman of about thirty or so who has recently joined us. She never comes till after lunch and arrives complete with a fetching chintz apron and cotton gloves. These she proceeds to don, looking with distaste at the rest of us, greasy and dishevelled, as we sit having our lunch in the sun (most of us now bring coffee and sandwiches so as to get on with the job). She then looks round, and carefully avoiding the spot where the dirty and heavy unloading of the rifles takes place, she advances on some elderly lady who has nearly finished the lock and stock job and sweetly enquires, 'Can I help by finishing that for you?' If she is lucky she gets away with it, and while her victim is handed a new dirty rifle she sits in the shade (complexion, you know!) and daintily fiddles about with the practically completed rifle with gloved fingers (we have all found it impossible to work in gloves). Her moment of triumph is when she hands the rifle over with a sweet smile to the sergeant.

Tuesday, 30 July 1940

I am delighted to see that people are getting wise to the wiles of Glamour Puss, as we call her. Today there was almost a fight when she tried to wrestle a nearly completed rifle from a frail old lady! The latter refused to let go of it, and others followed suit.

I took the opportunity of going up to Glamour Puss and, with a sweet smile, saying that as she had no job would she care to help me unload a case of rifles (which having lain for some time in the hot sun were in a particularly nauseating state of stickiness). When she saw it she blenched, but I propelled her firmly towards it, saying I knew she would be glad to help in any way, and after a glance at the grim countenances of the others, she decided it was best to comply – and we kept her at it till she staggered off, rather the worse for wear! That should learn her!

Wednesday, 31 July 1940

After a long hot day and a hot bath, after dinner I was invited to the pictures by Air Vice-Marshal MacEwen. He is in command of the staff of the RAF being trained here. He has rooms in the college just across the street and comes into the bar of the hotel each evening. I have discovered he is 'a bit of a lad' and find he is 'a bit of a wolf' too when we are in the cinema. I soon put a stop to <u>that</u> and we remain the best of friends! He now waves to me every morning from across the street!

I have introduced him to Rex, which has been a great success and has had the usual result where 'advances' are concerned.

Friday, 9 August 1940

The lovely weather continues, and so does the bombing. Churchill warns us of the dangers of invasion. The rifles are rolling along and we feel we are doing something that may help the country. Enquiries about the ammunition get the reply, 'It will be coming along.' My God, I hope so! Glamour Puss hasn't put in an appearance again. We just carry on as usual in our brewery yard and hope for the best.

Rex's sister, Gladys, has given us an introduction to a Miss Farnsworth, a friend of theirs from Nottingham. She called to see me and is so nice. She has invited me for a picnic on the river and as – after a fortnight of intensive rifle-cleaning – we first volunteers are being given an afternoon off, she will call for me tomorrow. It will be a nice change.

Saturday, 10 August 1940

Miss Farnsworth called for me in her car and drove us to the landing stage. Here we embarked and started to paddle up the river. Chaser came too. He doesn't awfully like the water and sits rather gingerly in the stern. It is all so lovely and utterly peaceful. The water gurgles, waterfowl scuttle into the reeds, stately swans eye us disdainfully, the birds sing and cows munch in the meadows. It is hard to imagine the horror and destruction going on just across the Channel. Beloved England, may you be spared the agony of invasion!

After a long paddle Miss Farnsworth – much to my joy as my back and arms are aching – suggests we stop and go ashore for tea. Choosing a likely bank we tie up to the branch of a tree and she springs lightly onto the shore, which is rather steep. Feeling I should do likewise I rise and place one foot on slippery mud and the other on the seat of the boat. The boat – with Chaser – floats away and yours truly falls up to her armpits into the river with a resounding splash!

Chaser, thinking I am drowning, gallantly flings himself into the river and adds to the confusion by trying to scramble over me onto the bank. A large spaniel now appears and also flings himself into the water with great zest, while Miss Farnsworth, kneeling on the bank, tries to give me a helping hand, but I am so overcome at my predicament I can do nothing but just stand there, shaking with laughter!

A large man (master of the spaniel) arrives on the scene and offers to give a hand. I hitch the now frantically struggling Chaser up first and my strong rescuer hauls me out, much to my joy. The bank is high and extremely slippery and I doubt if Miss F could have done it alone. It turns out our Good Samaritan owns a bungalow not far away to which he suggests we go, I dripping wet and covered in mud, while a sopping Chaser and the spaniel (now out of the river) proceed to shake themselves violently all over the dry members of our party.

At the bungalow the wife of our kind friend is most helpful. I am divested of my dress and undergarments, which are taken into the kitchen to dry, and clad only in my light summer coat (which mercifully I brought with me), Miss Farnsworth and I return to the riverbank, determined to have our picnic, come what may.

It is beautifully warm and we enjoy it very much, but when the time comes to get underway again we find that my clothes are far too wet to wear, so we tie them in a bundle and I embark, clad only in my coat. As it is the kind which has no fastening, this leads to some nervous manoeuvring when we reach the landing stage to disembark, and fully earns its title of a 'clutch' coat.

I am soon in a hot bath, and no harm done. The news tonight is that the Germans are launching a full-scale air offensive on Britain, their bombers coming over in swarms, preparatory to invasion.

Sunday, 11 August 1940

The Battle of Britain. Terrific air fights. The Germans are having a tough fight with the RAF. Rex is over in the evening.

The Battle of Britain, which took place between July and October 1940, was the name given to the effort by the Luftwaffe to gain air superiority over the Royal Air Force in preparation for invasion. Attacks on British ships in the Channel and ports moved inland to airfields and factories.

Monday, 12 August 1940

Back cleaning rifles. We return in time for the six o'clock news in the bar of the hotel. People come in from outside, including Vice-Marshal MacEwen and the RAF boys who are training here. We hear of terrific battles being fought over Britain. Our RAF is magnificent! In their Spitfires they have destroyed sixty-two enemy aircraft today. We sit and listen to the results, almost unbelievable when the enemy is so many and we are so few.

Wednesday, 14 August 1940

Score today – seventy-three destroyed. Marvellous RAF! How proud we are of you! Vice-Marshal's son was shot down but survived and trudged to the nearest RAF station with a request for an aircraft to go up and continue the fight!

Thursday, 15 August 1940

Rex to dinner. One hundred and eighty enemy planes destroyed today! It is a miracle of courage. God, how proud I am to be British!

Friday, 16 August 1940

Air raid over Croydon, waves of bombers, not one returned. Our log today: one hundred and seventy-six! Thumbs up! Rex stayed the night. Brigadier Gale has asked Rex to go to Scottish Command.

Saturday, 17 August 1940

This evening Rex took me to a concert at Madingley Hall. It is a most lovely place and is where Edward VII stayed when he was up at Cambridge. Rex is billeted in his Royal Suite which has a ceiling decorated with the Prince of Wales's feathers, all very palatial. It is beautifully furnished and the owner resides in part of it; they are very poor. Rex has ordered all the carpets up in the part occupied by the Army, and has had all the orderlies provided with carpet slippers to save the lovely parquet floors. The concert was very good and we all had drinks afterwards in the ballroom where I met a lot of Rex's brother officers. Home by moonlight with Rex – what bliss!

Sunday, 18 August 1940

The bombing continues, one hundred and forty-four enemy planes destroyed today. The 'Bomber boys' who are in training and come into the Bull for drinks are very glum and say that the fighters are 'having all the fun'. MacEwen assures them that their day will come.

Miss Farnsworth came to tea today. She is very relieved that I came to no harm through Saturday's escapade. Rex came to dinner and stayed the night. He was much amused to survey MacEwen's morning ritual of waving to me across the road from his bedroom in the college opposite. He kept well out of sight as he says he doesn't want to spoil the romance!

Tuesday, 20 August 1940

Cleaning rifles all day as usual. Rumours that the ammunition has arrived – and about time too! We feel that with the danger of invasion so imminent it would be a good thing if we could be instructed in rifle-firing – we feel we have now such an intimate knowledge of its internals that this seems the rational sequel. We suggest this to the sergeant and he says he will make enquiries.

Thursday, 22 August 1940

Air-raid warning at breakfast this morning. They have a proper air-raid shelter here, sandbagged and on the ground floor. We heard planes but they didn't drop any bombs. We went to the shelter and carried our tea or coffee; it only lasted about one and a half hours. So off to rifle-cleaning. The Germans are stepping up their attack. London getting it badly and Dover is being bombarded by huge guns from the French coast.

Friday, 23 August 1940

Rifle-cleaning finished! We shall have done ten thousand in this area – not bad going. It has been a most rewarding job and Rex says the completed rifles will soon be in the hands of the LDV. Half a million volunteers and only a portion yet armed.

Saturday, 24 August 1940

A lovely day! What a wonderful summer this has been – and so helpful to the Germans! Rex and I walked along the Cam to Grantchester and saw the vicarage where Rupert Brooke lived. It was beautiful along the riverbank and so peaceful, and lovely to get some exercise – and wear more civilised clothes.

Rex says the War Office approval has come through for him to go to Scottish Command. I shall be sorry to leave lovely Cambridge and my friends but so thankful I can go with him.

Sunday, 25 August 1940

Went to church. Rex came to say we go to Edinburgh on Friday. We had an air raid last night. Immediately the first bomb dropped Chaser retreated under the double bed and absolutely refused to come out (this showed sound common sense as it's the safest place). I, however, had promised Rex I would go to the shelter in the event of a raid, and with great difficulty lay flat on the floor and eventually fished him out and carried him down, equipped with torch, rug and cosmetic bag (for morale). Found everyone already assembled there and the management served coffee. Three bombs dropped near us. Chaser shivered violently all the time – not showing true British spirit, in spite of being a Scot! The all-clear came as dawn broke.

Evelyn accompanies Rex to Edinburgh, where they take a room at Thompson's Hotel in Drumsheugh Gardens. Rex goes to work at HQ each day but is home every evening. Evelyn has always been willing to follow Rex, even when it has meant uprooting herself from a place where she has been happy; it is something she discussed with Emlie before following him to the Far East in 1931, and that Emlie, despite her own distress at being parted from her daughter, wholeheartedly approved of.

Always able to see the bright side, Evelyn is in awe of the beauty of the Scottish capital, though less enamoured of its weather.

As Germany shifts its target to London and centres of population in its nightly bombing raids known as the Blitz, Evelyn extols the bravery of the capital's citizens and of the King and Queen, whose palace has been bombed but who refuse to leave their people. And she continues to sing the praises of 'our marvellous RAF'.

True to form, she finds a kindred spirit in her new home. 'I like her so much,' she says of Ida Coyle, the wife of Rex's brigadier.

Friday, 13 September 1940
Hitler proclaims that all his plans are complete for invasion (he seems to forget the Royal Navy). Wonderful news: there are new gun barrages in London and the raiders driven back! We are making the Nazis pay a high price. An air-raid warning after dinner. They are sure to try and get the ships in the Firth of Forth.

Friday, 27 September 1940
Germany and Italy sign a pact with Japan – they are certainly well matched. The massive air raids continue.

This alliance, known as the Tripartite Pact, was aimed at making neutral America think twice before entering the war on the side of the Allies.

Monday, 30 September 1940
Rex off to the Orkneys on inspection. Air raid on Edinburgh, bombs dropped, and we can see the whole sky red – thought the city was going up in flames. It turns out that a bomb was dropped on a whisky distillery, and pounds worth of valuable whisky for export have been lost – they say the firemen were quite tipsy with the fumes!

Monday, 7 October 1940

Rex back from the Orkneys. Says they are the most desolate islands, no trees – Chaser wouldn't like them! Brigadier Coyle has to go on a duty tour and Mrs Coyle is going with him and they have invited me to join them. It will be a wonderful chance of seeing some of the beauties of Scotland.

Sunday, 13 October 1940

My darling mother's birthday. Set off with the Coyles on a most perfect morning. A beautiful run to the Pitlochry Hotel, where the brigadier leaves Ida Coyle and me. We have comfortable rooms and the food is excellent. How I wish my Rex could be here with me!

Monday, 14 October 1940

Ida and I go to the Pass of Killiecrankie. Had lunch there and walked back along the pass, which was ablaze with glorious autumn colouring.

Tuesday, 15 October 1940

Rainy morning. Brigadier Coyle called for us. Back via Loch Tummel and saw some superb scenery. Picnic lunch and home. Lovely to see Rex again. Have joined the Lady Provost's comfort depot with Ida. The good ladies of Edinburgh, all superb knitters, want volunteers to pack the woollens and comforts in sacks to send to the Navy, Army and Air Force. Ida and I are the 'back-room boys'. The front room is filled with beautifully knitted pullovers, socks, jumpers, etc. and these are given out to us in accordance with lists sent by the would-be recipients. Our job is to assemble them and pack them into huge sacks, sew them up and sew the destinations upon them. We have some very awkward things to pack, such as dartboards and musical instruments and endless sea-boot stockings for the Royal Navy. As our room is unheated it is a good thing we have so much physical action to keep us warm. To our joy, we are joined by Nan Impey, the wife of Major Impey of the Lincolns, who was one of my friends in Hong Kong. Ida knew her when the Lincolns were stationed in Gibraltar. She is a darling and we are very lucky to have her with us.

The next days are employed in working at the depot. Rex back in the evenings, when we sit in the lounge after dinner. Edinburgh is full of Poles – refugees, who are fighting with the Allies. Many of them come into the hotel as guests of the residents and we sit and chat and listen to the nine o'clock news and have tea. Rex looks darkly on these handsome soldiers and deplores their charming custom of hand-kissing, which he think is rather 'sloppy'. (The female portion of the lounge is secretly in favour of this gallant habit!) One cannot but be heartsick at the stories they have to tell of the horrors of the destruction of Warsaw by the saturation bombing, and many of them have lost their whole families.

Saturday, 9 November 1940

The Germans have dropped a bomb on Edinburgh Zoo! This is on a high hill above the Firth. The poor animals are terrified but the only casualty is one of the budgerigars and the glass in the monkey house. We are amused to hear Lord Haw-Haw announcing this as 'the sinking of one battleship'. Rex and I went up to see the damage. We saw one chimpanzee carefully sweeping the floor of his cage before sitting down – he had evidently sat on some broken glass, poor dear! The lions now set up a terrible din when they hear the sirens.

Friday, 15 November 1940

Terrible raid on Coventry, the cathedral in ruins and appalling casualties. Later a severe raid on Southampton. Daddy had all his windows blown out from a bomb dropped only fifty yards away and shrapnel was blown across the drawing room. Thank God they were all in the Anderson shelter in the garden. Hugh is away with Daddy's old regiment, the Scottish Rifles.

Mussolini invaded Greece on 28 October.

Early December 1940

Snow in Edinburgh. Now I know that stories of the bitter east wind here are not exaggerated! Working hard at the depot as we have to get all the comforts off to the three services before Christmas. There is no one to clear the snow from the streets, which freezes into high mounds, and Ida and I have to pick our way home with torches in the blackout. We have bought ourselves lined bootees, which are a great comfort, and wear hoods.

We are very lucky in having been elected as members of the posh Ladies' Club on Princes Street. It is very exclusive and has a long waiting list, but for officers' wives they have waived this point, and we find to our joy that the secretary is none other than Jessica Cousins, daughter of Colonel Cousins, our neighbours at Harbour View in Hong Kong. She enrols us as temporary members, which is a joy; less so when we have to leave the very warm and luxurious surroundings of the club, with its deep chintzy armchairs and shaded reading lamps. We can also have lunch there if we want to entertain guests.

One night I have a nasty accident. We have only one reading lamp in our room and as I want to mend Rex's socks I move it from its place beside the beds and plug it into the socket by the fire. There is a blinding flash and a sort of explosion and I look down to see my left arm charred and have a most peculiar feeling. I must be dead! I feel no pain whatsoever. Chaser – who has immediately taken cover under the bed – now comes out and recognises me, but that gives me no assurance that I am not a ghost as we all know animals can see spirits! I commence to walk shakily downstairs, and by the time I have reached the hall a fierce pain all the way up my arm assures me I am still a citizen of this world. I walk into the lounge and am surrounded by sympathisers, all intent on their pet remedies for burns. Someone rushes off and returns and smears my arm with some Anti-Burn and then by a miracle someone remembers that a doctor is actually in the house seeing a patient, and he is fetched.

After this incident Evelyn laments the death on 9 November of former prime minister Neville Chamberlain, reflecting that though in hindsight he is now condemned, he 'did his best to save us from the horrors of war'. But another passing affects her more deeply.

I have lost a dear friend in the death of Colonel Michael Egan CMG, CBE. He and Ina had been friends of my parents from the Chatham days, when they were woven into the pattern of my life. Their son, Frank, a sub-lieutenant in the Royal Navy (he was my first love, when I was twenty), died when his ship was sunk in the Battle of Jutland. It was dear Michael who, in the absence of my father, gave me away at my wedding in St Martin-in-the-Fields in 1925, and he will leave a gap in my life and in my heart.

Thursday, 19 December 1940
Terrible raids on the Midlands. We have bombed Berlin again. I am thinking of our Bomber Boys at the Bull – they are having their chance now!

Friday, 20 December 1940
Receive the following:

'By the King's Order – The name of Lieut-Colonel H R Shillington, Royal Ordnance Corps, was published in the London Gazette as mentioned in a Despatch for distinguished service. I am charged to record His Majesty's high appreciation.'

David Margesson, Secretary of State for War.

A nice Christmas present!

Christmas was quiet but happy, as it is so lovely to be together. We were given haggis. Chaser had mine, which he seemed to like more than I did!

PART SEVEN

A warm handshake from over the seas

January–December 1941

Wednesday, 1 January 1941

General Wavell launches attack on Bardia in North Africa, where the Italians, under Graziani, are holding Tobruk. There is a massive air blitz on Tobruk in which my cousin Alexander Clifford (Dick to his family) takes part as a war correspondent. He was the first war correspondent in this war, going to France in 1939, and met Rex at his HQ near Arras. He and his great friend Alan Moorehead are covering the desert campaign – Alex for the *Daily Mail* and Alan for the *Daily Express*. They and the other war correspondents officially are a 'unit' under the name of 'public relations'.

Australian-born Alan Moorehead (1910-1983) would later also become known as a popular author of works of history, including The White Nile *and* The Blue Nile.

Monday, 6 January 1941

Snow and very cold. Working at the depot again.

Tuesday, 28 January 1941

Rex's mother seriously ill and he rushes off to Nottingham but had to return on the following Friday for an important conference at the War Office. She died on the Monday and Rex was so thankful that he had been able to see her but to his sorrow it was impossible for him to get leave to go to her funeral.

The fighting in North Africa continues; enormous Italian losses and many prisoners. Air raids over Britain continue.

Friday, 28 February 1941

General Gale has told Rex that the War Office have requested that Rex should be sent to take over Didcot Central Ordnance Depot (COD). General Gale says he much regrets losing Rex, as he had hoped he would accompany him to North Africa, but as the move will mean promotion to brigadier he would not stand in Rex's way. Rex is as sick as mud at not being able to go with General Gale (whom he likes so much) on active service. (Needless to say, I am equally overjoyed, though I conceal this from Rex.)

This means we shall be leaving Edinburgh in six days as Rex has to report at Didcot on 10 March. More packing up and more goodbyes.

Thursday, 6 March 1941

Packed up and ready to leave tomorrow. My future is a little dicey as there is no quarter for us at Didcot, it being occupied as officers' quarters, and officially I do not exist in wartime. However, I shall go to Reading with Rex and he has written to our good friends the Mermouds, from Bramley days, asking if they can put me up at the Great Western Hotel. They have replied that unfortunately the hotel has been taken over by the Paper Board, but assure Rex that they will find me accommodation somewhere.

Friday, 7 March 1941

Left Edinburgh. Touching send-off by a posse of charming Polish officers. Handsome and romantic-looking, they kiss my hand, expressing regrets at our departure and presenting me with gifts of chocolates and bunches of violets. Rex looks on in a somewhat jaundiced way; he thinks all this hand-kissing is 'tommy rot' and perhaps it is – but it's very pleasing!

We have a comfortable journey and arrive at King's Cross where we are spending the night at the hotel. Do hope we don't come in for one of the awful raids they have been having. The hotel is deserted and the service awful – but what can you expect?

Saturday, 8 March 1941

A quiet night, thank God! Took Chaser for a 'walkie' after breakfast and saw a notice saying, 'Road blocked'. This was an understatement if ever there was one. One side of the road had been blitzed to the ground – just one great heap of rubble – while on the other side the houses had either been reduced to rubble or had their entire fronts blown out. Here one saw the extraordinary vagaries of 'blast' – in all the devastation, rows of cups and saucers hanging on dressers totally undamaged. The ARP wardens and others were at work amongst the ruins.

This brings home the horrors of what Londoners are suffering very much more than any accounts or pictures can ever do and I return to the hotel sick at heart.

We arrive in Reading at about teatime and go straight to the Great Western Hotel. The Mermouds, who are still living there, give us a great welcome and are so distressed that they cannot offer me accommodation. However, they have booked a room for me at a place called Maiden Erlegh near Reading. They explain that this is a school run by a Captain Fox, but as he specialises in foreign pupils he has been badly hit by the war and is able to offer accommodation to people like myself. They assure us that I shall be comfortable, and after dinner Rex kisses me goodbye and goes off to Didcot after putting me, my luggage and Chaser into a taxi for Maiden Erlegh.

We take a turning off the main road into a very long (and by now) dark drive, lined with rhododendron bushes, and pull up outside an imposing door in a large building. Chaser and I get out of the taxi and the driver obligingly rings the bell, operated by a chain outside, and we hear it clanging away inside. Nothing happens. Chaser inspects the doorway. The taxi driver rings again and deposits the luggage (and Chaser's basket) on the doorstep. Beginning to wonder if we have come to the right place when we hear footsteps approaching the door, which is unbolted, and two forms appear.

To my astonishment they click their heels and bow in true Teutonic style, enquiring in strong <u>German</u> accents what is my business. For one wild moment I wonder if it must be a dream – the long dark drive, the huge hall (dimly lit), the colossal staircase I can just see and the two obviously German youths confronting me . . . All too like the opening of a horror film! An impatient cough from the taxi driver, however, curbs my impulse for immediate flight and I pull myself together and give my name. One of the youths says, 'Oh, yes, Captain Fox is expecting you,' and, seizing one of my suitcases, bows me in after I have paid the driver. Chaser and I follow him up the gigantic staircase, the other youth bringing up the rear with more cases. We walk along seemingly endless corridors (dimly lit), then a door is opened and I am ushered into a large, long room in which is burning – joy of joys! – a welcoming fire.

My escorts set down the suitcases and, telling me that the housekeeper will be along to see me, bow, click and leave. I inspect my new abode. It has two beds, dressing table, chest of drawers and wardrobe of light oak, and has obviously been one of the school dormitories. There are three windows but it's too dark to see anything outside. I look out along the corridor but there doesn't seem to be another soul on this floor – or perhaps they are all asleep.

Presently there is a knock at the door and a young woman enters. She is the housekeeper and asks if there is anything I want. She is very pleasant and says coal for the fire will be brought up. I tell her I have had dinner and want nothing so much as to get to bed. She shows me the bathroom and loo next door, which is reserved for my use. Chaser's basket is now brought up, and more coal, and he retires for the night. After the minimum of preparation, I do likewise.

Sunday, 9 March 1941

Wake to a lovely morning. The view from my windows is superb! From a wide terrace below, flights of steps lead down across lawns with beds of flowering shrubs to a lake set against thick woods. The air is filled with the sound of rooks cawing in the tall trees. I can hardly wait to explore it all and after breakfast Chaser and I set forth.

Maiden Erlegh was once the estate of the famous Solly Joel [London-born Joel made his fortune in diamond mines in South Africa], and here he used to entertain the cream of Edwardian society, including King Edward VII and the beautiful ladies with whom the monarch delighted to surround himself. The Italian terrace on which we presently find ourselves was built at the cost of thousands, Solly bringing over Italian craftsmen. The gardens surrounding the house are superb and famous for the shrubs of every description, which were Solly's delight.

The house and grounds of Maiden Erlegh school, Reading,
Evelyn's home for several months in 1941 when Rex, pictured on next
page, was promoted to the rank of brigadier at RAOC Didcot

The sun is warm, the air full of the scent of early spring flowers and bushes, and – oh! – the <u>warmth</u> of this lovely spot after Edinburgh!

We return to the house. This is enormous! On the ground floor in the centre is Captain Fox's apartment, his private sitting room and his office, and here I meet Captain Fox and his wife. He is a nice-looking military type and I like him. She is very tall and thin, with dark eyes and hair and a slightly vague manner. They are both very charming to me and hope I shall be comfortable and happy at Maiden Erlegh. My meals will be served in my private sitting room, which I find is rather disappointing being a small dark room on the ground floor, facing north and looking out on a large cedar tree. A cheery fire helps to dispel the gloom. It was, they tell me, Solly Joel's office and housed his diamond safe.

(Could there be possibly one tiny weeny diamond in the floor-boards, I wonder!)

Rex's arrival brings the sunshine, as far as I am concerned. We have lunch (a rather stodgy one of stew and steamed pudding) and then explore the gardens. Rex is as delighted as I am at the beauties of these and we later venture into the wild part beyond the lake, much to Chaser's delight.

There are bunnies, or so he thinks, judging by his delighted squeals and hysterical barks – calculated to scare any rabbit within miles. The estate seems endless and it is wonderful that it is ours to explore at will. Rex meets Captain and Mrs Fox later and is able to stay the night.

The news is grim: there was a dreadful air raid on London last night and many casualties. The contrast between the beauty and peace here and the horror and devastation not so far away is always there to haunt one. Oh, this ghastly war! How long will it go on? We were indeed lucky to miss this raid by one night.

Monday, 10 March 1941

Rex off early to Didcot. Much as he would like to live out here, it is too far away – he must be on the spot. The task he has been set at Didcot depot is a formidable one. It seems that the depot and its 'goings-on' are the talk of the neighbourhood. It is an enormous ordnance depot, packed with ammunition stores for all the war fronts, and vitally important. The Army personnel are at loggerheads with the civilian workers, who come under Whitley Council, which does not help matters. I suppose it is a compliment that Rex has been chosen, but it's going to be a tough job.

I have to be prepared to see very little of him, but this, I realise, is one of the times when wives must fade out of the picture and I am so lucky to be near him. I shall find some job to do as soon as possible.

Another lovely morning. I take Chaser out and then sunbathe on the veranda and meet members of another family who are living here in a suite on the first floor. They are Mr and Mrs Chotzner. He was a puisne judge in India and is a delightful old gentleman, very frail. She is much younger and a most attractive-looking woman. They live in a flat in Brighton and are here because of the air raids and Mr Chotzner's health. He has had a very serious operation and there is a nurse in attendance. It is nice to know there are some congenial people here as I shall spend a lot of my time on my own.

The German boys who welcomed me are explained. Captain Fox used to have a lot of boys from the continent here and these two have anti-Nazi parents who asked Captain Fox to keep them here before the war commenced, otherwise they would have been forced into the Hitler Youth. Mrs Chotzner says there are quite a lot of junior boys here too.

Tuesday, 11 March 1941

Last night as I was in my little sitting room Mrs Fox came in to tell me that Captain Fox had received a 'purple warning' from the ARP (he gets advance warnings because this is a school). She asked me if I would like to go down to the air-raid shelter. We went out into the hall where a procession of tousle-haired very sleepy little boys, carrying pillows, was straggling down the stairs to the cellars below. These turned out to be enormous, like everything here! I notice that all the central heating pipes run along the ceiling down here and decide I would rather take a chance above stairs than below. Though we are on the direct route to London, Mrs Chotzner says the chances of a bomb dropping here are slight, unless the German planes unload as they sometimes do when hard-pressed by our fighters. I make an excuse to Mrs Fox, and Chaser and I go back to the sitting room. Not so very long after, the dull menacing throb throb of the enemy planes can be heard as they fly far above us towards London in wave after wave. It is a sickening and horrible sound and one prays for all those who have to face this deadly menace night after night.

Wednesday, 12 March 1941

This morning I took Chaser out for a walk on a little common nearby and he engaged in a fierce conflict with another Scottie. Why do Scotties seem to have the fixed idea they are the only specimens of their breed that should be allowed to live? The din is dreadful and the Scottie's owner and myself fling ourselves into the mortal combat and at last succeed in separating our respective 'tykes'. Very hot and flustered, we at last face one another and discover that we know one another, she being none other than Topsy Glyn-Evans, wife of an Air Force officer, who came out to be married in Hong Kong in 1932. We are delighted to see one another but the intense hatred being displayed by our respective Scotties makes conversation impossible and we can only yell at one another at a safe distance, exchange addresses, and depart in opposite directions, dragging our canines with us.

Topsy and I can never take our dogs out together, Chaser and Hamilton having sworn a deadly 'clan' blood feud, but we get together and have a lovely natter about Hong Kong, mutual friends, etc. Topsy is a paying guest in a house nearby (like me, to be near her husband), and she tells me she has a job at the WVS depot in Reading, run by Lady Northampton, and suggests I might like to do likewise. It is the assembly point for all the clothing and comforts being sent so generously from the USA for the victims of the badly blitzed areas in the district – Southampton, Portsmouth, etc.

They need more volunteers to help with the sorting, so she says she will get me enrolled.

Sunday, 16 March 1941

Topsy and Glyn came over before lunch. They think this is a lovely place. The Chotzners join us and take us to see Solly Joel's swimming bath, which adjoins the house. It is quite palatial, and on the same scale as everything else here, surrounded by galleries from which Solly and his guests (including HM King Edward VII) would sit watching the beauties displayed in their Victorian bathing dresses disporting themselves in the water below! <u>Very</u> naughty indeed! (There is no record of Queen Alexandra ever visiting Maiden Erlegh!)

Monday, 17 March 1941

Went with Topsy to the Reading depot. She introduced me to Lady Northampton and the 'top brass'. It is a huge place, once a depository, now fitted up with shelves from floor to ceiling on which every conceivable article of clothing can be found. Coats, suits, jumpers and skirts, underwear for men, women and children, stockings, socks, mackintoshes, an American article called a Mackinaw (a short heavy woollen coat with a hood), and blankets. There are crates of rubber boots, shoes, and slippers of every size. There are most beautiful layettes for expectant mothers, and a whole section of children's clothes of every kind and size. Seeing this tangible and lavish evidence of the concern from our cousins across the pond warms my heart.

The work is very hard, as I find in the weeks to follow. I catch a bus into Reading after breakfast and report at the office. The organisation is conducted so that each emergency is dealt with as quickly as possible. They receive an SOS from some town that has been badly blitzed during the night and we are immediately detailed as to what is wanted – the bombed-out victims are often only in their nightclothes. We have to assemble the items and stack them on long wooden tables that run the length of the biggest shed. This is very heavy work – so many overcoats or blankets have to be lifted down from high shelves, and rubber boots and shoes collected. It can be back-breaking, but the need is so urgent that it is not until one gets home later in the day that one realises how sore one's muscles are and how one's back is aching.

All that we collect is listed, then we load it into the vans outside which are driven off to the stricken areas by the wonderful young women drivers who do these journeys in all weathers, often through the night.

I find that Mrs Chotzner also works here along with one of her two daughters, Vivian, a beautiful blonde, wife of Captain FitzClarence, now in Africa. Lunch at Heelas, the big store in Reading, and back to the job as soon as possible.

Tuesday, 25 March 1941

Have been working at the depot now for two weeks. Find it rather a lonely job. Topsy has left for another destination as Glyn has been moved. I know no one here except Mrs Chotzner – and she rushes back to be with her ailing husband – and the top-dogs (all in WVS uniform) are very snooty. One of them, Mrs Palmer (of Huntley and Palmers), really <u>takes the biscuit!</u> They give out orders and bustle about but it is we poor 'bods' who do the heavy work! When we get our lunch break and all go to Heelas, they sit apart at a table in isolated splendour and never think of inviting poor old me to join them. It would be different, of course, if I had a home to go to, or my Rex was with me, but night after night I sit in my dark little room and eat my solitary supper (usually a stew of some sort and stodgy pud) and the only visitor I have is Mrs Fox (to say there is a purple warning). And after taking Chaser out for a 'lift-leg' (kept strictly on a lead so as not to let him succumb to the temptation of a cat hunt) it is back upstairs along the long empty corridors to my dormitory, often with the horrible sound of the German bombers throbbing overhead on their way to discharge their deadly load of death and destruction.

Perhaps if I was not so tired I wouldn't feel so blue . . .

Saturday, 5 April 1941

Rex got over to see me this evening. He is having a tough job getting the depot into working order. Morale is practically non-existent, and the troops and civilians have cooked up a sort of code whereby a certain whistle alerts the workers in the big sheds that an officer is approaching, so that by the time he appears they have resumed the work they should have been doing.

The vastness of the depot – with railway lines and trains running through it – increases the task of supervision, but Rex is implementing a system to overcome the many problems that beset him. He has about two hundred officers under him, mostly civilians, and some very fine workers, he says, and knowing Rex I am sure he will be able to inspire them (and eventually the others) to really pull together and get cracking at the real job: to win this war!

With so many problems on his plate Rex is thankful for a few hours in this lovely place, though it is seldom for long, and he can only very occasionally stay the night, sometimes on a Saturday evening till teatime Sunday. The Chotzners then invite us in for drinks before lunch, and if it is fine Rex and I walk Chaser in the woods,

Sunday, 6 April 1941

Germany and Italy declare war on Yugoslavia. War news very bad: Germans making a big 'push' and the Greek flank exposed.

Wednesday, 9 April 1941

Rex took me over to have lunch at Didcot as General Body was coming down for inspection from the War House and bringing Mrs Body with him. Rex has a most palatial quarter here in the mess, but as that is sacred territory (men only) we cannot be entertained openly there and we are smuggled up the back stairs (and have a good laugh over this!). What would have been our official quarter were it not wartime is now a B mess ('B' mess as opposed to 'A' mess and not what you think!).

After our encounter with the back stairs we inspect Rex's domain while waiting for him to join us. He has a bedroom, large sitting room and bathroom – the latter in pale pink, even down to the toilet paper (not at all like Rex!) which he tells me is the idea of the devoted ATS who tend him and put fresh flowers on his desk! (Reflect gloomily that he will be impossible to live with if this continues ...)

Rex gives us sherry and an excellent meal is served, after which we have to suffer the indignity of being smuggled out of the sacred precincts again! This is harder because the place fairly swarms with ATS, some of whom look very feminine indeed in spite of their uniforms.

Thursday, 24 April 1941

The Greeks have had to surrender part of their army after desperate fighting, and the Germans have occupied Lemnos. The Allies are withdrawing from Greece.

Sunday, 27 April 1941

Churchill spoke on the nine o'clock news. A wonderful speech, nothing glossed over. We must be prepared for worse reverses but in the end the USA will help us win the war. Very bracing!

Monday, 28 April 1941

Letter from Ida Coyle. Their house in Parkstone was bombed in that last bad raid on Bournemouth. Some young officers nearby put out the fire, but much damage was done. She and Joe went down to see it and she says no one can imagine what it means to see one's home destroyed. The only consolation is that they were not in it.

The Blitz continues. Working hard at the depot.

Tuesday, 6 May 1941

Rex receives a letter from General Farquharson-Roberts (DDOS War Office) to say that in passing Didcot depot on the train he saw that a very great improvement had been made, and one from General Body, as follows:

> *My dear Shillington*
>
> *I should like you to know how very pleased I am with the way you and your staff have dealt with the recent issue of stores for units which had to mobilise at very short notice. I appreciate that you had a very difficult task to perform, and I am grateful to you for all the work which you have done.*
>
> *K. M. Body, War Office*

Rex says they are all very bucked and that they are the grandest lot and all anxious to pull their weight.

Sunday, 11 May 1941

Terrible raid on London last night. We could hear the bombers going over, wave after wave, with that terrible menacing throb which falls like a death knell on our hearts, and when I took Chaser out for his final airing I could see, far away in the direction of London, a deep red glow of fire. Went to bed sick at heart.

This morning we hear of the terrible damage and devastation – Westminster Abbey hit and St Paul's (miraculously spared) ringed by fire. The casualties are very, very heavy, but many of the enemy were destroyed. Our boys have paid back with heavy raids on Hamburg, Berlin and Bremen, so they are not getting it all their own way.

Tuesday, 13 May 1941

Rudolf Hess, Hitler's deputy, landed by parachute in Scotland to see the Duke of Hamilton! What on earth can he be up to?

Hess did indeed land in Scotland on 10 May 1941, apparently on a peace mission, though his reasons have never been fully explained.

Friday, 23 May 1941

Terrible battles in Crete. Germans landing parachute troops and hand-to-hand fighting – British, New Zealanders and Greeks.

Saturday, 24 May 1941

My birthday. Very sad news: the Cruiser HMS *Hood* has been sunk off Iceland and the German battleship *Bismarck* has managed to evade our blockade and is now out in the Atlantic with the Royal Navy chasing her.

Thursday, 29 May 1941
Bismarck sunk by the Navy! Hoorah!

Saturday, 31 May 1941
This has been a month of ghastly raids on London, Clydeside and Merseyside, and of serious reverses for the Allies in Greece and Crete. Also of reprisals on the part of the RAF, who are giving the Germans some of their own medicine.

Interspersed with the horrors of war, never long forgotten, have been golden hours spent with Rex, snatched from his arduous task at Didcot, in the beautiful surroundings of Maiden Erlegh. We have spent hours in the sunshine on the terrace or walking in the lovely woods beside the lake. The Chotzners have entertained us and we them, and there has always been the work at the depot, which grows more intense as the heavy raids continue. It is good to have some useful and practical work to do with the war news so bad.

The food here is very poor. I have made friends with the bursar, a nice young man called Nigel Headington. He comes in to see me after dinner sometimes which helps my lonely evenings. He likes Captain Fox, who has had a grim time with the war putting an end to his chief livelihood, and it seems that Mrs Fox is little help as a headmaster's wife. She is quite unable to organise, and now with such a depleted staff has duties she is incapable of coping with – the catering is an example. Not easy with rationing, of course, but I gather poor Captain Fox has much to put up with. I see very little of her, which does not break my heart! When she comes in to warn me that a purple warning is on she is in such a state of nerves, and jumps at the slightest sound, and this is the last time one wants to be regaled with stories of the awful damage and horrors we may have to face.

Friday, 6 June 1941

Working hard at the depot. Hitler is throwing in everything he has to break our morale – and is paying a heavy price for it!

Tobruk is still held by General Wavell and the Suez Canal is still open! The campaign in Greece – though the Allies were forced to withdraw – has seriously delayed Hitler's plan for conquest in the Middle East.

Sunday, 8 June 1941

Beautiful day. Rex brought Colonel Clarke over for lunch (arranged for a better meal!). Afterwards we went for a walk in the gardens and I suggested we should show Colonel Clarke the rose garden, which is looking lovely now. As we rounded a tall bay hedge from a secluded corner, a tall figure arises wrapped in a sheet from which protrude two white skinny legs. Clutching the flapping sheet to its breast and a very battered sunhat to its head, and emitting loud 'squawks' of dismay, this horrid apparition proceeds towards the shelter of the house in a series of awkward leaping bounds, to the great amazement of Rex and Colonel Clarke, while I, convulsed with laughter, explain to them that they have not disturbed the family ghost and that it is merely Mrs Fox, the headmaster's wife, who has been taking a sun bath!

The month is living up to its title of 'flaming June'. I wish I had more time to sunbathe in the garden. The swimming bath is festooned with a marvellous wisteria, which scents the air. I have been finding out a lot more about Maiden Erlegh in the days of Solly Joel. He was a real Jewish Cockney; his parents owned a pub, the King of Prussia, within the sounds of the Bow bells. He and his brother Jack made their millions in South Africa, but they never forgot the orphans of the back streets where they had been brought up.

His Mayfair mansion and Maiden Erlegh were filled with treasures chosen with the eye of a connoisseur. He bought Maiden Erlegh early in the century and nobody, even Solly himself, could estimate what he spent on this showpiece. It had fifty bedrooms, a road frontage of nearly a mile, and stood in 750 acres. Apart from the palatial £12,000 Pompeian swimming bath, it had lakes stuffed with trout, a cricket field, a polo ground, and a palm court with classical figures and marble columns (now Captain Fox's private apartment).

Solly had a great sense of humour and one story is of his suggesting to the ladies of his house party that they might like a swim, and for which he provided them with some very fetching bathing suits. One can imagine the enjoyment of the males present when the ladies jumped innocently into the pool, only to discover that their costumes began to shrink to practically nothing! (Was this thought up especially for 'Teddy', I wonder ...)

Even now, Maiden Erlegh is a fabulous place, and an aura of departed glory hangs about it, relic as it is of a day that has passed forever.

Sunday, 22 June 1941
HITLER INVADES RUSSIA.

Saturday, 28 June 1941
Over to sports day at Didcot; did my stuff, giving away prizes etc. – all very pre-war! It was nice meeting the officers' wives and they all say they wish I was nearer Didcot.

Sunday, 29 June 1941
The Russians are holding the Germans – each side making huge claims. Hitler always said he would never fight on two fronts ... perhaps he has bitten off more than he can chew.

Evelyn presents the prizes at Didcot depot's sports day, June 1941

Sunday, 6 July 1941

Hotter than ever – thank God for a day off from the depot! The raids continue.

Rex over to lunch and we sat in the rose gardens. These are red-letter days for us both, when we can be together and Rex can snatch a few precious hours and try to forget for a short time the pain, misery and carnage of this terrible war.

Monday, 14 July 1941

Russia becomes our ally.

Tuesday, 15 July 1941

When I was assembling children's clothes at the depot some time ago I noticed with what loving care the little girls' frocks had been made. In gay ginghams, they were beautifully smocked and trimmed with dainty lace or rickrack, with dear little pockets and belts. My eye was caught by a piece of paper tucked into one of the pockets, and I stuffed it into the pocket of my overall to read later. This is what was written:

Mrs Arthur Fisher, 3333 Jackson Street, San Francisco City USA
The women of America are with you in thoughts, prayers and hopes.

The message and its sentiments touch me deeply. I wonder to whom this dress will be sent, with its pretty trimming and its gay little handkerchief tucked into the pocket. To some distracted mother, wandering the shattered streets with her home destroyed – perhaps bereft of some members of her family? How can such people, bombed and shell-shocked, be expected to say thank you to their benefactors, however grateful they may be in their hearts? On an impulse I put the scrap of paper in my purse and in the rush and confusion of the next few days at the depot, forget all about it. Later one evening I come across it and answer it.

This morning I have received an answer to my letter from Mrs Fisher. She writes as follows:-

July 1st 1941
My dear Mrs Shillington,
My dear new English friend! I hope someday to meet my friend and that we may like one another.

When your most welcome letter came I was simply delighted to share it, not only with my friends, but also with the San Franciscan public. I showed it to Mrs St Aubyn, the President of our Northern Californian British War Relief Association since the resignation of Mrs Paul Butler, wife of the British Consul in our city.

Mrs Butler resigned on advice from Washington. Mrs St Aubyn fills the position marvelously. She thought, with me, that we'd show your letter to our chief reporter, and did she express enthusiasm at the idea of writing up the letter! Enclosed find a clipping from the San Francisco Morning Chronicle *[see following page].*

A great many people phoned to thank me, several wrote and expressed their appreciation of your letter. It certainly has been an inspiration to many of your American cousins!

I shall prize your letter along with some I received during the last war; Mr Fisher was then in France and this time, sadly, age and age alone keeps him from England. We both, as well as our son and daughter, are 'All for England'.

The little dresses I enjoy making are sent under the British War Relief Association of Northern California. I have almost finished my third hundredth.

Someday in the not-too-distant future when Hitler is out where he belongs and England is at peace again we would love to have some of the little children over here and have them roam over our hills.

Our hearts and thoughts are with you and soon we hope that England and America will be a real 'union' – as going a concern as our English-speaking union here in San Francisco.

Re-appreciatively yours
Eugenia L. Fisher

I am amazed at the response to my letter and touched by the warmth with which it has been received. I answered it at once.

This was the commencement of a warm 'penfriendship' between the two women, which lasted until Mrs Fisher's death some years later.

THE SAN FRANCISCO MORNING CHRONICLE
June 1941

From Somewhere in England
A Woman Says, 'Thanks, U.S.A.'

By ZILFA ESTCOURT

Here is a letter from England so gallant in its spirit, so brave in its attitude, that the San Francisco woman who received it in response to a little message sent with some contributions, has consented to share it with others of us who hope "There'll always be an England." The letter was written to Mrs. Arthur L. Fisher, 2200 Van Ness avenue.

"You will not know my name," the letter began, "but I am a member of the Women's Voluntary Service in Britain. When sorting out some children's frocks at our depot the other day, I came across the Christmas card with your name and address and also your message written on it from the women of the U.S.A.

Like a Handshake

"I feel I cannot let that message go unacknowledged. It was like the warm handshake of a friend from over the seas. In these dark days that is a very heartening thing.

"I often wonder if you in the United States can possibly realize what it means to us in the front line here to feel and know you are behind us in this titanic struggle for all we hold dear, not only for the vast material aid you are giving so splendidly, vital as that is, but for the great spiritual support which your co-operation is contributing— that is a tremendous force in this fight between good and evil, I am convinced.

"It is indeed good to feel that our two countries stand for the same great ideals and that we are prepared to stand by them, come what may. For to all of us, a world devoid of liberty of conscience is unthinkable!

"I would like you to know how much we in Britain appreciate all you are doing to help. When I stand in our depot and see the numbers of cases and bales of clothing sent us by the U.S.A. Red Cross to help our homeless ones, the innocent victims of Hitler's 'total war,' my heart swells with gratitude and affection toward you all.

A True Union Will Come

"Out of this horror and darkness and carnage of war there will, I feel, be born the real English Speaking Union—may we go forward together to build a better and saner world. We in Britain are not down hearted. The more the Hun batters us the more stubborn we become. I wish you could see for yourself the marvelous spirit of the people here—nothing written in the press exaggerates it. We shall hang on like true English bulldogs 'till your aid can really take effect. And every day, every hour brings that nearer. So, thumbs up!

With Good Wishes

"I think you would like to know that I sent those charming little dresses with your messages in them, off that very day to a badly 'blitzed' area, so by now some little English children are being made happy by them. I loved the gay little handkerchiefs."

The letter, sent with cordial good wishes, was signed by Evelyn Shillington.

The newspaper article inspired by Evelyn's correspondence
with Mrs Eugenia Fisher of San Francisco, pictured opposite
as a young woman, plus the note that started it all

Friday, 18 July 1941

Today I went up to London and took a bus to the City. It is impossible to describe the devastation around St Paul's. It is appalling! The whole area is in ruins which show evidence of the terrible fires which ringed the cathedral – and amidst all this destruction there it still stands, Wren's masterpiece, saved by a miracle!

I went into Westminster Abbey in the morning. A bomb had fallen through the roof and as I knelt to say a prayer a golden shaft of sunshine fell through the shattered timbers and shone, like a benediction, upon the Tomb of the Unknown Warrior.

Friday, 25 July 1941

Rex back, very tired. He has been on inspection all week.

Monday, 4 August 1941

The Russians still holding the Germans.

Wednesday, 13 August 1941

Dance given by the officers of Didcot mess. A thoroughly enjoyable evening, everyone very cheery. My partners all told me what a wonderful OC Rex is – they are practically all civilians and find him such a different commanding officer from what they imagined a regular brigadier would be. It is easy to see they both like and respect him and I am very proud to be his wife.

President Roosevelt and Churchill have met out at sea in the Atlantic.

Friday, 22 August 1941

The Germans nearing Leningrad. Reports of terrible battles and heavy casualties on both sides.

Monday, 25 August 1941

Stocktaking at the depot begins. Some bright soul has decreed that as all the goods from the USA are packed in tens, we ought to undo them all and repack them in dozens as the orders for them come in twelves! It is a ghastly job with the enormous number of different goods in the depot, and to my mind a ridiculous waste of time when it is vital to get the articles to the bombed areas. I counted over three thousand men's vests today and I am exhausted!

Monday, 1 September 1941

A new worry has arisen. Captain Fox's daughter has taken up residence here and she owns a very fierce Alsatian, who is kept chained up in the stables where the garages now are. One of the gardeners confides in me that the reason for this is that he is a killer of sheep and that he'd 'gobble Chaser up'. This is very worrying as occasionally he gets loose, and now I am terrified to take Chaser into the woods in case he should suddenly appear. Chaser may be gun-shy but he knows absolutely no fear where other dogs are concerned and would tackle one three times his size without hesitation if he were attacked. This would mean disaster with the type we now have here. It does seem such a pity there should be this anxiety to spoil the pleasure of this lovely place, but there always is something, it seems, in this life – nothing ever is perfect.

Tuesday, 2 September 1941

This morning I received a letter saying that they are reorganising the depot and that my services are no longer required. Not a word of thanks for all the hard work I have put in since I volunteered! It seems they are recruiting the younger women – girls now being called up – who are snaffling these sorts of jobs in order to avoid compulsory service. They certainly made use of us older 'girls' to get that loathsome repacking job done!

I shall be very lonely if I can't get another job. I see so little of Rex; he has such an onerous job and finds it very difficult to find time to get over to Maiden Erlegh. I realise now how lonely I am here.

Friday, 5 September 1941

Rex over to dinner and to stay the night. We had a talk and he is going to see if he can find somewhere in Didcot where I can live. This has cheered me up a lot.

Sunday, 7 September 1941

I went over to attend the National Day of Prayer at Didcot and stayed to lunch with Rex. I am just praying he will be able to find somewhere there for me to live.

Tuesday, 23 September 1941

Wire from Percy Hutchison saying he has a booking for *The Luck of the Navy*, my mother's First World War play, at Glasgow for 13 October (my mother's birthday) and suggesting I go up for the opening as there may be work for me to do on it. This is the naval spy play which ran for over a year in London, had three touring companies and was played in South Africa and in Canada, and which I worked on when I was staying with the Hutchisons at Edenbridge. It is my revised version which is being played in Glasgow. Rex says I certainly should go, I have nothing to do here and it really is important I should be on the spot in case any alterations are necessary in the script. He is so frantically busy he doesn't see much chance of getting over to see me and by the time I return he may have found accommodation for me in Didcot. Chaser will live with Rex at his quarter.

Saturday, 11 October 1941
Up to St Pancras where I met Percy and Nella, who took me out to dinner, then back to St Pancras by Tube from Piccadilly. The platforms are crowded with people – old folk, women and children – who take up their station to sleep during the dark hours of Hitler's now nightly visitation. What a sight this is! All along the platforms they congregate, whole families, all tackling this strange new pattern of existence with true British phlegm, with so much courage and cheerfulness that it brings tears to my eyes.

Percy had booked us sleepers, the train is in, and we say goodbye to Nella, who is staying at home with John. Soon tucked up in my bunk, the train pulls out on its way to Scotland.

Sunday, 12 October 1941
Arrived in Glasgow. Percy and I have breakfast at the Station Hotel and Percy puts me into a taxi to take me to the hotel which the advance agent has booked for me. This turns out to be a commercial hotel not too far from the theatre. The proprietress is a typical Scot body, very kind, and at once takes me under her wing, shows me into my bedroom and tells me that they have 'snacks' I can have before the theatre and a late meal afterwards.

There are quite an assortment of commercial travellers in this hotel. I appear to be the only woman.

Monday, 13 October 1941
Percy picks me up early for rehearsal. (It's a bit of a thrill to see my name up outside: 'Revised by Evelyn Shillington'!) He tells me the

theatre is booked out. Remembering the huge success it was, I feel a bit queasy when I think of the opening tonight . . .

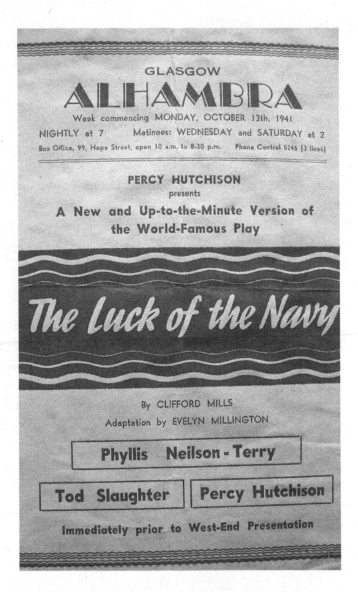

Cast photo from the Glasgow production of *The Luck of the Navy*,
adapted by Evelyn from her mother's play, signed by its stars
Phyllis Neilson-Terry, Tod Slaughter and Percy Hutchison

At the back of the stage the usual chaos reigns! I am introduced
to Phyllis Neilson-Terry, who is playing the part of Mrs Peel,
and who is complaining about her dressing room. Tod Slaughter,
a veteran of touring in his own company as *Sweeney Todd the
Demon Barber of Fleet Street*, is on the top of a high ladder doing
some vital alteration to the set as there is no one else to tackle it.
There is a desperate shortage of stagehands, owing to the war, and
so the cast is helping to set the stage for the rehearsal to begin.
Percy informs me I must take a taxi into town and buy dresses
for the leading lady and the 'flapper' and get them to the theatre
as quickly as possible. This takes some time and what with one
thing and another I begin to wonder if the curtain will ever rise

to time on the play tonight. But true to theatrical traditions it does, and to what a spectacle: the Royal Navy in full splendour and a full house.

Our good pal, Colonel Geoffrey Love, has come over from Edinburgh to escort me – and a fearful rush it has been for me to return to my hotel to get a snack and into my glad rags before he called! – and he is as thrilled as I am at the reception the play receives. A really wonderful evening. The Loves have invited me to stay with them in Edinburgh next week.

Tuesday, 14 October 1941

Excellent notices of *The Luck of the Navy* – 'A rattling good thriller containing many moments of genuine excitement – a play for the hour' (*Evening Times*) – and business is excellent. Percy is delighted and revelling in his part of the naval hero, Stanton VC, which he played in the 1918 version.

Thursday, 16 October 1941

I am very comfortable in my hotel. I have made friends with a real dyed-in-the-wool old sea-salt of a Scot Merchant Navy sailor. He talks with a strong Scot's accent and regales me with stories of the perils of the convoys which carry our vital food supplies under the constant threat of Hitler's submarines. They are a gallant lot and pay dearly for keeping our nation alive, and I take off my hat to him and those like him.

The play continues to draw full and enthusiastic houses, but there is trouble as Tod Slaughter is hitting the bottle! He gives an excellent performance as the chief German spy when he is sober, but when he has 'partaken' – phew! The other night he got all mixed up in Schaffer's speech to Mrs Peel about the big net of British freedom, 'in which the little German fish swim in

and out,' which came out something like, 'the little fishing ...
hic! ... German schwimming ... hic! ... in and out'. Percy is
frantic!

Sunday, 19 October 1941
Over to Edinburgh to such a warm welcome from Jill. Geoffrey is
away on duty so Jill and her two daughters and self have the house
to ourselves.

Monday, 20 October 1941
Gosh, this house is so cold! It is up high above the Firth of Forth
(lovely views) and because of the air raids the Loves are living in
the basement. My room is three floors up – I should have a lovely
view if they bomb the Firth!

Friday, 24 October 1941
Have a lovely time seeing my pals, Ida Coyle and Nan Impey,
friends from the Lady Provost's depot when Rex was at Scottish
Command. I must say, I find it a bit hard to leave the nice warm
basement where Jill and her daughters are cosily embedded and
climb up three flights to my solitary and bitterly cold bedroom, and
shan't be sorry to get home.

Have caught a nasty cold and have been fighting it all the time.
Thank goodness there have been no air raids while I have been
here.

Friday, 31 October 1941
Jill saw me off on the train to London; a long journey, and cough
and chest very bad. Back to Maiden Erlegh. Rex came over in the
evening. So lovely to see him – and Chaser!

Tuesday, 4 November 1941

Up after three days in bed feeling very rocky. My small dark study is very depressing now the November evenings are drawing in. Even in the daytime the very large cedar tree which grows so close to the window, dripping rain, obscures what light there is, and except for the Chotzners, whom I see very seldom, there is no one to talk to. Most welcome are the short visits of Nigel Headington, who very kindly calls in to take Chaser out for his bedtime 'walkies'. Then off Chaser and I go up the huge staircase and along the empty corridors to bed.

Tuesday, 11 November 1941

Here I am most unexpectedly in Brighton! *The Luck of the Navy* is being played at the Theatre Royal and Percy suggested I might like to join him, Nella and little John at their hotel, and Rex will try and get down for the Saturday matinee. Ina Egan is coming too.

Saturday, 15 November 1941

Rex joins us today. It has been a nice break and the play is going rather well, but the news that little John, who has been ill all week, has developed whooping cough has rather spoilt the party, especially for me as I have never had the complaint – so far at any rate!

Monday, 17 November 1941

Back at Maiden Erlegh with Rex – he had to return to Didcot. Feeling much better for the change.

Tuesday, 25 November 1941

Letter from Percy: Nella has whooping cough!

Thursday, 27 November 1941

Rex's birthday. He came over for dinner. So thankful we are to be together, but sad news of the loss of the battleship *Barham*, which has been sunk by a Japanese submarine off the coast of Singapore with the loss of over five hundred men. A sombre birthday indeed.

Rex has some very good news for me. He has heard through Nella's sister, Audrey – now married to Guy Fossick, who lives in Sutton Courtenay, quite close to the Didcot depot – that a Mrs Sinclair is anxious to have an officer's wife as a paying guest. She has this large house, Lady Place, in which her three grown-up children, two sons and one daughter, have each their own suites, and is terrified, now they are no longer at home, that she will have evacuee children billeted on her.

She has suggested that I should go over to Sutton Courtenay next Monday to meet her.

Monday, 15 December 1941

Moved from Maiden Erlegh today. Rex sent an Army lorry for my baggage and I went down to the study to superintend the removal. When I returned I discovered that my regimental brooch, which I had left on the dressing table prior to pinning it on my felt hat, had disappeared. The only person on that floor is a maid who has already started to sweep the floor of my room. When questioned she says she has never seen it.

I go and see matron and she is not at all encouraging, saying that 'things have disappeared', including her nice fountain pen. I ask if she is accusing the boys of the junior school, to which her only reply is a shrug.

I am terribly upset. The brooch is one of my most treasured possessions, Rex having had it made as his wedding present to me, so that it is doubly precious.

I cannot hold up the soldiers and the van, which is now fully loaded, and have to get miserably into the car waiting to take me to Lady Place. Here Mrs Sinclair welcomes me, and I tell Rex, who has come over to see me in, of my loss. He says he will immediately notify our insurance company in Reading and that they will notify all jewellers in the district to whom the thief might take it.

We have lunch with Mrs Sinclair in the large dining room, waited on by a very ancient butler, who seems to suffer with his feet. Afterwards, coffee in the drawing room, which is beautiful, with large French windows opening onto the garden. Mrs Sinclair comments on the size of the garden and the lack of gardeners, with a speculative eye on Rex. I fear her hopes, if any, that he will spend his few hours of leave working on her lawns and flowerbeds are doomed to disappointment!

As there is no heating in my bedroom Rex makes a note to have an Aladdin lamp sent over from the depot. I see him off with a happy heart as now we shall see so much more of one another and I shall be able to get over to Didcot and take part in the activities at the depot with the other officers' wives.

Thursday, 25 December 1941

Rex fetched me in his car for service in the garrison church and I met several of the wives afterwards. Then, as Rex had to stay to do 'dinners', I returned to Lady Place and he picked me up later to have dinner with Guy and Audrey Fossick. Guy is a prosperous businessman, exempt from active service, and they have a baby son called William. I remember when I was living with Percy Hutchison at Edenbridge that Audrey was a bit of a problem, and what a relief it was to Nella (and Percy) when Guy fell in love with her and married her. She now seems very happy and has everything she wants.

Alas, Christmas has been marred by the terrible news coming in of the fall of Hong Kong. Lovely island of sweet waters, what will be your fate at the hands of the Japanese conquerors? And even the news in the Middle East that Benghazi is now in our hands does little to lighten our mood as the Japs sweep on into Malaya. Will Singapore be able to hold out?

PART EIGHT

Long days at the office

January 1942–December 1943

Thursday, 1 January 1942

The year opens with renewed activity at the depot. Rex shows me round and I am amazed at how enormous it is. It is of course the Central Ordnance Depot and its vast lines of sheds, full of stores for every requirement of the Army, stretch away in every direction while railway lines run through them which connect with Didcot Junction.

In addition to the supplies being built up for our Army in North Africa, there is a large quantity of stores marked 'Hong Kong' and 'Singapore' which, alas, will never now reach their destinations.

Rex, it seems, has managed through discreet and understanding meetings with Whitley Council to smooth over the difficult problems and animosity which existed between the civilians and the military. Discipline has been tightened up and the practice whereby look-outs gave warning of an officer's approach by whistling has been completely wiped out. But best of all, a new spirit of co-operation and willingness to get on with the job of winning the war has been established.

Friday, 2 January 1942

We are having a very cold spell and I am thankful for my Aladdin oil stove which warms my bedroom and provides hot water for my bottle and a drink at night. Mrs Sinclair is a real Spartan! In this very cold house she scorns the shivers of lesser mortals like yours truly. We sit in state for meals in the arctic dining room at an enormous table, suitable for her large family, waited upon by the very old butler, Carter; all very incongruous for our sparse rations.

Mrs Sinclair keeps an eagle eye on any wasteful practices and I am called over the coals for putting marmalade onto my plate – it should be put straight onto my toast, thus ensuring that not a cat's lick is wasted!

No fire is lighted till 4 p.m. sharp when a match is put by Carter onto the fire in the drawing room where I join Mrs Sinclair for tea (far too late to warm the large room, of course).

Monday, 5 January 1942

I am bidden by Mrs Sinclair to take a doll to a Mrs Freedman which is to be raffled for the local hospital. Mrs Sinclair says I shall find her very charming and that she and her husband, Louis, are always generous to all war efforts. I arrive on the doorstep of Priors Close, their charming house, and find Ruby Freedman is all that Mrs Sinclair claimed for her. She and Louis are Jewish and most hospitable. She gives me coffee and a most generous contribution.

Wednesday, 7 January 1942

Very cold! Life is still settling down here. As the aunt of Sir Archibald Sinclair [Minister of State for Air], Mrs Sinclair is fully aware of her social status and is very much the 'Queen Bee' of the village. Amongst other good works she has a working party here at Lady Place once a week, to which I have been introduced. We sit in the large and very cold library, heated by a one-bar electric fire, and cut out, machine and hand-sew various garments. I find the company very friendly and it is nice to get to know people who live in the village.

Thursday, 8 January 1942

Rex took me to the depot to a coffee party to meet the officers' wives. They were all very charming and said how glad they were that I am now living near enough to take part in the activities there. We have planned a working party to take place once a week.

Mrs Sinclair's son, John, now in North Africa with his regiment, has left his spaniel at Lady Place. He is very fat, has worms, is vastly lazy and rejoices in the name of Blood.

It seems that John has always called his spaniels by names that commence with the letter B, and having exhausted all he can think of was forced to give this sanguine hound this strange name. Blood is definitely the bane of my existence! He loathes all forms of exercise but whenever I take Chaser for a walk Mrs Sinclair insists that Blood should come too.

In vain I creep downstairs hoping to leave the house undetected, but Mrs Sinclair has ears tuned to the smallest sound, and the command, 'Please take Blood with you,' always dashes my (and Chaser's) hopes of a carefree walk.

Blood, who has sensed the prospect of a hated 'walkies' and has hopefully concealed himself, has now to be found, and the task of getting him out of the house commences. This entails dragging him by the chain on his collar while he makes disgusting choking noises and tries to impede our progress by sitting down whenever possible and refusing to move!

When Rex is with me his solution is to wait until we are well out of sight of the house and then to remove Blood's chain, whereupon he immediately takes the shortest route home as fast as his avoirdupois will let him. (Rex's name for Blood is best left to the imagination!)

Sunday, 15 February 1942

News of the fall of Singapore to the Japanese. This is terrible news, remembering the tales of the appalling atrocities inflicted on the British in Hong Kong as well as the loss of prestige in the East. One can only pray that many were able to escape to Australia before the occupation.

Monday, 16 February 1942

We have had a thick fall of snow on the top of freezing ice. I go to take Chaser out and I am bidden, as usual, to take Blood with me. I drag the unwilling creature to the front door, put his chain on and open it. A freezing blast enters and Blood gives one stricken glance outside and refuses to budge. Propelling his considerable weight onto the top step I manage to close the door behind me whereupon Blood does an about turn and, twisting his chain round my ankles, brings me down on my right shoulder. An appalling pain shoots through me and as I rise and manage to disentangle myself, Blood, taking advantage of my discomfort, makes a dash for the back door, trailing his lead.

Tuesday, 17 February 1942

Had a restless night and my shoulder is very stiff and painful, but I get no sympathy from Mrs Sinclair who, with a cold blue eye and chilly manner, treats me to a description of how she, with a fractured collarbone and broken arm, carried on and fulfilled all her duties without a murmur! This reduces me to silence and I try to bear my apparently slight injuries with a brave smile.

Sunday, 1 March 1942

Bitter east wind! I have now met two of Mrs Sinclair's family. Her eldest son, Hugh, is a professor at Oxford and generally comes to dinner on Sundays. He is very tall and very pale, probably due to the fact that his speciality is 'diet' and he uses himself as a guinea pig in his experiments.

Mrs Sinclair's daughter, Margaret, is also very tall and an officer in the ATS. She comes when her duties permit and has her mother's rather awesome presence and must, I am sure, exercise most excellent discipline on her subordinates.

You might think that these visits would add to the gaiety of Lady Place – but no! We all sit round that large dining table in complete silence, like monks in a Trappist monastery. This is quite weird and has an awful effect upon me. I feel I must giggle or break the awful silence with a rude word, but one glance at Mrs Sinclair's marble countenance is enough to reduce me to suitable decorum.

As soon as the meal is over they all retire to their respective suites before leaving, and I can't for the life of me see what possible pleasure or indeed 'contact' of any sort can come from these visits.

Monday, 9 March 1942

Mrs Sinclair announces at breakfast that she is expecting another paying guest today. She arrives in time for lunch. Her name is Betty Craig and she is the young wife of one of John Sinclair's brother officers now on active service with the Buffs [Royal East Kent Regiment] in North Africa. She has a baby boy of eighteen months. She is Irish and most attractive-looking, with dark hair and blue eyes, and we become friends at once.

Sunday, 15 March 1942 – National Day of Prayer

Went with Betty Craig to the garrison church service at Didcot.

Afterwards visit the ATS camp with Rex. The commandant told me how grateful they are to Rex for all he has done for them. His predecessor hated women in uniform and they were made to feel his displeasure, whereas Rex has done all he can to make life easier for them. She points out the improvement in their living quarters and how much they have appreciated the flowerbeds outside the mess he has had planted. It is good to hear how much he is liked and esteemed by all of them.

Rex's 'devoted' (Evelyn's description) ATS on parade in Didcot

Betty is a great joy! She has a delightful sense of humour and she soon sums up the atmosphere of Lady Place and shares my view that it is rather like being at school!

Her time is pretty well taken up with her small son, and I am away a lot at Didcot, but I usually return in time for tea with her and Mrs Sinclair in front of the drawing-room fire, so welcome in this cold house!

Mrs Sinclair is very lucky to have staff in this day and age: a cook (never seen but doubtless very elderly), the butler Carter (creaking), and the housemaid Ethel (elderly but nice). There is a part-time gardener still able to walk and bend (all able-bodied men being in the Forces). Our Mrs Sinclair is really a remarkable woman and my wonderment increases when I discover she thinks nothing of going out to post her letters in the box down the road in this freezing weather in a chiffon blouse! This all takes a lot of living up to, unless you are to be classed as a cissy!

Monday, 23 March 1942

Mrs Sinclair, having announced she is leaving for a week's visit to her married daughter, who rejoices in the name of Mrs Haddock, departs after breakfast this morning. Betty and I are delighted – it is as if a dark cloud has lifted. The change in the house is remarkable, and to our astonishment, when the time came for us to have dinner, Carter appeared and suggested that we two ladies might prefer to have our meal served in the drawing room before the fire, which we noticed was banked up high, not as Mrs Sinclair would have it. We spend the evening in a state of related joy and thankfulness.

Friday, 27 March 1942

The past few days have gone all too quickly! Betty and I, waited on by Carter and Ethel, who seem only too anxious to fulfil our slightest wish, have completely succumbed to this life of disgraceful luxury and are revelling in our freedom. Blood, too, rejoices in a life completely free from exercise – much to his liking! But this delightful existence is rudely shattered today when Carter informs us that on Sunday Dr Sinclair will be coming to dinner and will be bringing four fellow professors with him. All joy departs as we face the prospect of a meal in that freezing room in company with a 'pride of professors', all doubtless as grim and forbidding as Dr Sinclair has proved to be – and all probably hostile to females. A gloomy prospect indeed.

Sunday, 29 March 1942

The dreaded day dawns! Betty and I carry out our plan to let Dr Sinclair and his friends have their sherry in the drawing room and to make our appearance just before the gong sounds.

Dr Sinclair introduces us and we take our places round the dining table – and here a big surprise awaits us. Instead of the dull, awkward meal we expected, these dreaded men of learning, led by Dr Sinclair, turn out to be the greatest fun, full of jokes and laughter and obviously not at all averse to female company! It is not long before we are all on the best of terms and when they depart to return to Oxford we are very sorry to see them go.

What strange spell is it that Mrs Sinclair casts over her son to turn him from the genial and amusing man of today into the morose zombie he becomes in her presence?

There is a large oil painting of Mrs Sinclair at the time of her marriage to Mr Sinclair, a much older man. She wears a ball gown and with her fair hair dressed high she looks quite human. One can but wonder what can have produced the Mrs Sinclair of today, or what sort of a childhood her children must have had.

Monday, 30 March 1942

Mrs Sinclair returned today and life at Lady Place returns to the pattern as before. My right arm and shoulder are still very painful. All efforts to trace my regimental brooch having failed, the insurance company have paid the claim. I am heartbroken at its loss.

Monday, 13 April 1942

Rex moved into Lady Place today. They are terribly short of quarters for the officers at the depot, so Rex has given his up. It is lovely to have him here.

Monday, 20 April 1942

A massive raid by America on Tokyo and Kobe. [The USA had entered the war after the attack on Pearl Harbor, 7 December 1941.] Only last Monday Rex moved into Lady Place and today Mrs Sinclair announces that she will be closing up the house early in May as she intends to give the staff a holiday. We shall have to find other accommodation until she returns from staying with her daughter, Mrs Haddock, who is having a baby. This is quite amazing! She knows well enough how very difficult it is to find anywhere in the village and that Rex must be on the spot, and the idea that we should turn out for a period to suit her and return when she decides graciously to open the house again is 'just not on' for Rex, who sets out at once to find us suitable permanent accommodation.

Monday, 4 May 1942

Rex has heard of accommodation in a house in the village here. It is owned by a Mrs Webster, whose husband is in the Royal Air Force. The house is close to the river and has a nice garden. We go to see her and she shows us a double bedroom and a small sitting room (used to be her dining room) which we can have, and a shared bathroom and kitchen. Rex arranges that we shall move in next Monday.

Monday, 11 May 1942

Moved into my new accommodation. When Rex told Mrs Sinclair he had found accommodation for us she asked him for how long.

Rex said, 'Forever' and I have never seen anyone more flabber-gasted. She certainly had never expected this!

Saturday, 16 May 1942

Glorious weather. Sutton Courtenay is a dream in its spring garb. There is a beautiful white magnolia out in the garden here. Mrs Webster has a small son of two and a half years and her husband comes down at weekends when he can get leave. The atmosphere here is a marked improvement on Lady Place.

Thursday, 21 May 1942

My dear friend Jane Hadden comes down to Sutton Courtenay and we find accommodation for her as a paying guest with Mrs Spencer, whose husband is in the Forces and who has a large house in the village here. She has five children (all at school) and another one on the way.

The air raids on London continue and one night Jane and I, out in the garden, hear the steady throb throb of aircraft – it is our bombers at last going out to give the Germans a bit of their own medicine. Good luck to them and God bring them safely back to us!

Sunday, 24 May 1942

My birthday. Went to church in the lovely old church here. Asquith, once our prime minister, is buried in the churchyard. Dined with Rex and Jane at the Freedmans', who are becoming very good friends of ours.

With the help of Rex, who has found an empty shop in Didcot, Jane and I have opened a branch of WVS and the Citizens Advice Bureau, and with the aid of the Didcot wives I also run a weekly sewing party in another empty shop, where in the shop window, exposed to the view of all and sundry, we sit and mend soldiers' socks. The first job we have is a large sack delivered by an orderly which turns out to be socks from the Pioneer Corps and which I find to my disgust are not only full of enormous holes but unwashed too! My work group recoils in horror and I send a stiff request by the orderly that we cannot attempt to darn them until they have been washed.

Next week the sack is sent down to us and again it is full of the noxious and quite stiff socks. I have had enough! Rising in my wrath I return the socks to the orderly and, climbing into the vehicle in which he has brought them, instruct him to drive me to the office of the OC Pioneer Corps.

We sweep into the Pioneer camp and I demand to see the officer in charge. I am duly ushered into a large room where the officer in question is seated at a large desk. He raises his eyebrows when I am announced and rises to his feet, but before he can say a word I produce several of the most odorous specimens I have selected for the purpose and spread them out upon his desk, asking if he thinks them fit to be sent to us to mend. Taking a hasty step back and turning somewhat pale he stammers his apologies and, turning to the orderly, demands that an enquiry be made immediately. I am escorted back to my faithful band who are overjoyed that the matter has now been settled. Rex is tickled pink at the whole affair!

Getting to the WVS office every day means catching the bus at 9 a.m. with sandwiches and coffee after Rex and Chaser have departed in great state in Rex's car.

It is interesting work, especially the CAB, where we are expected to be able to answer all kinds of questions. Every day we have to read up the official memoranda concerning the latest rules etc., and the information covered can be very widespread indeed.

We are instructed never to admit we don't know an answer, but to request the caller to ring again later. Then Jane and I indulge in a frantic search for the required information so that we shall be able to deliver it when the call comes through.

The WVS work is often connected with the depot.

Tuesday, 26 May 1942

Today we are told that we have to fix up an ATS private who has been dismissed from the service. The culprit duly arrives under escort with a sergeant and turns out to be a most unrepentant sinner, who has obviously been a 'tart' of the first order.

Under the stern and disapproving ATS sergeant, Jane and I commence the task of fitting the delinquent out with civilian clothes before she is put on a train at Didcot. We have a fair selection of all sizes to choose from, but we have not bargained for the taste of our fair lady! Obviously she is delighted to be returning to her former way of life and has no intention of not looking the part. With scorn she rejects the garments we offer her till, quite carried away, Jane and I find ourselves behaving like anxious shop assistants offering all we have to tempt her choice, till an infuriated cough from the scandalised sergeant brings us to our senses and our 'floozy' is marched off, protesting indignantly at what she calls an unpardonable infringement to her liberty at not being allowed further time to decide whether a red or green gown suits her best.

Wednesday, 27 May 1942

Rommel has attacked in North Africa and the British Army has been forced back after fierce fighting. My cousin Alexander Clifford and his war correspondent friends are in the thick of this, risking their lives to send us news.

Wednesday, 10 June 1942

Today was the day the fishmonger opened in Didcot! This is one of the excitements of life at the office and only happens occasionally and always quite unexpectedly. Like the Indian grapevine, the news will suddenly spread and before you can wink an eye the street is full of eager beavers all intent to take their place in the queue. The fact that all we shall get (if we are lucky) is a slab of hard-frozen and quite tasteless Icelandic cod never dampens our spirits, so welcome is anything which helps out our meagre rations.

Jane and I cannot leave the office unattended so one of us rushes up the street to take our place (or plaice) and hopefully to return with a portion each in triumph.

Sunday, 21 June 1942

Tobruk has fallen to the Germans under Rommel and our Eighth Army is forced back to El Alamein line. This is a terrible blow!

Saturday, 11 July 1942

As the summer rolls on I am finding life here not so easy. Maggie [Mrs Webster] has now no help as all able-bodied women have been called up and I have to take my part in the cleaning of the house. I am away all day at the office from 9.30 a.m., not returning by bus till after 6.30 p.m. Today, as the office closes at 1 p.m. on Saturdays, I decide to tackle washing the kitchen floor. Its vast area is covered with squares of black and white linoleum. I am convinced I can tackle this job successfully – have I not seen it done many times before? I collect my pail of suds and scrubbing brush and start off with vigour. All goes well until I discover that I have succeeded in marooning myself in the middle of the room with a nicely scrubbed clean floor all round me – and no way of withdrawal left open!

Life is rather difficult in other ways. Sharing a kitchen is always a problem but this is made more difficult because I find Maggie less than co-operative. She knows that I have to give Rex his breakfast before 8.30 a.m., when his car comes to take him to Didcot, but every morning she makes it her business to get down to the kitchen if possible before me and to put a saucepan of porridge on one gas ring and a kettle to boil on the other. As she never gives her son, Laurence, his breakfast till after Rex has left I can see no reason for this except to embarrass me.

On the Sundays when her husband is here we have an arrangement that she should have first use of the oven. This would be all right if she didn't leave the dirty pans in the sink, full of greasy water, so that I have to clean them all before I can get our lunch. Ugh!

Laurence is a real terror. Very plain with a large mouth, usually open, he has a huge clown's grin when he has pulled off some particularly naughty piece of mischief and he delights in thinking up some new annoyance. Like turning on all the bath taps or, one morning, standing stark naked at the bathroom window and throwing medicine bottles down on the heads of the scandalised spectators below. But to me his least endearing activity is his habit of waiting till one has scrubbed the horrible red-bricked floor of our large scullery and then to come in from the garden, where he has collected a bucket full of earth and debris, and with a huge grin, emptying it all over the floor!

He nearly drives his adoring mother crackers trying to get him to eat. She sits for hours coaxing him to swallow the meals she has so lovingly prepared, and at night when she has put him to bed and retired, hopefully, to her sitting room for a little rest, no sooner is she settled down than loud roars from above will send her flying in case some calamity has befallen him, only to find the scamp

standing at the bottom of his cot with a chortle of glee! And this is
repeated again and again. What Master Laurence needs is a nanny
of the old order!

Monday, 10 August 1942
Rex has seven days' leave and we have decided to travel down to
Cornwall to the Boscarn Hotel at Looe. This hotel is situated right
on the beach and we have a lovely view from our bedroom. The
Fossicks are here too.

Wednesday, 12 August 1942
The weather is lovely and we have found a very nice bathing beach
further along the coast.

Walks are somewhat restricted by barbed wire on the cliffs,
and another reminder that we are at war is the daily bayonet practice on the sands, where troops charge swinging dummies with
ferocious cries. There are no holidaymakers in Looe owing to the
tip-and-run air raids carried out by the Germans in their endeav-
ours to locate and destroy the corvettes [a small warship] being
built in well camouflaged inlets on the upper reaches of the river.

In the evenings we have often taken a boat across to the
Fisherman's Arms, a delightful pub, where in an atmosphere redolent
of tobacco, Rex stands the customers pints of beer. These sturdy
fishermen are terribly cut up at the news just in of the disastrous raid
on Dieppe, where many of their relatives and pals lost their lives.

These men are the real 'sea-dogs' of England, and when I
hear one of them solemnly declare, 'Every drop of my blood
belongs to Nelson!' it seems, in this atmosphere of oaken beams
and tobacco smoke, to be entirely in keeping. Tomorrow we go
to Polperro.

Two photos taken on Evelyn and Rex's holiday in Looe, summer 1942

Thursday, 13 August 1942

This Cornish fishing village, set in deep cliffs with its picturesque harbour, is enchanting. We have Polperro practically to ourselves and wander along its narrow streets which are flanked by fishermen's cottages. We spend some time in the museum, where they display pottery, 'pixie' charms and relics of the wreckers who used to lure ships onto the cruel rocks with lanterns.

Monday, 17 August 1942

Back in Sutton Courtenay, all the better for the short Cornish break. Rex immediately immersed in conferences and I back to Jane and the office.

When Rex has to go away Chaser has to stay with me. I take him to the office, but sometimes it is not possible. Today I shall not be away long, but it means I shall have to go through the process every dog lover knows well, of breaking it to him that he is not coming with me.

He is at present lying in his basket, apparently asleep. This is only camouflage. His ears are attuned to my slightest movement; I could no more take up my hat or reach for my gloves (lying on a chair nearby) without his instant attention.

I try to fool him by walking round the room and surreptitiously pick up my hat and gloves and tiptoe to the door, but with one bound he is out of his basket and beats me to it, his entire small body registering his delight that we are 'going walkies'. I motion him from the door, saying, 'Basket!' in what I hope is a masterful tone. The light fades from his eloquent brown eyes and his tail, so gaily wagging, hauls down its flag of happy anticipation as he turns upon me a look of heart-breaking reproach.

Hardening my heart I explain to him that it is impossible for him to come with me today, and indicate he must be a good dog and await my return. Although he knows perfectly well what I mean, he chooses to interpret this as a return of hope and rushes to the door again, giving little yelps of joy and tail-wagging – this is to undermine my willpower. When he realises all is lost he collapses on the floor in depths of dejection.

Hardening my heart anew I pick him up and deposit him firmly in his basket, admonishing him to be a good dog and to wait (two commands he perfectly understands), and make a dash for the door, only winning by a short head as he hurls himself at it despairingly.

I walk down the front garden path feeling like Brutus and every low heel in history rolled into one. I picture the poor little fellow left alone, his little black nose pressed to the door (he will probably catch a cold in his eye) and my heart fails me. Despising myself for my weakness I tiptoe round to the back of the house and peep cautiously through the window. Chaser is busily employed in making a bed for himself on Mrs Webster's chesterfield. He has selected the largest and most downy cushion and is now completely absorbed in the task of prodding and thrusting it with his nose in order to place it just to his liking. This accomplished, he climbs upon it and executes a series of rapid convolutions before he finally settles down to sleep in his cosy nest with a sigh of contentment. All this is strictly forbidden, as well he knows, and I feel it is something in the nature of a reprisal for my leaving him. Ah well, I reflect, as I turn from the window, the vision of the faithful hound fading away, Scotties are known to be proverbially tough and may not be as sentimental as other breeds, but my, oh my, aren't they little twisters!

And off I go happily to catch my bus!

Monday, 2 November 1942

Montgomery has launched an attack on Rommel's Army. This attack, under an elaborate cover plan of dummy vehicles, tanks and guns and dummy pipelines to deceive the enemy, is fully covered by my cousin Alexander Clifford and his correspondent friends.

Tuesday, 3 November 1942

After fierce fighting, news that Rommel has been forced to withdraw from El Alamein and the Eighth Army is sweeping on; there is no doubt that Montgomery, with his genius and supreme self-confidence and his gist of the 'common touch', has inspired the Desert Rats, who have fought so long and so bravely against the fabulous Rommel. The Eighth Army has covered seven hundred miles in fifteen days to Benghazi. This is splendid news! Rex thinks this is a turning point and we need to push on now.

It is interesting that Evelyn calls Rommel 'fabulous'. Myths had grown around the man they called the Desert Fox, so much so that Claude Auchinleck, Commander-in-Chief of the Middle East forces before Montgomery, had written to his men: 'There exists a real danger that our friend Rommel is becoming a kind of magical or bogey-man to our troops, who are talking far too much about him. He is by no means a superman, although he is undoubtedly very energetic and able.'

Sunday, 8 November 1942

The Allies make a landing in North Africa and Rommel's Army, with reinforcements denied to him, is relentlessly pushed back.

The dark days are lengthening, and getting to and from the office at Didcot is an ordeal, with a long wait in the cold at the station to catch the bus to Sutton Courtenay. My right shoulder and arm are increasingly painful and keep me awake at night.

Saturday, 12 December 1942

We have only a small one-bar electric fire in our sitting room, which has to do for breakfast, but in the evening I light the fire. This is one of those 'olde worldly' iron basket types, and if we have run out of coal it means getting more from the coal shed across the kitchen yard, now deep in snow. However, when it is at last burning and Rex returns, all is well!

The Freedmans have invited us and Jane to stay with them for Christmas. Their only son, Neil, is in Cairo and I think they are glad of our company. They haven't heard from their son for weeks now and are constantly hoping for news.

Monday, 28 December 1942

Back at Maggie Webster's. What a contrast to the luxury of Priors Close, where we were given breakfast in bed!

On Christmas Day we attended the Divine Service at the lovely old Saxon church and after a relaxed afternoon we assembled in the drawing room where several officers and their wives joined us for cocktails and a very nice Christmas dinner, and afterwards the men went off to play billiards. So passed a happy day, and how much we all appreciate the love and hospitality with which Louis and Ruby surround us.

Thursday, 31 December 1942

New Year's Eve is spent with the Freedmans and Jane. They have received good news regarding their son and we all face the new year with brighter hopes and – though we know that the way before us will be hard and long – thanking God, above all things, that we are all together.

Friday, 1 January 1943

The year opens much more cheerfully, far more so than we could ever have hoped last year. The Allies are now on the offensive and Russia is doing marvellously well. The situation in the Pacific is easier and the Japs have been nearly driven out of New Guinea. The enormous losses of the Germans in Russia must be draining the lifeblood of Germany, the USA output is increasing every day and our air superiority is a great asset. The good news has acted like a tonic and we all face 1943 with confidence. Please God, may Churchill's 'bright gleam' [speech of November 1942] broaden into the dawn of true victory!

Thursday, 7 January 1943

Jane and I over to the WVS rest centre and stores at Blake's Buildings. We find they are in a dreadful state – the clothing all mouldy. Send in our report to HQ. Sewing party in the afternoon.

Sunday, 17 January 1943

Up to London for Rex to attend a conference at the War Office and stay the night at the Regent's Palace. We dine with the Freedmans at the Hungaria and take them to see *Arsenic and Old Lace* at the Aldwych – a very happy evening.

Sunday, 31 January 1943

The Germans surrender Stalingrad to the Russians after terrible battles and heavy casualties on both sides. The sufferings and losses of the Germans are appalling as they retreat, the Russians steadily pushing them back, aided by their great ally, 'General Winter'. Hitler has good cause to regret, as Napoleon did, that he attacked the Russian Bear.

Life here is not improving, due to the hostile attitude of Maggie

Webster, which is difficult to understand. Rex and I have done everything in our power to create a friendly atmosphere, but to no avail. Inhabitants of the village tell us that Maggie has a chip on her shoulder due to the fact she is a tradesman's daughter (her father is a corn merchant in Abingdon) and it may well be that some of the Sutton Courtenay elite have made her feel this way. But it is certainly not the case with us. Rex has always gone out of his way to be helpful; she has a pass to the depot; I have babysat for her and she has always been invited to any social functions at the depot – none of which she has accepted.

From the beginning, although she was glad to have us as paying guests (and we pay well), she has made things difficult for me. She has a huge refrigerator which I am not allowed to use (on the grounds of Laurence's milk) although it could well accommodate far more than my needs, and insists that all my stores should be kept in a circular brick larder built out from the kitchen, which I soon discover is so damp that anything kept in it goes mouldy – which is why, of course, she never uses it herself! And she continues to make difficulties over the use of the oven, etc.

I am having a lot of pain in my right shoulder and arm, the result, I fear, of that fall last February at Lady Place, and the cold weather doesn't help. The one bright spot is when Rex can snatch some time off and we can spend part of it at Priors Close with Ruby and Louis Freedman. Jane comes too, and their home is a haven of rest and relaxation for us all. Ruby insists in sending us and Jane a large basket of vegetables from their garden every Saturday morning, a great help, and which I always share with Maggie.

Monday, 22 February 1943
Rex is due seven days' leave and we go down to Brighton and stay at the Dudley Hotel. While we are there we get some first-hand

views of the almost daily 'dog-fights' between the German daylight raiders and our Spitfires. It is thrilling in the extreme to watch. No sooner do the Huns appear than our boys are off like hounds from the leash and into the attack, and we can see them diving and manoeuvring until they all disappear in the distance.

Our hotel is comfortable and we have splendid weather, but our holiday is overshadowed by the illness of our little Chaser. No longer does he want to go 'walkies' and he leaves his food untouched. It breaks our hearts to see him. We take him to a good vet who prescribes pills for him but we return home very sad indeed.

Our anxieties over Chaser increase as we take him to our vet in Oxford. He fears a malignant growth and we have to face the loss of our little companion or letting him suffer, as we can see will be the case. These are dark days for us.

Wednesday, 10 March 1943

Took Chaser to another vet, well recommended, in Oxford. Alas, he diagnosed the disease as Parkinson's disease, a fatal cancer of the glands. There is no hope of recovery and we love him too much to let him suffer.

Friday, 12 March 1943

Our beloved little Chaser was put to sleep today. It was evident he was suffering and so Rex arranged for one of the officers to take me over to Oxford and I had the heart-breaking job of saying goodbye to this beloved little companion. The vet was so kind, and I know it is for the best, but I returned thoroughly miserable and Rex is terribly cut up too. We shall miss him horribly. Rex is arranging for him to be buried in the garden at Didcot, opposite the mess, where he loved to go with his master.

Monday, 15 March 1943

Bitter east wind. Utterly miserable. Miss Chaser so much. Have lost my voice completely. Feeling so down.

Thursday, 18 March 1943

Voice better but shoulder very painful and I now have a neuralgic pain in my right arm which keeps me awake at night. I am thankful I have work at the depot to keep me occupied, but going home without Chaser is rather grim and I can't face his favourite walk along the bank by the weirs where he used to hunt imaginary bunnies with such zest. I expect to see his little black body emerge from the bushes and rush to follow me along the path.

Rex is trying to find some other accommodation for us. This is not easy as it has to be within easy distance of the depot, but we live in hope.

We have given Chaser's basket away to a dog-owner, but Rex decided to have his collar with its tail-wagger medal and his leash buried with him in the big flowerbed opposite the mess. Rex also decides he should have a memorial and he commissions the master carpenter at the depot to carve a suitable one, just to mark his grave, which he gladly assents to do, having been fond of Chaser. He tackles this job with zest but is carried away by his emotions and Rex is somewhat taken aback when he produces a large wooden cross, about two feet high, on which is inscribed, 'In Loving Memory of Chaser' and the date of his death.

It is obvious that this is a real labour of love and that the carver has put his heart into this sad task, and that to spurn it would cause much pain, and all that is Irish in Rex rises to the surface. A ceremony is held in which Chaser's collar and lead are buried with all due respect, and the next time I go to the depot Rex points out to me with some pride this memorial to our beloved pet, on whose grave it is now the habit of the children of the depot to place flowers. And whatever the depot may think of it, no one has the temerity to show it – Rex can be formidable when he chooses!

Some weeks pass and then General Body comes down from the War Office on one of his official visits.

On leaving the mess after lunch with Rex his eye is caught by the sight of an unfamiliar object in the big flowerbed. Striding across the lawn to inspect it he is heard to utter a muffled, 'Good God!' and on returning to re-join Rex remarks something like, 'Dog lover myself – but a cross! A little excessive, don't you think?' before he enters his car and is driven away, somewhat glassy-eyed.

Nothing further transpires, but later Rex tells me that General Body has insisted that when he leaves Rex will have the cross removed. And so it has come about that there are now two graves within the precincts of the RAOC depot at Didcot. One is that of a Roman soldier which was discovered beside one of the roads, and the other is that of a little Scottie, the beloved pet and faithful companion of a British officer. RIP.

Wednesday, 7 April 1943

Rex has heard of a cottage in Blewbury to be let furnished and we go over to see it.

Blewbury is an enchanting village, not too far from Didcot, and the cottage, Green Bushes, is lovely. We meet its owner, Mrs Gifford, a very attractive woman whose husband was secretary to the White Rajah of Sarawak. It seems there has been some domestic trouble and she and her husband are now separated and she is anxious to get away from Blewbury and its associations. As we fall in love with the cottage we then and there agree to take it when she leaves on 20 May.

Rex is anxious to move out of Maggie Webster's as soon as possible, and as my arm and shoulder are now so painful I can scarcely raise my right arm, we decide that Rex will return to the mess until 20 May and I will take the opportunity to go and stay in Oxford and make an appointment to see Mr Girdlestone, the famous orthopaedic surgeon at the Radcliffe Hospital. I shall stay at the East Gate Hotel and it will give me a rest, which I badly need. Jane will hold the fort at the WVS and CAB offices with the help of one of the officers' wives from Didcot till I return.

Friday, 16 April 1943

Doing the last of the packing up. It has turned intensely hot and Maggie does nothing to help. I have all our stores, comforts, etc. to pack and should be glad of a little assistance with the latter as my arm is so painful.

Rex came and saw me off on the train to Oxford. I have a very small room but I am thankful to be here and after dinner go to bed early.

Saturday, 17 April 1943

Very hot indeed. Sat in Magdalen College gardens by the river and let the peace and beauty sink into my soul. It is marvellous to be able to rest.

Rex came over after tea. The company at the theatre here are putting on a show at Didcot depot for charity and Rex has two tickets for me and himself for the dress rehearsal of the musical *Hi-de-Hi*.

This is great fun and a beautifully mounted show, with Flanagan and Allen and Arthur Askey, and we thoroughly enjoy our evening. Wilson, Keppel and Betty [a popular music-hall act] do their amazingly funny sand-dance; Eddie Gray, another of the Crazy Gang, adds to the hilarity; and Gwen Catley and Florence Desmond do the singing and dancing. The song 'Easter Parade' about a lady in her Easter bonnet was particularly beautiful.

Wednesday, 28 April 1943

Easter is over! In spite of the heatwave and the fact that my small room is very hot indeed, I am thoroughly enjoying this time of rest and relaxation. The hotel is comfortable, the food excellent and I explore this ancient and beautiful city – the water meadows where fritillaries grow; the colleges with their superb gardens and grey walls up which wisteria climbs. I treasure time spent in these gardens, where the busy throb of the traffic is muted and only the song of the birds and the occasional deep throb of a mellow bell is heard ringing out the hour as it has done down the centuries. I explore the antiques shops and the innumerable bookshops and worship in the lovely old churches; and at night the students come in for coffee and sit on the lounge floor and discuss everything under the sun.

Jane, Ruby and Louis have been over to lunch and Rex pops in whenever he can, but always – and shattering the peace one seeks – rises the strident voice of Hitler, furious that his vaunted *blitzkrieg* has failed to fulfil its purpose to smash our morale. Now he threatens to destroy utterly our places of historical interest and to flatten our beauty spots. These have become known as the Baedeker raids, after the famous guidebooks, and it is terrible to think that any night all this beauty of our national heritage may be reduced to a heap of ruins. Please God this will never come to pass!

Monday, 3 May 1943

My appointment with Mr Girdlestone, a very, very busy man, as he informs me. Having made me feel suitably grateful that I have been granted this interview he examines me and advises an operation, and with a gleam in his eye says he will 'just nick a piece of bone' out of my shoulder. When I ask if my shoulder will be all right he says, 'Oh, yes, for all you'll want of it,' which is hardly reassuring. (I don't feel he likes me and I most certainly don't like him.) I return to the doctor through whom I got my appointment, where Rex is waiting for me, in a depressed mood and wondering why he said my injury was 'the result of a misspent life'. Can't for the life of me see how taking Blood out for 'walkies' can fit into this assumption!

Wednesday, 12 May 1943

End of the war in North Africa. Tunis is occupied and the Eighth Army, the Desert Rats, meet the First Army. My cousin Alexander Clifford, reporting the advance of the Eighth Army, has an historic meeting with Ward Price, who is reporting the advance of the First Army. [George Ward Price had been the *Mail*'s reporter in Berlin before the war when the paper was the only British newspaper to consistently support the German Nazi Party. He was granted privileged access to Adolf Hitler, and wrote about him and Mussolini in his 1937 book, *I Know These Dictators*.]

Ward Price sends a letter to Alex's mother, my aunt Marian, enclosing some photos of Alex driving his captured German car in Algiers. He also expresses his delight at getting to know my cousin better, comments on his popularity with all the correspondents and says he believes Alex to be the most able of them all.

We go over to meet Mrs Gifford, the owner of Green Bushes, again, and are more than ever enchanted with the cottage. She has perfect taste and has furnished the long sitting room, which stretches the width of the cottage, with rugs, off-white covers on the chesterfield and armchairs, and chintz curtains at the two windows at opposite sides of the room.

Evelyn's cousin, the war correspondent Alexander Clifford,
at work during the war

There is a big fireplace which she has fitted with a Courtier
stove, which she assures me I shall bless her for (how right
this proves) and the staircase to the upper floor rises from
the living room leading to two good-sized bedrooms, one of
which Rex will use as his dressing room and the other will be
our bedroom. These have built-in wardrobes and beds with

Vispring mattresses. There is a nice kitchen with an electric cooker, a boiler and a refrigerator – which lives in the downstairs bathroom!

The back garden stretches down to a 'whoopee room' which they have built for parties and extra guests. This is large with a parquet floor and its own water supply. I notice on the wall a glass cabinet in which are displayed the stars and high honours bestowed by Queen Victoria on the famous General Gordon of Khartoum. They are most interesting – and of course most valuable – and we express some trepidation at taking over such a responsibility, especially as they are so far from the cottage, but Mrs Gifford pooh-poohs any idea of danger to them so they will have to stay put.

She tells us where to shop in the village and other useful information, and all seems to be going well when she pauses on the doorstep saying goodbye to inform me nonchalantly not to take any notice if her husband should call at the cottage. 'He may have a revolver,' she says, 'but don't worry, he is not likely to use it.' I try to look as if such occurrences are quite normal in my life; all the same I am glad Rex, who has gone on down the garden path, has not heard, and also as she is tall, slim and has dark hair and eyes, her husband is unlikely to mistake me for her! There is some comfort in this.

Friday, 28 May 1943

Move into Green Bushes. Rex will come later. Ruby has sent two lovely hydrangeas, blue and pink, and Mrs Gifford has filled the cottage with roses. It is a golden day and my heart is full of gratitude to God for this lovely home. Rex arrives later and I have a nice dinner for him and we drink to our new abode, so thankful to be alone at last together.

Rex and Eve with friends in Green Bushes, Blewbury, and, top,
Rex and colleagues outside the cottage

The village – where *The Wind in the Willows* was written in a fairy-tale cottage – is delightful. Many of the cottages have lovely gardens, filled now with bulbs and spring flowers, and interesting people live in them. The Saxon church lies at the heart of the village and the various lanes lie in a sort of spider's web around it, threaded with crystal-clear watercress-bedded streams. G.B. Stern [Gladys Bronwyn Stern, playwright] lives in a cottage here, and so does the painter Sir William Nicholson.

The jockey Steve Donoghue [six-times Epsom Derby winner and ten-times Champion Jockey] lives and has his racing stables here and the first sound in the mornings is that of the horses' hooves as the string moves past the cottage on its way to exercise on the Downs nearby.

Evelyn at the window of Green Bushes

This is the centre of white-heart cherry country, and I shall always remember the unearthly beauty of the cherry orchard by moonlight – a lovely sight.

The one snag is my difficulty in getting to Didcot to do my jobs there. Rex goes by car but I have to walk quite a distance across the village green to catch the bus, and have a long wait for the bus home, which means I don't get back till the church clock is striking seven. Jane has decided to move out of Sutton Courtenay to live in Didcot where she is on the spot for the office and nearer to me in Blewbury.

We soon get to know people in the village and Steve Donoghue invites us to cocktails and shows us round his stables. He is organising a charity concert for the war effort and looking for a suitable place to hold it, and is delighted when Rex offers him the garrison theatre at Didcot. This takes place before we move to Blewbury and the cast of *Hi-de-Hi* come over from Oxford under the patronage of Lord Nuffield and put on a marvellous show, ending with a charity auction in which Arthur Askey and Flanagan and Allen auction off some marvellous gifts. There are bottles of brandy, whisky and gin donated by Louis Freedman, amongst others, all to benefit the war effort. Rex puts on a splendid display of refreshments afterwards when we meet the cast and are introduced to Lord Nuffield and his nice wife. I shall remember how sad he looked when he told me that he would gladly give away all his millions, for this great philanthropist, who has done so much to help those who suffer, is himself denied the blessing of good health.

Saturday, 12 June 1943

Steve Donoghue has organised a donkey derby to help raise £5000, the price of a Spitfire, for the Wings for Victory week. This took place today and was a huge success. Perfect weather and the onlookers had the unique opportunity of beholding Steve Donoghue,

Gordon Richards [knighted in 1953, British flat racing Champion Jockey twenty-six times] and Michael Beary [St Leger and Derby winner] mounted on donkeys in the full glory of their racing colours, competing against one another.

The sight of these famous jockeys urging on their unaccustomed steeds, who with traditional obstinacy absolutely refuse to budge

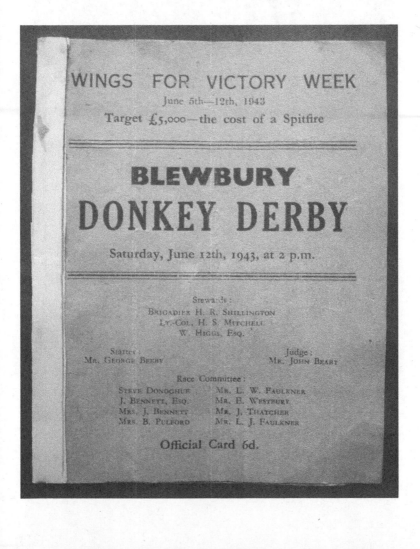

Rex, left, Louis Freedman behind him in hat and belted coat,
at an event for Spitfire Week

and in one case, having got off the mark (with the aid of a carrot),
turning round and returning to the starting point, has the spectators in stitches. Gordon Richards was actually 'unhorsed' – or
should that be 'undonkeyed'.

Later a grand auction was held in the village hall, to which many
valuable gifts had been contributed, and a good sum was raised for
the cause.

*With the exception of a short entry on 10 July about the RAOC
sports meeting in Didcot at which she presented the prizes, Evelyn's
diary entries until 19 September are observations on the war in the
Mediterranean, some of which were clearly added much later. Evelyn
was working long days in the shop, Rex likewise in Didcot, so perhaps
she had little time or inclination to write about her own day-to-day life
during this period.*

Ruby and Louis Freedman look on as Evelyn, top, presents
the prizes at Didcot depot's sports day, July 1943

The Allied victory in North Africa allowed the invasion of Sicily to take place, and Evelyn had a special interest in this campaign – her cousin, Alexander Clifford, was covering it for the Daily Mail, *while his fellow journalists Christopher Buckley and Alan Moorehead were doing the same for the* Telegraph *and the* Express. *She rejoices at news of the arrest of Mussolini, a man 'corrupted by power'. With Sicily fallen, Allied troops invaded mainland Italy, which surrendered on 8 September. Meanwhile, Alexander, unhappy at not being permitted to take part in the Salerno landings, had decided to 'go it alone' with Moorehead. Evelyn describes how they borrowed a truck from a film unit and set off hard on the heels of the retreating Panzers. In the town of Vallo on the main road to Naples they drove to the HQ of the carabinieri, who, apparently, 'promptly surrendered the town to them'. The following day they were able to inform the hard-pressed Fifth Army that Montgomery's Eighth Army was not far behind – and contact was made between the two sides on 16 September.*

Sunday, 19 September 1943

The fifth anniversary of the founding of the ATS was celebrated with a parade service held at Didcot in the presence of Chief Controller Knox. This is a great occasion for our ATS, who parade before the saluting base where Controller Knox takes the salute with Rex. Then on to the field where all the troops are assembled and where a very lovely service takes place, before Rex escorts Mrs Knox to the mess where we all meet. She is beautifully turned out and attractive-looking, and she inspects the ATS quarters – which Rex has done so much to improve – before she leaves. In due course Rex receives the following letter from her from the War Office.

Dear Brigadier Shillington,

May I say how very pleased I was to meet you and Mrs Shillington on the occasion of the church parade yesterday. I am indeed grateful to you for the help and co-operation that you have shown on all sides and which helped to produce such a happy spirit throughout the day and made my visit to Didcot so very enjoyable.

With best wishes

Yours very sincerely

Jean Knox

Jane and I are still running the WVS and CAB office and I am coping with the task of getting there and back, and indeed enjoy my morning walk through the winding paths over the watercress beds. Now that the evenings are getting chilly I appreciate fully Mrs Gifford's foresight in having installed the Courtier stove in the sitting room. There is peat in the garden stacked up and all I have to do is feed the stove with Coalite [a brand of low-temperature coke] and cover it with peat, then when I return hours later just riddle it and put some logs on it and it gives out a cheerful glow under which I can roast potatoes for our supper.

We have made friends in the village, and Michael and Daphne Sieff (of Marks and Spencer) have rented G.B. Stern's cottage nearby; when there is time we entertain one another.

Rex has got a young girl from the village who comes in and cleans the cottage as I am away all day, and life goes on in a peaceful pattern till the end of October, when Rex comes back one day to say he has been appointed to DDOS Eastern Command HQ. This will mean yet another move and I shall have to stay on here till he can find somewhere for us to live together again.

The news that Rex is leaving Didcot brings many letters from both the military and civilians saying how sorry they are that

Chief Controller Knox with Rex at the fifth anniversary of the founding of the ATS, September 1943

he has to go. One from Didcot Hospital Committee says, 'Your memory will always be associated with all you have done for the hospital', and wishes him the best of luck in his new appointment.

Another, from one of his civilian officers, gives an insight into just what sort of commanding officer Rex is:

Dear Sir,

I trust you will pardon my writing to you, but I hear you are leaving Didcot.

May I take this opportunity of expressing my very grateful thanks for all the many kindnesses you have accorded me while

serving under you at Didcot, and here's wishing you the very best of
luck in your appointment. An understanding mind with some of us
inexperienced officers meant so much in the earlier days. Many of us
will long remember your keen understanding of human nature and
patient consideration when we've come to you thinking everyone but
ourselves was wrong.

I appreciate for one the difficulty of having to try and mould
an inexperienced 'civvy' like me to be of use to the country. Any
advancement I made I owe in no small way to you teaching me the
pitfalls.

Thank you
Yours very truly
C Yerling

Monday, 25 October 1943

Rex will have to wait until he gets to Eastern Command before
he can make any arrangements as to where we can live. They have
taken over Luton Hoo, the home of the Wernhers, as their HQ.
(She, Anastasia, was the daughter of Count de Torby, and I remember her during the First World War selling programmes with her
sister Nadia at the war charities performances.)

Friday, 12 November 1943

Rex left today to take up his new appointment and I am left alone
in Green Bushes. Please God we shall be together soon again.

Monday, 15 November 1943

The autumn chill is in the air and the cottage, so perfect in
summer, is proving a somewhat different proposition now the cold
weather has set in.

The attractive oak-beamed walls of lath and plaster are little protection against cold and damp, and the heating system, so proudly pointed out by Mrs Gifford, does not work. Luckily I am at Didcot most of the day and the Courtier stove, banked up by peat and Coalite, keeps the sitting room warm, but I have only a small one-bar electric fire in my bedroom, and returning after dark to a dark and empty cottage is not very pleasant.

I have no near neighbours and the back of the cottage looks out across the garden to an orchard. There is something a little creepy about this old cottage at night and I could wish when going up the staircase to bed (which leads straight to my room) that I had a door I could lock. There are all sorts of queer creaks and groans I never noticed when Rex was here, and one night I have a real scare when I hear stealthy footsteps under my bedroom window, which I find out in the morning belonged to thieves stealing turkeys from the farm at the back of the orchard!

Wednesday, 1 December 1943

Rex is living in Luton but is not at all enthusiastic about it and feels it will be better for me to remain in Green Bushes until he has made enquiries in the neighbourhood for somewhere better for us to live.

I have asked Jane to come and stay with me until I can join him. She is as sad that I am leaving as I am to say goodbye to her. The next commanding officer's wife will take over the WVS and CAB office and Jane will stay on for a bit, but doesn't want to stay permanently now I am going. We have enjoyed working there together and have had many a good laugh – one of the best was when Lady Reading, head of the WVS, came to carry out an inspection. Jane and I cleaned up the office and were all ready to receive her when a car drew up and out got the heads of the WVS depot for which I had worked when I was living at Maiden Erlegh – Mrs Palmer and co. They were in full WVS uniform and although they had never set foot in the place, proceeded to drape themselves outside the office and when Lady Reading arrived, they welcomed her and showed her the interior as if they were the ones who had done all the work, making sure that Jane and I were kept well in the background. Rex, when he heard of it, was furious, but Jane and I were really amused as the cars drove away with the Reading lot very pleased with their morning's work and Lady Reading's kind words of congratulations!

Saturday, 4 December 1943

SNOW! The plumbing system freezes up! We phone for a plumber only to be told there is not one in the village (don't you know there's a war on!). We phone frantically around but the only one in the neighbourhood is up to his eyes with emergency calls and can give us no hope of a visit in the future. Things are getting desperate when a kind neighbour, hearing of our plight, comes to the rescue and takes us into the garden where he shows us how to deal with the sump, which will relieve things temporarily (if not too pleasantly) until the plumber can come.

Really, living in an ancient cottage in the country in wartime has its problems, and I am not sorry when Rex writes to say he has booked us a room at the Glen Eagle Hotel in Harpenden, not far from Luton Hoo, and will be sending someone over to fetch me in a week's time.

So once again it's a case of packing up, and as I have acquired extra linen, etc. and have the 'comfort trunk' to fill as well as everything else, I am thankful to have my Jane to help me. Our hearts are heavy at parting but we shall be meeting again for Christmas with the Freedmans.

Wednesday, 15 December 1943

At last the day of my departure has arrived. Rex sent a van over for our baggage and a car to take me to the Glen Eagle and I say farewell to Jane and to lovely Blewbury. I shall never forget Green Bushes and this lovely bit of England – the lovely old church, the winding lanes where a witch once lived in one of the cottages and where King Hal [Henry VIII] had a hunting lodge. Along the road past the Barley Mow, Rupert of the Rhine chased Cromwell's 'crop-ears' and here the Blewbury miser lived, a man so mean he stole clothes from the scarecrow! Near the inn called the Load of Mischief, with its sign depicting a man with a woman on his back, is where the stocks once stood and a cottage where *The Wind in the Willows* was written.

But most of all, my memories will be that night in June when the moonlight drenched the cottage in a frame of white cherry blossom.

Thursday, 16 December 1943

The Glen Eagle is a large pleasant hotel and we have a good-sized bedroom looking over the garden. There seem to be quite a few residents here. Sam Harris, the Jewish proprietor, gives us a warm welcome and it is so good to see Rex again after all this time.

Friday, 17 December 1943

Unfortunately I have gone down with a flu bug, great timing as usual. Rex is extremely busy at Eastern Command and says there's lots to be done. The hotel is splendid – I do not miss the temperamental plumbing and heating system of Green Bushes!

Saturday, 25 December 1943

Recovered enough to come down to Priors Close to spend Christmas with dear Ruby and Louis and Jane. How we shall miss all these dear friends of ours!

Louis and Ruby Freedman, Eve and friend at the
Freedmans' home, Priors Close

Friday, 31 December 1943

A New Year's Eve ball given by Eastern Command at Luton Hoo.
This is a marvellous house set in extensive grounds. The treasures
have been removed by Sir Harold and Lady Wernher but one can
imagine how splendid it must be when the art and antique furniture are in place. It has a great hall and a beautiful staircase, and
the fine apartments and antechambers in which we danced and had
our refreshments were impressive. In one room there was a lovely
portrait of Nell Gwyn, which cheered me up a lot as of course I
know no one here yet.

At midnight Rex and I, in company with this large assembly of the armed forces, welcome in the new year with fervent hopes for the future. What will the next twelve months bring, I wonder?

PART NINE

These dark days of war

January 1944–December 1945

Saturday, 1 January 1944

The set-up at this hotel is rather queer, to say the least. Sam
Harris is a somewhat flamboyant little man. We are not here long
before we discover that Gracie the housekeeper, a most attractive
and capable woman, is Sam's mistress, a fact they do not try to
disguise, leaving their bedroom door, with unmade double bed,
wide open for all to see! We find that the hotel bar is always full
in the evenings and before lunch with Americans from the nearby
HQ of the United States Eighth Army Air Force, and that some
of them stay here for weekends when they are granted leave. They
bring their girlfriends of the moment with them as a rule, but still
proudly show one photos and snaps of their wives and families at
home.

They are engaged in the heavy night-bombing of Germany,
and every day accounts come in of the terrible raids on Berlin,
Hamburg, the Ruhr, etc. I shall never forget the sight of these
weary young men, returned from the hell over Germany, their
eyes ringed with fatigue, or the tension when we heard the throb

of the returning planes and wondered how many were missing. It was pathetic to see the anxious faces of the girls they spent the few hours of leave with, trying to keep up a brave front before what so often proved to be a final farewell, or to witness the agonised waiting for news of a safe return, often so tragically ended in the news of yet one more man 'killed in action'.

The Germans – hard hit by the massive Combined Bomber Offensive – have retaliated and launched a renewed bombing attack on London and our cities. 'Retaliation' is hardly the right word as it was Hitler who began the bombing of open cities and defenceless civilians.

Tuesday, 4 January 1944

Went up to London to see a matinee performance of *Where the Rainbow Ends*; found the house sold out and had to sit on the top step of the dress circle as so often before. Went round to see Italia Conti, who produces the play, and Roger Quilter, who wrote the lovely music – but perhaps the best music of all was the happy laughter of the many children and the ringing cheers as St George vanquished the dragon in the everlasting fight between Good and Evil. How very poignant in these dark days of war. The national anthem was sung with such passion, and I left the theatre thinking how lucky we are to have Mr Churchill as our present St George.

Wednesday, 12 January 1944

News of the opening of a Russian offensive to the west, breaking the ring of Germans round Leningrad. Hitler has his hands full now with his forces facing pressure on many fronts.

Monday, 24 January 1944

News that the Allies have landed at Anzio and that a desperate battle is raging against the German forces under Field Marshal Kesselring.

Friday, 4 February 1944

Desperate fighting around the monastery at Monte Cassino where Kesselring has set up his headquarters.

Tuesday, 15 February 1944

Cassino destroyed by bombing. The destruction of this beautiful old monastery is sad news, which was inevitable when Kesselring chose it for his HQ. The Germans are still firmly entrenched in bunkers and strong-points in the massive ruins.

Rex is so busy at Eastern Command that I only see him late in the evening. He often has to go away to attend conferences in London or elsewhere. We are a conglomeration of residents here: two elderly couples (one with a very spoilt Peke called Maisie); a nice young nurse called Paddy from St Alban's Hospital; a nice man, unfit for the Forces, who is working at some civilian establishment and who is showing me how to do the *Telegraph* crossword puzzles; and a Free French officer with his blonde wife, much younger than he is.

We have also made friends with Peggy and Douglas Gluckstein. Douglas is at Luton Hoo with Rex and he and his wife, who is a rabbi's daughter, come sometimes to stay the weekend here. She is a delightful girl, very attractive, who lives in London. Nan Gluckstein, Douglas's mother, also comes down for weekends; her husband, Douglas's father, was killed in the First War World.

Saturday, 26 February 1944

Rex is to get some leave and we have decided to spend it at the Tregenna Castle Hotel in St Ives. The weather is bitterly cold here and it should be warmer down there in Cornwall. Much looking forward to it, and Rex is too.

Sunday, 27 February 1944

Life here at the Glen Eagle Hotel continues to be eventful, with various comings and goings. My crossword skills have greatly improved and I am getting quite addicted to my daily puzzle. Guy, my tutor, has been transferred to another establishment in London and I will miss him dearly as he was good company. I speculate on the nature of his occupation as he never openly stated just what it was, although I think it was definitely 'hush-hush'.

The open affair continues without shame!

Evelyn with hair in scarf, Rex behind her next to proprietor
Sam Harris (with cigarette) on terrace of the
Glen Eagle Hotel, pictured opposite

Tuesday, 4 April 1944

Here we are at Tregenna Castle and it is all we had hoped for!
Set high above St Ives bay in extensive grounds and woods, we
have a large sunny room on the ground floor with French windows which lead out to the woods at the back of the hotel where
we can wander. The daffodils and narcissi and rock plants are all
in bloom and we find spring already here in contrast to wintry
Hertfordshire. The hotel is very comfortable indeed. It is filled
with residents here to escape the bombing, and the food is very
good.

Wednesday, 5 April 1944

Today we took the bus to Penzance and another to Lamorna Cove. The walk down to the cove was exquisite, with blossom hanging over the stream and masses of wild daffodils at our feet. The cove itself, set in granite cliffs, was being used by Commandos practising a landing. It was thrilling to watch them scale the high cliffs, but even more so to watch their rapid descent, practically running down the steep sides with a rope wrapped round them. Rex and I walked on round the headland and came upon a most lovely sight: masses of golden daffodils on the grey granite against the deep blue of the sky and sea. Lovely Lamorna Cove, I shall always hold you in my memory.

Thursday, 6 April 1944

Today we decided we would take the cliff walk to St Gurnard's Head. We started off all right, but alas, the path soon deserted the cliff edge and we plodded through what seemed to be endless cabbage fields intersected by granite hedges and innumerable stiles! After a considerable time of this very boring ramble, I stopped and told my better half, who takes all this sort of thing (literally) in his stride, that I would go no further. His reply was that he was determined to continue but I could turn back if I liked, and on reflection on what this would mean (endless cabbages and no Rex) I decided to continue with my lord and master (as well he knew I would!). I was rewarded in the end when we reached St Gurnard's Head, a most impressive headland jutting out into the Atlantic, where we sat high above the sea, watching the waves beat on the formidable rocks far below us, while seabirds of all sorts screamed and wheeled beneath us.

Then off again to be rewarded at a friendly inn with a ploughman's lunch and beer for Rex, and cider for me, and best of all (as far as I was concerned) with news that a bus would shortly be passing the inn which would take us back to Penzance.

Saturday, 8 April 1944

We wave farewell to our Cornish resort and its glorious scenery. Rex has to go to London on Monday for a meeting at the War Office and will be staying overnight. I amuse myself with an evening watching American airmen trying to impress a group of girls – with a limited rate of success.

Monday, 10 April 1944

Odessa liberated. Russian offensive in the Crimea.

We shall have spring all over again! The daffs and rock plants are only just coming into bloom. They have quite a nice garden here. Marguerite Nangle, who is living here with her husband, Colonel Nangle, is a keen gardener and we do a little work on it, with Sam's consent; it is much neglected. Colonel Nangle, who is years older than his wife, was in the Indian Army in Intelligence and used to go off on missions disguised as a native. He should have been a good spy as he is very thin and wiry and can sit for hours squatting on his heels in native fashion. This comes in very handy when he helps us weeding the lawn! They have a Scottie called Hamish who reminds us of our dear and sadly missed Chaser.

Tuesday, 9 May 1944

King Victor Emmanuel of Italy has abdicated in favour of his son, Umberto.

We have a new resident, a tall man with very blue eyes and a gentle manner. He turns out to be John Logie Baird, the brilliant inventor and pioneer of British television and coloured TV. His house in Sydenham has been badly damaged by blasts in an air raid which has forced him to send his wife and two children to Cornwall. He has left his faithful friend and assistant to look after his priceless apparatus and equipment and come to live at the Glen Eagle. He is naturally extremely anxious about the risk of another raid destroying his life's work. He tells us that a disastrous fire in 1936 at the Crystal Palace – in which his apparatus was stored – cost him thousands of pounds and all his precious blueprints. Another blow was when the rival firm, Marconi-EMI, was awarded the coveted BBC contract, and the final disaster was the declaration of war in 1939 which forced the Baird company into liquidation.

It is soon clear to us that Logie Baird, like many men of genius, has no head for business and a total disregard for money and that he has been cruelly exploited. No one could help admiring this gentle giant and we pray that fate may spare him further calamities.

Sunday, 4 June 1944

The fall of Rome, and Kesselring falls back 150 miles to the Gothic Line.

Tuesday, 6 June 1944

Awakened before dawn by the steady throb of countless aircraft flying in wave after wave. Then comes the news over the radio that the Allies have made a landing on the coast of Normandy! I pray to God that all our men are safe and that the inevitable casualties will be fewer than expected.

Rex off to Eastern Command, where so much of this preparation for Operation Overlord has been planned. All day reports come in of airborne landings and bridgeheads being established from which the Allies fight their way through the German defences.

Monday, 12 June 1944

Montgomery welcomes the Prime Minister, Winston Churchill, with CIGS Sir Alan Brooke, to his HQ at Creully.

The invasion of Normandy is only six days old when Hitler launches his 'secret weapon', the deadly V1, on Britain. The news of these new weapons is daunting. They are pilotless flying bombs, aimed to 'cut out' over their target, exploding with devastating effect.

The Battle of Normandy is developing, waged in the worst weather in living memory. These desperate battles are reported by my cousin Alexander and his associates, and their reports are all we know of the appalling conditions and the bitter fighting, with heavy casualties on both sides.

The Doodlebugs, as Hitler's flying bombs are called, continue to spread destruction over Britain.

Poor Logie Baird is frantic in case one is dropped on his house in Sydenham. He has taken us to see his laboratory there and a wonderful experience it was! The house is badly shattered, shuttered and boarded up, thick with dust and fallen plaster, but he took us down to the basement, and opening a door, told us not to enter until he gave the word. When we do we see ourselves advancing into the room on a screen, not only in colour, but in three-dimensional TV. As we advance over the floor – avoiding the cables which lie about and the wires which descend from every angle – he explains how we are some of the very first to see this miracle.

No wonder, then, that he spends his time in a state of nervous agitation lest this priceless and quite uninsurable invention be destroyed any day or night.

Every morning after breakfast he rings Sydenham to hear if his brainchild is still intact. This he will not do in the hotel, and he comes out into the garden, where I am often sitting, to pace restlessly up and down until the time comes for him to phone, when off he goes, having shed his coat, his braces off his shoulders and wearing his bedroom slippers! The perfect picture of the absent-minded inventor of fiction!

Returning, relieved that all is well, he resumes his pacing up and down, contemplating the heavens, that brilliant brain of his evolving heavens knows what scientific wonders, till the moment comes when he stops and enquires of me if I can lend him a pencil. This has now happened so often that I always have a second one in my bag.

Logie Baird is not a fit man. He is on a stringent diet and badly misses his wife and family. He loves to come up to our room after dinner to hear the news, and always asks for 'Dragon's Blood'- his name for the cup of Bovril I give him. This gentle lovable man deserves better than the treatment his ungrateful country has given him.

On 9 June an article appeared in the *Daily Mail* under the heading 'Waterproofing the Army', describing the immense task the RAOC was set in equipping the tanks, armoured cars and supply vehicles so that they could get through water, and the assembly and issuing of half a million components to some 5,000 different depots. This task, involving Britain's entire steel industry (sheet rolling), was one of the greatest rush jobs of the war. Time was so short that 280 works, scattered from Scotland to Cornwall, were engaged on the job. No wonder Rex has been busy!

Tuesday, 27 June 1944

The Americans capture Cherbourg.

We are getting a nasty taste of the Doodlebugs. So far none have fallen on Harpenden but they come over us on their deadly mission. They seem to have no military target – just dropping and exploding at random and designed, obviously, to break our morale. One is supposed to take cover when one hears the ominous 'phut phut' of their engines, but personally I always seem too paralysed to do anything during the short period before the explosion – which tells one it has fallen elsewhere. The casualties since these 'secret weapons' were first launched are as heavy as during the Blitz of 1941 and Hitler loses no pilots.

Rex has received a letter from General Williams.

> *Controller of Ordnance Services*
> *The War Office*
> *Whitehall Place*
> *20th June 1944*

Dear Mr Shillington,

Now that the campaign in Europe has begun, I would like to thank you and your staff, military, ATS and civilian, for the magnificent job you have done in equipping the Expeditionary Force and in getting ready the thousands of stores required to maintain it in the early stages.

The work has been hard and the hours long and the task is not yet over, but it will be a source of extreme satisfaction to everyone who has taken part in the preparation of the Force to know that all Commanders, from the Command-in-Chief down, have expressed their opinion that never has an Expeditionary Force been so well and completely equipped before. I attach a copy of a letter I have received from the Commander of the 2nd Army, which is typical. I should be glad if you will convey this message to all the members of your staff.

Yours sincerely,
L. R. Williams

As stated, General Williams enclosed a letter expressing the same thanks and appreciation from General Sir Miles Dempsey, written on the eve of D-Day.

Sunday, 9 July 1944
Caen falls to the British.

Saturday, 15 July 1944
Rommel attacked by fighters and his car crashed into a tree. He is reported seriously wounded.

Thursday, 20 July 1944
Hitler reported wounded in a bomb plot on his life by his Generals, unluckily unsuccessful. The Allies have landed in the South of France.

Monday, 28 August 1944
The liberation of Paris! This wonderful and moving occasion is brought home to us vividly by our Free French officer, Lieutenant Otten, who was living at the Glen Eagle Hotel. He invited us up to the Free French Forces HQ in St James's Square, and it is impossible to describe the atmosphere of joy, relief and emotion which was felt by all as General de Gaulle led the Free French Forces through the Arc de Triomphe at the head of the Armies of Liberation. How wonderful to know that Paris is at last free from the German occupation under which she has lain for so long.

I have managed to get up to London to meet Louis and Ruby for lunch, and entertain them and Jane and other friends in the lovely Ladies' Room of Rex's club, the Junior United Service Club in Lower Regent Street. There is also a beautiful drawing room, full of lovely flowers and periodicals to read, where one can have tea. When Rex is able and has to visit the War Office he joins us, but his duties at Eastern Command keep him very busy.

One evening we are invited to meet Douglas Gluckstein's grandmother, and he and Peggy drive us up to dine with her in her beautiful flat in Berkeley Square.

She is a wonderful and charming old lady and most interesting. She tells us how the Lyons teashops started. It was the idea of her husband, who was horrified at the idea of young women (just then beginning to be employed as 'lady typewriters') having nowhere to get a meal except at the city chop houses, frequented entirely by men. The idea of a chain of shops selling tea but no alcoholic liquor was born, but he did not feel it suitable that the name Gluckstein, associated with the cigarette firm of Salmon and Gluckstein, should be used for the new project, so the name of a cousin, Joseph Lyons, a dilettante and free from the stigma of smoking, was chosen. Mrs Gluckstein told us how she sailed in a boat with her husband to Ceylon where he bought the tea plantation for Lyons tea, which would become so famous, and how the first teashop was opened in Piccadilly. We also met Peggy's parents, her father a rabbi and a most delightful man.

Friday, 1 September 1944

The Allies take Dieppe. Everything seems to be going wonderfully well and all seems set for a clear sweep to the Rhine.

Now Rex is able to snatch a well-deserved leave and we are told of the Ferryboat Inn at Helford Passage which is situated right on the estuary.

Monday, 4 September 1944

Antwerp is liberated.

Rex and I go to the Ferryboat Inn, which is delightful. We are intrigued to see, moored in the passage, one of the huge Mulberry harbours (Churchill's brainchild), which played such a vital part in the Normandy Landings. [An initial design for a temporary portable harbour had indeed been sketched by Churchill back in 1917.]

We are hearing now something of this gigantic operation in which forests became ammunition dumps, and tented camps (well camouflaged) for a thousand men covered acres. It was in vast holes on the side of the Thames that thousands of men worked to construct these great Mulberry harbours to be towed across the Channel and thus enable the armies to land where the Germans least expected them.

All this was carried out in the greatest secrecy. No part of the country escaped and by spring the whole of England seethed with men and machines.

We soon discover for ourselves what a terrific effect this strict security has had upon the people in this area. It is quite impossible to obtain any directions from the locals who, when we enquire the way to the nearest cove (Durgan), where we want to bathe, treat us with a blank stare and a flat denial of any knowledge of such a place!

Looking at the Mulberry harbour brings back to Rex memories of the tremendous task it was to equip the armies for Operation Overlord before the landings. These armies had to be maintained at a rate of 750,000 tonnes of supplies a month, covering everything from ammunition to a toothbrush; from tanks, guns, trucks and rifles to toilet paper! Every soldier even had to be supplied with a vomit bag in case of seasickness!

The thought of war, however, is soon forgotten in the sheer beauty and peace of this lovely corner of Cornwall: the walks across the estuary, where herons wade, and onto the cliffs at Nare Head, or down to Frenchman's Creek of Daphne du Maurier's novel. One day we discover a beautiful little church still decorated for harvest festival, with stooks of corn and leaves and fishermen's nets, and instead of the organ the hum of the bees.

Here, as we kneel in the golden shaft of sunshine, surrounded by the fruits of men's toil in thanksgiving for God's gift of 'harvest home', one feels the 'peace which passes understanding'.

Saturday, 9 September 1944

This morning Rex received a telegram recalling him immediately to duty. This blow comes quite out of the blue, but a rumour that Hitler has launched his second 'secret weapon', the V2, on London may have some bearing on the matter. Rex goes straight upstairs to pack his things and I want to go back with him but he points out that our booking is for another five days and it would be a pity to waste it, and most reluctantly I am persuaded to stay on.

I try and make the best of the lovely weather and I go for walks and swim in the cove, but the joy has gone out of the holiday and I find the evenings, surrounded by happy holiday families (and too timid to go to the bar by myself), very lonely indeed and am thankful when at last I find myself on the train for home.

It is quite true that a new and terribly destructive weapon has been launched in Hitler's V2. Stories of the destructive quality of this huge rocket, which has a much longer range than the V1, come in as more of the deadly objects fall on England.

Monday, 18 September 1944

The fall of Boulogne and Brest.

Saturday, 30 September 1944

Calais is now in the hands of the Allies. News of my cousin Elizabeth Clifford's engagement to an actor, Gordon Davies. I pray to God that they will be happy.

This is the same Elizabeth who inherited Evelyn's diaries after her death, later passing them on to her daughter, Jacy Wall.

Thursday, 5 October 1944

The British land in Greece. Hungary asks for an armistice.

I am in my bedroom when there is a terrific explosion and blast waves which tell us that we have had a visit from one of Hitler's V2s. As our windows are still intact it is evident that it must be some distance away, in the direction of Luton, and as Luton Hoo is considerably nearer that town than we are I spend an anxious time till we hear it has actually fallen on Luton itself and Rex comes home to dinner with reports of the terrible devastation and heavy casualties.

Every day now we hear of this deadly weapon against which there is little defence.

Friday, 24 November 1944

The Russians have crossed the Danube. But things in France are not going so well, and as autumn deepens into winter, so our hopes of an early victory fade with the falling leaves.

Life at the Glen Eagle leaves much to be desired. The hotel – as far as the residents are concerned – has deteriorated a great deal since Sam Harris became so deeply involved with the USA Eighth Army Air Force stationed nearby.

They now use the hotel increasingly, especially the bar, and while some are splendid fellows, others are often the worse for drink, and in the evenings the din rises even to our bedroom. Luckily the bar closes at ten o'clock, but the Yanks now come to stay weekends and there is an element that bring their 'floozies' with them and throw wild and noisy drinks parties till all hours of the night.

It is useless to complain to Sam about this. He is doing very nicely, thank you, with the proceeds from the bar, and he now serves meals to the Americans in the bar after drinking hours.

He cuts down our meagre rations to the bone and it is hard for us to see (and smell!) the large juicy steaks being served to the Americans as we cross the hall to eat our scanty meal. Of course Sam is quick to point out to us that the Americans supply the steaks themselves, but it is easy to see that as he and Gracie also profit from this boost to their meat ration, he is not likely to do anything to upset them by complaining of their behaviour.

Saturday, 16 December 1944

The Germans have launched a strong offensive against the Americans in the Ardennes. The news coming in of the desperate fighting shows that they are by no means beaten and that there are many battles yet to be fought.

Sunday, 24 December 1944

News that the Germans' Panzer Army is now in sight of the Meuse and of heavy fighting and casualties. Not much joy for Christmas!

Monday, 25 December 1944

Sam put on a party with long tables at which we all sat, and asked some of his cronies to it. We and the other residents joined in but it soon became rather smutty and noisy, so Rex and I went up to our room with some of our friends to try and forget the shortcomings of our hotel and to remember how blessed we are to be here together.

There is also much to be thankful for, this Christmas of 1944. The successful Normandy landings, the liberation of Paris and

Rome, the Russians across the Danube; and in the Far East the Japanese driven by the Americans out of Assam and forced to retreat from Imphal and Kohima. We still have the V2s with us and there are many desperate battles to be fought, but we can at last feel that the tide has turned and can look forward with renewed hope to whatever the new year may bring.

Wednesday, 3 January 1945
Montgomery has launched a counter-attack against the Germans in north Alsace.

The V2 blitz still continues. When I go up to London I can see, as the train draws into the station, the appalling destruction which these terrible weapons are inflicting on our city. Huge areas are completely demolished; piles of rubble mark where buildings used to stand.

The bombing of Germany continues and it's some little comfort to know that the Germans are getting some of their own medicine.

Friday, 12 January 1945
The Russians have launched a strong offensive and Hitler has been forced to order a retreat on the Western Line as the Russians' offensive demands more troops.

Wednesday, 17 January 1945
The Russians have entered Warsaw! Hitler must be really regretting having to fight on two fronts.

Thursday, 18 January 1945
On the Western Front, the Armies are engaged in a battle for the Rhine; bitter fighting is taking place in waterlogged country against fierce German resistance.

Sunday, 18 February 1945

Glorious day! The hottest for this time of year for forty years! Up for the first time after a bad bout of flu, feeling rotten.

Tuesday, 20 February 1945

News from Aunt Alice that my cousin Alexander is to be married on Thursday! His bride is Jenny Nicholson, a brilliant journalist whom he met when they were both covering the liberation of Paris. She is the daughter of Robert Graves, the poet, and Nancy Nicholson, the daughter of Sir William Nicholson, the artist, who was one of our neighbours in Blewbury. For some reason neither mother nor daughter have chosen to be known by the name of Graves, famous though it is! Anyway, Graves and Nancy are now divorced and he is living on the island of Majorca.

Alice also writes that she is very anxious about Uncle Harry. His faithful housekeeper of many years, Miss Moore, is retiring, and in spite of Aunt Elsie's efforts to find a suitable replacement she has had no success so far.

As Harry will be all alone in his house, Rothbury, when Miss Moore leaves, Alice is moving in to stay with him and she asks if I can possibly go to Storrington to help them until a new house-keeper is found. I have written today to say of course I will go.

Thursday, 22 February 1945

Alex and Jenny were married today at the Savoy Chapel before a gathering of their many friends. Apart from Alex's own family none of the other members of the family were invited.

Wednesday, 28 February 1945

Flying bombs still falling. Rex away for three days on conference in London. I pray to God that he will be safe from the danger of the

V2s. So far we have been spared these terrible destructive weapons in Luton, but again London is taking a pounding.

Thursday, 1 March 1945

Up to London to see Kilham Roberts about *Rainbow* [Denys Kilham Roberts was a barrister as well as an author and editor, but the purpose of the visit is unclear]. Went to Knightsbridge afterwards and was very distressed to see what one of the beastly 'buzz bombs' had done to the Bunny Dell, demolishing the lovely may trees under which the nannies used to sit with their little charges (often with coronets on their prams). It looks like a battlefield, torn and scorched and devastated. While I was in Woollands [a Knightsbridge department store] they had warning of yet another approaching and we were all shepherded down into the basement where we sat till the danger had passed.

Tuesday, 6 March 1945

The Allies take Cologne. Things are certainly moving now! Alice wrote yesterday that Miss Moore has left and she has moved into Rothbury so I shall be off there tomorrow.

Thursday, 8 March 1945

Here I am in Storrington, Alice and Harry very pleased to see me, as I them. It has been arranged that I shall sleep in Alice's cottage, Merryfield, and take over the shopping for rations, etc. and do the cooking: a midday meal for Harry, Alice and self, and snack at night.

My heart sank when I saw on what I was supposed to cook tasty meals: Harry's gas-cooker is a 'vintage' model and ought to be in a museum! Harry, a real miser (bless him!), surrounded by his treasures, remains blissfully unaware of the barest amenities for running a house. I have seen him dole out the absolute minimum from a shabby old purse to poor Miss Moore for such essentials as new sheets and towels, and he would most certainly have a fit if asked to invest in a new cooker!

Monday, 12 March 1945

The last enemy rearguards, fighting furiously, have been driven back across the Rhine and now the British, American and Canadian forces lie upon its western bank.

My battle with Harry's cooker continues! My day is passed as follows:

Up and get my breakfast, then to Rothbury, doing any necessary shopping en route. A warm welcome from Alice and Harry, who expects his lunch to be on the table by 12.45 p.m. sharp! After coffee with Alice and Harry I enter the kitchen, don my apron as if it were warpaint, and say, 'Let battle commence!'

The first struggle is to light the old thing (the cooker, not Harry!) and after several attempts – resulting in it popping out and a most unpleasant smell of gas – I am ready to cook. There is absolutely no way whatever of regulating the temperature – the gas seems to fluctuate (doubtless dying of old age) – and the fact that dear Harry is by now, watch in hand, pacing back and forth in the dining room, is hardly likely to soothe one's nerves!

I am also finding it rather scary having to return to Merryfield after dark along the blacked-out lanes by torchlight and let myself into the dark empty cottage, which having been unheated all day is very cold and unwelcoming. I get upstairs and into bed with hot-water bottle as fast as I can! Still, it is so worthwhile to feel I am being of use to these two dear relatives of mine who are so appreciative of my help in this emergency.

Tuesday, 13 March 1945

Elsie's efforts have been successful and, all being well, I shall return to the Glen Eagle on Thursday. Out of the frying pan and back into the fire!

Wednesday, 14 March 1945

Harry's new housekeeper arrived today. Her name is Mrs Hardy (descendant of Nelson's Hardy, she tells us). She is small, grey-haired and very genteel and I just wonder how she will stand up to the introduction to Harry's cooker ... May the blood of the Hardies sustain her!

Thursday, 15 March 1945

Returned to the hotel. Rex off to Colchester tomorrow; he is frantically busy and I am thankful that we managed to have dinner together.

Tuesday, 20 March 1945

Mandalay captured.

Friday, 23 March 1945

Wonderful news! Montgomery, with that old war-dog Churchill by his side, has crossed the Rhine! At last the Allies are on German soil!

The Russian armies too have swept across the Oder and Neisse Rivers and joined hands with the Western Allies. Can this be the beginning of the end?

Saturday, 24 March 1945

Letter from Daddy. My half-brother Hugh, who joined Daddy's old regiment, the Scottish Rifles (now with the Mountain Battery, incorporating many regiments), is taking part in the fighting.

Evelyn's father, Harold Clifford, his wife, Eva,
son Hugh and a friend

Friday, 30 March 1945
Heidelberg and Danzig have fallen and our tanks sweep on!

Thursday, 12 April 1945

Very sad news today: President Roosevelt, our great friend and ally, has died suddenly of a cerebral haemorrhage. He will be greatly mourned and it is ironical that he, who has played such a great part in this war, should not have been spared to see its victorious end. He is succeeded by his vice-president, Harry S Truman.

Tuesday, 17 April 1945

Rex has seven days' leave from tomorrow and we are off to Tregenna Castle once more. I hope we can enjoy a full holiday this time – and avoid the cabbages!

Tuesday, 24 April 1945

This has been a lovely holiday, once more in lovely Cornwall. We revisited Lamorna Cove, went to Kynance Cove with its marvellous colouring, and took walks along the cliffs. The Cornish lanes with their granite hedges are alight with spring flowers and gorse.

Thursday, 26 April 1945

Collapse of all German resistance in Italy!

Sunday, 29 April 1945

Mussolini has been murdered in Milan! His body and that of his mistress were taken by the enraged Italian mob and strung up, head downwards, in the square in front of Milan's railway station. This is the end of the strutting dictator who has caused the deaths and misery of thousands of his countrymen.

Tuesday, 1 May 1945

Hitler, hiding in the bunkers beneath the German Chancellery in Berlin, with the Russians on the outskirts of the city, has committed suicide. With his world collapsing about him he first married his faithful Eva Braun and then shot her and himself. It is almost impossible to digest this news – so long has the world shuddered to hear that raging, ranting voice and the throb of his aircraft and secret weapons as they dropped their deadly missiles, while country after country fell under the occupation of the German Panzer Armies.

What utter desolation and destruction he has left behind him – to his own country as well as many others – in his mad dream of establishing a *Reich* 'which would last for a thousand years'. All to end in a Berlin bunker.

Wednesday, 2 May 1945
The fall of Berlin. As the British armies and the Russian army meet on the shores of the Baltic, the survivors of the Berlin garrison surrender and Goebbels and his family commit suicide.

Friday, 4 May 1945
Today in his caravan on Lüneburg Heath, Montgomery accepted the unconditional surrender of the German forces. So ends the holocaust of the past years of this terrible war in Europe.

Tuesday, 8 May 1945
Today was signed in Reims the official document which formally concluded the war in Europe [actually signed morning of 7 May]. The end of the war was celebrated quietly in Harpenden, but in London the joy and relief of the Londoners broke all bounds and they flocked, as they always do in time of national crisis, to Buckingham Palace, and there on the famous balcony the Royal Family, accompanied by Winston Churchill, stood to acknowledge the cheers of their faithful subjects, who together with them had shared the dark days of the war.

The end of the hostilities will mean a change at Eastern Command. Luton Hoo is returning to its owners, Sir Harold and Lady Wernher, and Rex will get a new posting. So yet another move in the offing! I wonder how many times during this war I have moved, and how many friends I have left behind.

As the summer comes, it is still hard to realise that the war is over and that one can sleep quietly in one's bed.

Monday, 23 July 1945

The war in the Far East is far from over. The Japanese have proved themselves masters of jungle warfare and it seems this could drag on and on. They have a great many prisoners who they treat with the utmost cruelty, especially those who were forced to work on the infamous Burma Road, where so many perished.

Monday, 6 August 1945

The Americans have dropped an atomic bomb on Hiroshima causing terrible devastation. This terrible weapon, developed in secret by scientists, explodes in a mushroom-shaped cloud which rains down appalling contamination on all beneath it.

Wednesday, 8 August 1945

The Russians have declared war on Japan.

Thursday, 9 August 1945

Another atomic bomb dropped on Japan, on Nagasaki. Reports coming in of more terrible devastation.

Tuesday, 14 August 1945

News today of the unconditional surrender of Japan! This is to spare their country from total destruction by this terrible new weapon, which inflicts not only devastation on vast areas but also ghastly injuries of burning and deadly pollution of the atmosphere. [Surrender actually took place on 15 August.]

Monday, 20 August 1945

In the meantime Rex has got his posting with Eastern Command to Wentworth, near Windsor, and it means finding somewhere to live in the neighbourhood.

Thursday, 23 August 1945

We have been told of an excellent hotel at Englefield Green, near Wentworth, and as Rex is frantically busy winding up his office at Luton Hoo, I set off today to inspect our future abode. The hotel is a little way out of the village, set on the edge of the green, and is a large very pleasant house with a fine garden. I am most favourably impressed with it. The proprietress, Miss Hilda Downey, tells me she can offer us a double room on the first floor on 15 September, and although I can't see it I feel that I should book it then and there, and when Rex hears about it he agrees I did the right thing. He is very anxious to leave the Glen Eagle as soon as possible and as he has to take up his appointment at Wentworth on Monday, 3 September, he rings up Douglas Gluckstein, who is demobbed and now the manager of the Cumberland Hotel, Marble Arch, and books us a room there.

Sunday, 2 September 1945

The surrender of the Japanese signed in Tokyo Bay.

We go to London for the Freedmans' party. Louis has taken rooms for all his guests in Jermyn Street and we meet dear Jane again. It is grand to see Louis and Ruby once more and to meet Neil, their son, back from Cairo, and some of his young friends.

We have a superb dinner at Ciro's with champagne and then all walk to Piccadilly Circus to join the huge crowds assembled there around the statue of Eros (sandbagged) to watch for the magic moment when the lights go on again in London. As the singer's voice floats out from the Criterion restaurant balcony, all the lights and neon signs, darkened for so many years, blaze out once more to the deafening cheers of the crowds.

Then off with many more to the palace where thousands are already calling for the Royal Family, who repeatedly appear to acknowledge their cheers. After a struggle we manage to fight our way back to the West End to a nightclub where we see a cabaret and, fortified by more champagne, dance into the small hours of the morning. Quite a night!

Monday, 3 September 1945
Rex collects our baggage from the Glen Eagle and we move out for good. We have a very nice bedroom at the Cumberland (with private bathroom) and the Glucksteins have filled the room with flowers. They give us a warm welcome and insist on our dining with them.

Tuesday, 4 September 1945
Breakfast in our room, then Rex's car calls for him and he goes off to Wentworth. I go shopping and on to Harvey Nichols for lunch – it is wonderful to be in London again! Rex back in time for dinner. What a relief to be out of the Glen Eagle!

Wednesday, 5 September 1945
The British re-occupy Singapore.

Thursday, 6 September 1945
Dined with the Freedmans and Neil at Ciro's.

Friday, 14 September 1945

The Glucksteins dined with us at the Hungaria.

Saturday, 15 September 1945

Rex off early to Wentworth and I will follow by train and meet him at the Lodge Hotel this evening. First of all I went into Hyde Park to watch the flypast of the Battle of Britain pilots in their Spitfires over Buckingham Palace. It was a lovely clear morning, and as the crowds waited, gazing into the sky, we heard in the distance the throb of the planes and suddenly there they were, flying in perfect formation to execute a victory roll over the palace where the Royal Family were on the balcony to greet them. It was a most moving sight and our hearts were full as we saluted the last of those gallant few who fought against such dreadful odds to save England in her hour of peril.

In my taxi on the way to Waterloo I pass the captured V2 rocket, a most sinister sight, and a reminder of yet another peril thankfully passed.

Arrived at the Lodge Hotel. Our room is not very large but has a nice view over the gardens. Rex joins me and we have an excellent dinner and feel we are very lucky to be here.

Sunday, 16 September 1945

Rex takes me over to Wentworth where his office is situated in the golf clubhouse, now taken over by the Army. Set in pine and heather country, all around are the fine houses of the rich tycoons, members of the famous golf course. The surroundings of the hotel, in Englefield Green, are very pleasant too, high up above Windsor and just on the edge of Windsor Great Park.

Monday, 1 October 1945

The Lodge Hotel is most efficiently run by its owner, Miss Hilda Downey. She is a somewhat daunting personality, very fat and bouncy, and sports a mass of auburn hair (I suspect a wig). She has a sort of 'boudoir' off the hall, where she sits, rather like a spider at the heart of its web, fully alert to everything that goes on in her domain. She is extremely efficient. Every Thursday a car comes for her, and in full warpaint, Miss Downey drives off to Fortnum and Mason, to return in the evening laden with goodies for the table. She has a special clientele of customers in the parents of boys at nearby Eton College who come down to visit their offspring on Sundays and who appreciate the excellent food they get here. She has an excellent cook and all the vegetables come from her garden.

There are a nice lot of residents here. One is a widow who has a niece in Australia. She shows me snapshots of her very attractive niece, and points out a tall young man amongst her many boy-friends, telling me that he is Prince Philip of Greece. He is very handsome and I ask if perhaps her niece will marry him, to which she replies, 'Good heavens, no! He hasn't a penny.'

Another resident is an attractive redhead (another Evelyn). She was born in Shanghai where her father was in the Diplomatic Service. Her mother, a widow, stayed on in Shanghai and was imprisoned by the Japanese, with many dying of starvation. She was liberated and is now slowly recovering in England.

Evelyn is in the throes of an affair with the son of a diplomat and confides in me how 'very special' he is. She is divorced and has a son at school and he is unmarried, but younger, I think. She goes up to London to meet her beloved and returns either in seventh heaven or in deep despair, and I must confess I find it all rather boring.

She and a friend of hers who comes to stay are the envy of us all as they have real silk taffeta petticoats which <u>rustle</u> as they walk! Most of us have very tired crêpe de Chine – dress coupons being so scarce.

Englefield Green is an attractive spot and now Rex has more time he and I take long walks in Windsor Forest – so lovely! I go in to Windsor for my hairdresser and Ina Egan, who lives in Windsor, comes over sometimes for lunch here.

Sunday, 14 October 1945

Rex and I had a glorious walk in the forest to Virginia Water, and there in the golden sunshine we walked under the chestnut trees by the lake, the 'plopping' chestnuts the only things falling from the skies now.

Miss Downey is a real martinet! She loves to entertain the guests in her boudoir in the evenings, and although Rex often comes in from Wentworth tired and not feeling sociable, we soon discover that the invitation is in the nature of a royal command!

One of her idiosyncrasies is to insist on the front door being always kept open. Now it is the autumn and when the east wind blows it makes the hotel (though centrally heated) very cold. On enquiring of the residents why this has to be, we are told that it is Miss Downey's decree and that it is best not to cross her. They tell us of a couple of residents who did this and were escorted to the front door (which was of course open) where with a sweeping gesture she informed them, '*There* is the great outdoors – it is all yours from tomorrow.' It is therefore best to remain on the right side of this formidable lady and we have so much to be thankful for here – excellent food, good company and lovely surroundings. I get up to London to see my friends by Green Line Bus which passes the hotel, and we have every comfort.

Tuesday, 25 December 1945

Christmas Day. Church with Rex and the Fosters. They are very nice; he is a doctor and his sister, Aileen, married to a man in ICI now out in Australia, becomes a good friend of ours. Miss Downey puts on a real Fortnum and Mason display of Christmas cheer and we play mahjong after dinner.

Monday, 31 December 1945

And so the year of victory draws to its close, but at what cost of lives shattered by the loss of dear ones? I pray to God another such war will never happen again and wonder how long the peace will last. In an Army life one never really knows.

PART TEN

Halcyon days

July–December 1946

Evelyn's first diary entry of 1946 is not until March, when we learn that Rex has a new appointment: Director of Ordnance Services for the British Army in Europe, taking over from General Geake. The post will be based at the Palace of Caserta near Naples, headquarters of Allied Command and scene of the signing of the surrender of the German army the previous year. Rex leaves on 6 May, and, while she is waiting for news that she can join him, Evelyn fills her time visiting friends and relatives – her beloved Jane and aunts, of course, but also Marjorie, the friend she made at the Clifton Hotel in Southport when Rex was posted to Burscough in 1938. Once Evelyn makes a friend they are a friend for life.

On 2 July she finally sails for Italy on the SS Ranchi, whose passengers consist mainly of Italian prisoners of war returning to their homeland.

True to form, Evelyn makes friends amongst the Army wives on board, and in particular with one of her cabin mates, Lita Staunton, wife of the senior chaplain to the Forces, who is also travelling to Naples. Lita is 'a grand travelling companion', writes Evelyn, 'with her enchanting Irish brogue and delicious sense of humour'.

The Italian diaries see Evelyn doing what she does best: describing the idiosyncrasies of the human race with her amused and sympathetic eye. If

they lack some of the drama of the war years, they are just as fascinating,
for Evelyn's enthusiasm for her new surroundings is so infectious. And so
she offers us a privileged glimpse of life in a conquered nation, while never
ceasing to be hugely grateful for the opportunity she has been given to escape,
for a while, the austerity of post-war Britain.

We pick up the diary again as SS Ranchi sails into the Bay of Naples.

Thursday, 11 July 1946

One of the happiest days of my life! First of all it is a glorious day of
blue sky and sunshine and very warm. Lita and I finish packing and
join everyone else on deck to watch Capri rising out of the mist
on our right and the island of Ischia on our left – then the cone of
Vesuvius raises its head and we are entering the Bay of Naples.

It is all and more than I expected: the deep blue of the sea across
which Vesuvius rises in majestic grandeur, and on the hills lovely
villas set in gardens. Which, I wonder, is ours!

We approach the harbour and it is possible to see the damage
done by the Allied bombing – many buildings on the docks are
mere shells and derelict ships lie half-submerged, rusted and
twisted, evidence of the accuracy of the bomber's aim.

As we enter the harbour the excitement of our Italian prisoners
rises to a crescendo. They crowd on the rails of the ship, exclaiming
and pointing. Now we see streams of excited Neapolitans rushing
madly down the wide streets to the quayside while a brass band
stationed on the jetty bursts forth in a gay tune. It looks as if the
jetty will soon be overrun by the hordes gathering to welcome the
now frantic prisoners home, but they are dealt with efficiently by
the military police and remain outside the dockyard gates.

But now we Naples wives are straining our eyes for the first
sight of our husbands as the *Ranchi* comes slowly alongside the
quay. Lita and I stand side by side – this at last is journey's end and

The view of Vesuvius and the Bay of Naples from La Loggetta,
Rex and Evelyn's home during the summer of 1946

we can scarcely contain ourselves as the gangway goes down and
the military police, embarkation officers and medics come aboard.

But where are they, those stalwart figures we thought would be
waiting impatiently for our arrival? No sign of them!

A sense of anti-climax sweeps over us – we feel forlorn and
deserted – then Lita gives a little cry and points. A long line of service lorries are careering wildly down the hill to the quay, followed
by several gleaming limousines, and out tumble some very flustered
individuals in shorts and tunics – our missing husbands at last!

They rush wildly along the quay, their eyes fixed on the ship's
rail, and I quickly pick out Rex's tall figure, followed by a slight,
dark officer. 'D'Arcy!' cries Lita, and they spot us and make their
way to stand beneath us, shouting out words of welcome and that

they are late because our ship arrived thirty minutes earlier than expected and that they were in the club having a 'quick one' when they suddenly heard that we had docked.

It is tantalising to stand there unable to meet. Nobody is allowed on or off the ship till the disembarking formalities are ended and as conversations carried on at that distance are impossible, it is decided that our husbands should go and have a snack at the club while we have lunch on board – which Lita and I are far too excited to eat.

Lunch over, we go to change our English money into lira (900 lire to £1) and then check our various piles of luggage on deck; then at last, all formalities over, we are free to join our husbands, now waiting on the quay. In a moment I am clasped in a pair of strong arms and a voice I have been longing to hear says, 'Darling!' A good moment this! When I can disengage myself I notice how brown and fit he is looking. Lita now introduces me to the Reverend D'Arcy Staunton, her husband, and then she is spirited off in his care to Caserta, where they are to live in a bungalow in the married quarters.

Meanwhile my baggage is being loaded on to a large Army lorry Rex has brought with him for the purpose. Eight huge, bronzed Germans are handling this job with true Teutonic thoroughness. Rex explains that these are SEPs (non-Nazi Surrendered Enemy Personnel) who do not wish to return to their country, as distinct from ordinary POWs. He says they are very well off here working for us, getting better food than we get in Britain, and are most obliging and efficient. They are also most carefully screened before being allotted to officers' homes. Nevertheless, I gaze at these, the first Germans I have seen since the war, with some trepidation.

At last the operation is over to the satisfaction of Sperry, Rex's batman, and they spring on to the lorry and are away.

It is terribly hot down on the quayside with the Italian sunshine beating down on us and I am thankful to get into Rex's Humber Pullman, complete with soldier-driver, and to leave the docks for the busy streets of Naples.

I am immediately assailed by a host of new impressions: the high, shabby buildings, like tenements, many defaced with monarchist or communist slogans, the aftermath of the recent elections; the crowds of dark-skinned Neapolitans; the overloaded trams, to the outside of which little boys cling like flies. There are kiosks draped with festoons of oranges and lemons, and carts drawn by small donkeys wearing ornaments of brass with tinkling bells. And over all the blazing hot sunshine.

Now we are on the Via Roma, the shopping centre of Naples, and my eyes open wide. Here are shops simply crammed with goods we have not seen for years in England! Nylons, soaps, perfumes, shoes and sandals and lovely lingerie vie with shop windows stuffed with radios and cameras, while there are sweets, pastries, cheeses and cakes in abundance. Remembering the queues of British housewives at home waiting patiently to collect their meagre rations, one wonders rather bitterly where is the penalty of being a conquered nation – and where the fruits of victory!

We swing out of the crowded Via Roma and pass a great church before which a hearse is drawn up – six coal-black horses with sable trappings and plumes, the coffin draped with sweeping black coverings. Then through a crowded marketplace with stalls piled with fruit and produce, on past high buildings where dark-eyed children play in the dust; up and up, always up, through winding roads to Vomero, high above the Bay of Naples.

Now the road is bordered by high white walls, over which wisteria and purple bougainvillea spill in a riot of colour, and one glimpses white villas and an occasional flash of blue water. Then suddenly we stop outside a graceful grilled gate set in the tall arch of a terracotta wall. Above it in a niche stands the carved figure of a woman. On the wall is an inscription, 'La Loggetta', and Rex says, 'Here is your villa.'

The driver swings back the gates and we enter the drive. On our left is a pale pink-washed lodge, in which, Rex tells me, the owner of the villa, Signor Cenzato, now resides with his wife. We pass on down a winding drive, fringed with oleanders and flowering shrubs on one side and on the other by sloping gardens, disclosing enchanting glimpses of the bay beneath.

Then we round a bend – and there is the villa! Set high on the side of the hill, it is built of pale terracotta stone and designed on the plan of an ancient Roman villa. It has balconies and loggias and tall white colonnades that lead to formal terraced gardens, ornamented with classic statues of bronze and in which fountains play. Below these the ground falls away steeply, covered with vines and olive groves, and far below lies the panorama of Naples.

The car draws up before an imposing entrance under a high pediment, and we alight and enter the hall. My immediate impression is of the gracious coolness after the heat and dust of Naples, and the sound of many tinkling fountains.

We cross the hall, which has a paved marble floor and a fountain playing into a low marble basin, and passing an alcove leading into a charming small library, enter the main living room of the villa.

Very spacious and of lofty proportions, what strikes you as you enter are the immensely high windows set in arches, the central one with glass doors folded back leading onto a spacious patio outside.

The room is decorated in palest hand-painted pastels depicting the fable of the sea-nymph Parthenope, said to be buried beneath the waters of the bay, and of Ulysses, tempted by the Sirens.

Rex has filled the room with vases of flame-coloured gladioli and bowls of roses and jasmine, and I am quite speechless, never having imagined anything like this! But it is as one advances into this lovely room that its full beauty is revealed, through the high central archway. Across a spacious loggia with a mosaic floor depicting the signs of the zodiac rise two tall double colonnades of white stone, covered in wisteria and climbing roses, which flank a broad paved walk to the verge of the hillside and frame, between their last white columns, a superb view of Vesuvius across the blue waters of the bay.

It is some time before Rex can tear me away from this enchanting prospect.

Sperry appears to tell us that tea is served on the patio. I am truly thankful for this interlude – I am feeling a little stunned by all this and welcome a chance to catch my breath, as it were, to try and assimilate my fairy-tale surroundings.

Rex is looking very fit indeed, in spite of the heat and his very strenuous job at GHQ. As we have our tea he tells me more about it, and it is certainly no sinecure. As DOS CMF (Central Mediterranean Forces), he is responsible for all Army establishments in a district including not only all of Italy, but extending as far as Vienna in Austria, with Trieste thrown in for good measure. [The strategically located city of Trieste, which had been under German rule after the collapse of the Fascist regime in 1943, was briefly taken over by Yugoslav Communists in 1945 and was now under joint British–US military government.]

He leaves every morning after an early breakfast for Caserta, twenty-one miles away, and does not get back until just before dinner time. He says Caserta, which used to be a royal palace, is terribly hot and dusty, and that although it means a drive of three quarters of an hour each way, it is well worth it to return to the coolness and peace of the villa.

I ask him to tell me something about the Cenzatos, the owners of the villa. He says they are very charming people and have been most helpful in every way. The villa was built by Signor Cenzato to his own design as a summer residence from the heat of Naples, where they also have a flat. Being a very wealthy man (he was director of all the electricity works in Naples) he was able to indulge his taste and that of his wife. Since the villa was occupied – first by the Germans and then by the British – he and his wife have been living in the lodge near the gates. I am horrified at the thought that Signora Cenzato, used to the luxury of this exquisite home, should be cooped up in that small house and forced to endure the humiliation of seeing us in occupation of the villa. However, Rex tells me they are hoping very much that when the British Forces leave Naples they may get their home derequisitioned, and Rex has assured them that he will do all he can to bring this about.

Our bedroom, which is decorated in pale green, has a huge window, eight feet wide, with a wonderful view of Vesuvius and the bay. There I make the acquaintance of Maria, who Signora Cenzato has sent to be my personal maid. She is a plump, pleasant-looking little body, and immediately breaks into voluble Italian. As she can speak no English and I no Italian it is some time before we get sorted out and I manage to make her understand that I do not wish her to unpack for me. At last she departs and I am left in peace to fend for myself, have a wash and change into a cool dress for dinner.

We have our drinks on the patio and Rex tells me about the staff for this amazing villa. I have already met Lewis, Rex's driver, and Sperry, the batman, who besides valeting Rex waits at table. Up to now he has been in complete control of the rest of the staff. As well as Maria there are two cooks, Oscar and Leo (the undercook) who are Sudeten Germans, Francesca the washerwoman, and six Croat guards who in patrols of three, guard the villa day and night. Rex says this is necessary as the Neapolitans are the most awful thieves. They sleep in the basement, which is very large and airy, and at night patrol silently in rubber-soled shoes, armed with powerful torches.

This seems an awful lot of staff to me, but Rex proceeds to tell me that there will be a lorry full of Germans arriving every morning from the POW camp to work in the villa and to tend the garden. Rex says the latter was terribly neglected and that they have worked wonders. It seems that Oscar, the cook, is somewhat temperamental, but he certainly can cook! We have coffee on the patio and afterwards I am thankful to retire to bed as I feel it has been quite a day.

During the night I sprang up in bed, awakened by the most fearful din! Imagine I am back in the war and an air raid is in progress, but it is only a fiesta! Rex says this is the month when the priests collect money to buy fireworks and illuminate their churches, each district vying with each other to produce the best (and noisiest) show. All the inhabitants assemble in the plazas, brass bands play and fireworks are let off, to the huge delight of all. But I do feel that they really don't know where to draw the line if this has to happen at five o'clock in the morning. Heaven knows when they sleep! Rex says most of the afternoon. We compose ourselves for slumber again and are soon fast asleep – fiesta or no fiesta!

Friday, 12 July 1946

Wake to a glorious morning – very relieved indeed to find yesterday was not all a dream! Maria enters with morning tea, which we have sitting at the table in the window, enjoying the marvellous view across the bay. What a difference to the scenes I left behind in London.

Sample the sunken bath and I am relieved to find that hot water to fill this luxurious affair is forthcoming and there is no water-level mark to worry about. Descend to breakfast in my turquoise and rose housecoat (purchased at great cost and eleven coupons) feeling rather like a film star. This is excellent for the morale after years of austerity England!

I am very glad Rex has arranged for the day off duty. I need his support in these rather bewildering first hours of adjustment to a new and strange way of life.

After breakfast we go out to the patio. The morning is still cool and fresh. Little lizards are basking in the sun on the marble verges of the beds of roses and pinks at the base of the colonnade. The scent of wisteria and roses fills the air and great butterflies sail by. If only it were possible to transplant my friends in England here, how perfect it would be!

Rex suggests that I meet the rest of the staff, and, collecting Sperry, we set out for the kitchen quarters. These are spacious – a large kitchen complete with two electric cookers and an enormous refrigerator, a scullery and wash-houses, and another large room where the staff eat. There is also a staff sitting room. All these look out onto the fruit and kitchen gardens at the back of the villa.

As we enter they all rise, the Germans standing stiffly to attention, while Sperry introduces them to me. First Oscar, the head cook. He is short, dumpy and rosy faced, with a sulky expression. Leo, the undercook (and Oscar's friend), is tall, lean and good-looking. They bow in the most correct manner. Maria now brings forward Francesca, the washerwoman, a thin woman with a cadaverous face. I learn with dismay that none of them can speak English and wonder how on earth I shall manage! Rex, however, assures me that Sperry will interpret for me – like most of our Tommies who fought in Italy he has picked up some of the lingo.

He orders Oscar to show me the cooking arrangements. Oscar, very sullen, does so, showing me the cookers, opening the ovens and exhibiting a large quantity of cooking utensils. I enquire about the stores and rations and I am told that the Army rations for the entire household arrive three times a week by lorry from the depot: meat, bread, butter, potatoes, vegetables, cheese and tinned milk – the only sort safe to drink here.

On the way to lunch at the San Carlo Club, now an officers' club, we call in at the BOD where I meet Major Lee-Wood, who is very charming. He suggests I might like to enlist the services of his Italian secretary, 'Jane', with whom to go shopping, and it is arranged he shall bring her to cocktails at the villa on Sunday.

We call at the Married Families' Shop in the Via Roma next. This is full of Army wives, and seems amply stocked with everything one could desire in the way of tinned goods, drinks, cigarettes, cosmetics, etc., and I feel more in wonderland than ever! Passing through the Via Roma I have a glimpse of the shops and look forward to sampling them when I go shopping with Jane.

Naples is indeed very hot and dusty and we are glad to get to the San Carlo Club, where a cool drink is called for.

After tea, as we are sitting on the patio, Signor and Signora Cenzato come to call on us. They are both so charming and make me so welcome that any sense of awkwardness one feels at being in possession of their home is quite dispelled. The *signora* is a most attractive woman, elegant and most beautifully dressed all in white. She is slight with dark hair and eyes, and is a Venetian. She can only speak a very little English and her husband interprets for her. He is short, slim and has beautiful manners.

He explains how happy they are to have a British officer and his wife in the villa. When Italy surrendered and the Germans moved into Naples, they behaved, he says, most brutally to the Neapolitans. The villa was seized and the Cenzatos had to take refuge in the porter's lodge (where they are now) as their winter apartment down in Naples had been damaged by bombs.

We serve them drinks, and as we sit and talk we offer them the hospitality of the garden whenever they care to make use of it, and express the hope that they will often come and see us. Rex takes Signor Cenzato to see the bowling green at the side of the villa. It was in a derelict state and Rex has had the SEPs working on it. When they leave I feel much happier about it all than I did before.

We have a delicious dinner. Oscar, Rex tells me, used to cook for the German General Staff, and was highly recommended for his culinary abilities when Rex got him out of the 'pool' in the POW camp. An assortment of most delicious Viennese pastries make their appearance with the coffee on the patio, and though fully aware what these can do to the figure I just can't resist them after having been deprived of this sort of thing for so long.

Later as we go to bed a moon is throwing a silver path across the bay, and I still can't help feeling it must all be a dream.

Saturday, 13 July 1946

After an early breakfast Rex sets off for Caserta and I am left alone in my glory.

Maria comes to ask if there is any laundry I want done. She is responsible for Rex's and mine only. The household laundry is done by Francesca – and a pretty formidable task this is with four-teen people sleeping in the villa! She must have been busy washing down in the basement since early morning, for now she is out in the kitchen garden spreading out sheets on the bushes to dry.

I realise that having a personal maid presents a problem where 'undies' are concerned. Mine are at a very low ebb owing to coupon shortage, and like everyone else's at home have been darned and patched up. I scrapped my most shameful 'make-dos' before sailing to Italy, but having met Signora Cenzato I am sure her undies must be divine and realise that I shall have to get down to the shops as soon as possible and stock up if I don't want to lose face with Maria, who has been her personal maid.

I wander out into the garden and come upon one of the Croat guards. He is exceedingly handsome, with fine features and flashing dark eyes, dressed in khaki shorts and tunic and with a beret set at a jaunty angle on his head. When he first sees me he stands to attention, then bends and picks a red rose from a bush at his side, and with the superb grace of a romantic actor offers it to me with a dazzling smile. The whole episode – set against the brilliant backdrop of the bay and Vesuvius – is such that I almost expect an orchestra to strike up and for one of us to burst into song! But pulling myself together, I accept the rose graciously and pass on with what I hope is the correct degree of dignity – not having been conditioned to this sort of thing.

I notice a large lorry coming down the drive. It draws up and out jump eight stalwart SEPs from the POW camp, who Rex has told me come each day to work in the villa and garden. They are magnificent specimens of Hitler's 'Aryans', all blond and bronzed, and the sight of them makes me feel quite queer. They split up into groups under one who appears to be their foreman – one group marching off towards the bowling alley and the other round the back of the villa. I have asked Rex to arrange that they should only work on the ground floor of the villa as somehow I don't fancy Germans in our bedroom; so Maria is detailed to clean and look after the bedrooms on the first floor – which shows my ignorance of the Neapolitan idea of cleanliness.

I return to the villa and later watch the Germans at work on the lounge. It is an education to see them turn it out. Every chair and couch is turned upside down, brushed and dusted; the furniture and floor polished till they shine. They are extremely 'correct' and whenever they catch sight of me they click their heels and bow. This is rather trying as I am constantly coming into contact with them.

This morning there was a most awful fuss and fracas in the staff room. I enquired from Sperry what it was all about and he says that someone has been pinching the sugar ration. Sperry accused Oscar, and Oscar, almost in hysterics, accused Maria, who equally hysterically accused Oscar, and it developed into a first-class row.

Leo and Oscar with Rex's batman, Hopwood, centre,
beside Rex's official car

Evelyn's 'rosenkavalier' – as she calls him in her own caption –
between two fellow Croat guards at La Loggetta

I gather that there is no love lost between the Germans and
Italians – the Germans despising the Italians for being cowardly
fighters who betrayed Germany to the enemy by their surrender,
and the Italians loathing the Germans and all their ways. Reflect
that this is hardly likely to make housekeeping here a bed of
roses!

Spend the morning unpacking the case of table linen I have
brought out with me for dinner parties. Siesta after lunch, then tea
on the patio and letter-writing until Rex returns just before dinner,
tired after a long hot day at Caserta and more than ready for a cool
drink.

It is very funny to see his arrival home! For some reason most of the staff feel it incumbent to welcome him. As he alights from the car they all spring stiffly to attention and salute the arrival of 'Signor General' as they call him. I watch this performance with awe, reflecting what a change from England where he used to get up and light the boiler of Green Bushes!

Sunday, 14 July 1946

After breakfast, it being Sunday, it occurs to me that Maria might want to go to Mass. Try to convey this to her by sign language, giving what I imagine is a graphic interpretation – kneeling down and praying. This she interprets as a desire on my part to go to bed, and with delighted cries of, '*Si, si, signora!*' she rushes to the bed, turns down the bedclothes and advances on me with the intention of undressing me. I have the greatest difficulty in making her understand that I do not wish to '*dormire*' at this hour of the morning!

She is most attentive to me, dogging my footsteps, and will try to undress and dress me before and after siesta unless I manage to creep to my room while she is otherwise employed. I am not used to the attentions of a lady's maid and find this a nuisance and must try and train her just to attend to my clothes and mending and otherwise leave me alone!

We go for a drive to Naples and up to Posillipo – it is beautiful and there are some lovely villas there. On the way back we stop at a flower stall and buy armfuls of flowers. This evening Brigadier and Mrs Ford and Major Lee-Wood came to cocktails. Major Lee-Wood brought Jane with him – everyone seems to call her this and I never did find out her surname! She is an attractive Neapolitan girl, a civilian clerk employed by the Army, and speaks perfect English. It is arranged that she shall call and take me shopping tomorrow morning, Major Lee-Wood providing a car from the BOD for that purpose.

Monday, 15 July 1946

At about eleven o'clock the BOD car arrives with Jane and we set out for Naples. When we arrive at the Via Chiaia (the Bond Street of Naples) we get out and walk so that I can see the shops. They are enchanting, especially the undie shops, and after I have bought some of these we go on to the Via Roma and I purchase a pair of white sandals and a pair of bedroom mules. Being Neapolitan, Jane does not feel the heat, which is getting me down (along with the masses of jostling people crowding the pavements), and I insist that we go to the San Carlo Club to get a cool drink before lunching there. After this she drops me at the villa on her way back to the BOD.

After a siesta I am relaxing on the patio after tea when Sperry appears with a very conspiratorial air and says he wants to speak to me. 'More trouble,' he hisses in my ear, in a somewhat sadistic manner. When, alarmed, I ask what it is, he informs me that Oscar has given notice. This shakes me badly (which I have a suspicion was his intention). What worse calamity can befall a household than for the cook to leave? And with a household like this! The fact that I suspect Sperry wants Oscar to quit and is enjoying this makes it worse.

When Rex arrives I rush to break the dire news to him. He is just having a much-needed whisky and soda and looks at me with incredulity. Realising that he must be stunned by the calamity, I repeat, 'Oscar has given notice.' He gives a shout of laughter. 'Good God! The man's a prisoner of war – he can't give notice!' <u>What</u> a relief!

After Rex has dealt with Oscar, he and I discuss the question of my not being able to talk directly to him. It is obviously impossible for things to continue as they are, and Rex suggests that he should arrange for an interpreter to come down with the SEPs from the

POW camp each day so that I can take over the household management and not be dependent on Sperry, who has got much too
big for his boots. This will certainly ease matters.

Tuesday, 16 July 1946

Today Rex sent his car back to take me to Caserta to lunch with
Lita Staunton. The road runs through olive groves, fields of hemp
and tobacco, and vineyards, the vines trained in graceful festoons
from tree to tree. The agricultural implements the peasants use
are as primitive as those in China, and the method used to draw
water from the wells with the help of a donkey harnessed to a
long pole, who walks round and round, is exactly the same as that
employed there, only in China it is the water buffalo who does
the task.

We approach the Palace of Caserta along a wide and imposing avenue. Built by Charles of Bourbon, King of Naples, it was
commenced in 1752 and was to be the greatest palace in Europe,
surpassing El Escorial and Versailles, but unfortunately the money
ran out before it was finished. Even so it is immense, built round
four huge courtyards, with a portico supported by a hundred columns and a vast hall from which rises a staircase twenty feet wide,
flanked by marble lions said to represent Victory and Defeat, but
so depressed and bilious-looking it is impossible to tell which is
which!

Now the palace houses both the British and American headquarters and the huge courtyards are full of Army transport. Rex
introduces me to his secretary, a charming South African girl
named Margaret Piert, and suggests that she shows me something
of the palace before taking me to Lita Staunton's quarter.

The whole palace, with its vulgar ostentation, seems to me the
acme of bad taste and I am not sorry when we emerge into the

open and cross the courtyard to make our way to the married families' quarters. These are set in the gardens some distance from the palace, under some trees. They consist of wooden Army huts set in rows, separated from each other by strips of lawn and with a communal bathroom and lavatories at either end of each group. There are small gardens in front in which asters and roses are making a brave attempt to survive the dust and heat. It is certainly airless here, cut off from any breeze at one end by a hill with ornamental terraces and an artificial cascade of water flowing down it.

Lita gives me a warm welcome and morning coffee is waiting for me. She shows me over her domain, which consists of three rooms, which she has made very attractive with flowers and chintzes, but even Lita, never one to complain, admits the communal arrangements are trying. I feel ashamed to think that I find even the villa hot at times, and wish so much that I could share it with her. They have a swimming pool and an open-air cinema, which is some compensation, as well as expeditions to the club at 22 Beach, where she says the bathing is marvellous.

It has been grand seeing her again. How I wish we were nearer! Transport difficulties make meeting regularly impossible, but she will be coming over to see me soon, I hope.

Wednesday, 17 July 1946

This morning when the lorry arrived with the SEPs an interpreter came with it. He is a typical German, blond with glasses, and very correct, clicking his heels and bowing on the slightest provocation, but it is a blessing to be able to make myself understood at last.

I have a few words with him and then we all march into the kitchen – myself, the interpreter and Sperry – where we find Oscar and Leo lined up, Oscar very sulky as usual.

I told the interpreter I wished to speak to Oscar alone, and Leo and Sperry withdrew. Then I got down to the truth. As I suspected, Sperry has been treating Oscar very badly, bullying him and keeping all the rations under lock and key, compelling Oscar to ask for every little thing and doling them out bit by bit.

During this recital Oscar became very voluble and excited, interrupting and gabbling away in German, and I had to ask the interpreter to cut him short and to tell him that in future, if he had any grievances, he was to tell me through the interpreter and that he would get consideration and justice, but that in return I expected politeness and co-operation from him. I said that in future all the rations would be checked on delivery by myself and Oscar, and that he would then be responsible for them. At this he became frightfully emotional, and the interpreter explained that he was afraid I should blame him if anything disappeared because he was a prisoner of war. I replied that to be a prisoner of war was a misfortune but not a disgrace, and could happen to anyone, and that as far as I was concerned I would trust and treat him exactly as I should anyone else – unless I found my trust was misplaced.

This seemed to impress Oscar, who calmed down, and for the first time I saw his round rosy face without its habitual scowl. The scowl, however, seems to have transferred itself to Sperry, who is going about shaking his head at my foolishness in trusting Oscar. Well, we shall see. I couldn't possible have gone on with things as they were. We shall have quite a lot of entertaining to do and everyone knows what that's like when the cook sulks!

Tonight we have a dinner party: Rex's New Zealand friend, Brigadier Clump, and Brigadier Bilderbeck, an old friend from Hong Kong days. Rex has arranged for Jane to come up in a car from BOD to take me shopping.

Rex, right, and his friend Brigadier Clump, Italy 1946

We go to the market and get enough whitebait for four for 80 lire (about 1s 10d), also melons and fruit, cheese and flowers. It is marvellous to be able to buy without a ration book!

Thursday, 18 July 1946

I have acquired three very important words in Italian: '*sporco*' which is dirty, '*lavare*' which is to wash, and '*stirare*' which is to iron. Tried them out on Maria with success. She washes and irons beautifully, and also sews and mends, being convent-trained; but I have not been at all satisfied with the household linen washed by Francesca – very *sporco*!

Explored the lower regions where Francesca does the laundry and discovered that she washes everything in cold water (a Neapolitan custom). No wonder it never looks clean! When I told Rex he says he will arrange for some Army boilers to be installed in the basement.

Friday, 19 July 1946

Things very much easier in the kitchen now. Our rations arrived by lorry today and I went through them with Oscar, who is now responsible for them, with the exception of the purchases I make from the Married Families' Shop, such as tinned fruit and extras (which Oscar calls the 'reserves') which I shall keep in my private store-cupboard.

Oscar is transformed, his rosy face wreathed in smiles, and so is his great friend Leo. This morning they asked permission, through the interpreter, to go shopping to 'trade' our surplus bread and other rations for extra eggs, etc. Having got permission from Rex, I see them setting gaily off up the drive with a large covered basket, Oscar's little legs twinkling in the effort to keep up with Leo's long loping stride.

Rex has put Leo in charge of the bar and he takes great pride in it, polishing the glasses and shelves and always appearing on duty before Rex returns from Caserta in the evening ready to serve us drinks on the patio.

The only discordant note has been Sperry. In a private talk with the interpreter, Rex has discovered that, in addition to bullying the staff, Sperry has been cheating the Germans out of their official cigarette ration (which is very small) and as Sperry's attitude is now anything but co-operative Rex has decided to replace him. A new batman has arrived today. His name is Rouse and he used to be General Geake's batman and knows Oscar and Leo, so let's hope things will be easier now.

By the way, the missing sugar has been discovered hidden away in Maria's chest of drawers – several pounds of it! When confronted with her crime she did not seem to be unduly upset – stealing to the Neapolitans is as natural as breathing. In spite of their religious fervour it does not seem to be counted as a sin; certainly nothing to be ashamed of.

Sunday, 28 July 1946

Met Brigadier and Mrs Heywood last night at the Park Club. She has just come out to join her husband. He is tall and good-looking and she is most attractive and blonde; beautifully dressed – her evening dress is a dream. I liked them both very much and after dinner we joined up with their party and danced till quite late.

At the Park Club one sees quite a lot of the 'fratting' (or fraternisation) which has been going on with our officers and the less respectable Italian girls. Mary Heywood and I were disgusted to see two officers (old enough to know better) with a pair of tarts of the waterfront, terribly made up and very 'sexy' indeed. They pawed the men quite openly, putting their arms around them and gazing into their eyes until we wondered what would happen next! One of the officers (unfortunately in our corps) is, Rex tells me, a married man with two grown-up children. What amazes me is that he should be so lost to all shame as to behave like that right under the eyes of his senior officer!

The temptations for men parted from their families may be very great, and this was, of course, going on long before the families were allowed to come out; but many homes are being broken up because of the liaisons formed with these women. The Italian girls will go to any lengths to hook a British officer, and British Tommies are marrying them at the rate of eight a week, sometimes knowing no more than their Christian names!

D'Arcy Staunton told me this, and being senior chaplain to the Forces, he knows what he is talking about.

Tuesday, 30 July 1946

Rex has sacked Francesca, the washerwoman. Her washing (even with the hot water provided) left much to be desired, but the final straw was that we discovered that she was consumptive and Maria, who shared a room with her, complained that she spits over everything. This has been confirmed by the rest of the staff and Rex had no alternative but to get rid of her. Rouse says he knows of an excellent washerwoman who will come in her place.

Saturday, 3 August 1946

This morning Oscar, through the interpreter, asked if I would like him to make a pastry with a long German name, which I had never heard of. The interpreter said that Oscar had often made it for the German General Staff, and that it was a particular favourite of Herr Hitler.

While secretly longing to sample it, I felt this would never do, and told the interpreter, with great dignity, that that was hardly a reason to recommend it to a British officer's wife, and to Oscar's disappointment it was banished from our board. How patriotic can you be!

The last two days the heat has been terrible. I went down to the hairdresser's and came out dripping and must have got a chill as yesterday I had a temperature of 101° and a pain across my back and stayed in bed.

Even up here at the villa our bedroom was 92 degrees last night, and not a breath of air with every window open. It does not help having to sleep in our sandfly 'room' [like a mosquito net] with the curtaining all around us; but this is a precaution we have to put up with or risk sandfly fever.

Thank goodness I am better now as tonight Rex has arranged for the Army Mobile Cinema Unit to pay us a visit, and as we have a dinner party they are to give us a movie after dinner. After tea they turned up and with great dexterity rigged a huge canvas screen across the outside of the glass doors leading to the patio so that the audience can sit in the open and catch any vagrant breath of air that may be stirring. We have invited the Cenzatos and their friends, and of course the staff will be there, though what they will make of it I can't imagine!

Sunday, 4 August 1946

Everything went off splendidly last night. The film was *Blythe Spirit* – very good indeed. Still not feeling too good; it's probably the heat. It's too hot to even go for a drive or out to the Park Club for dinner. The Cenzatos, being Italian, evidently do not feel the heat as we do, for as we lie on the patio, sipping cool drinks, we can hear the sound of the clash of bowls as Signor Cenzato entertains his friends to a lively game. They often troop down in the evening, and one of the 'buddies' is exactly like Mussolini!

Monday, 5 August 1946

Lewis, Rex's driver, has been taken ill and has to go to hospital. Rex has arranged for a temporary driver in his absence. It is hotter than ever and I have lunch and tea on the patio.

There is scarcely a breath of air, and as I lie in a deckchair, too lazy even to read, a barefoot peasant woman followed by three little bambinos approaches from the garden slopes. She advances timidly, then as I smile at her she comes up onto the patio. I recognise her as one of the peasants who live in the house up the drive; she has been pointed out to me as having been once known as 'the Beauty of Naples' and in spite of the many children she has borne and the hard life she has led, there are still traces of the beauty that has made her a legend. She is tall and graceful and has enormous eyes of deep and liquid brown, and her hair, though streaked with grey, is thick and lustrous. She is incredibly dirty, as are her three bare-footed offspring, who gaze at me timidly out of luminous brown eyes with much the same expression as we turn upon some strange animal in the zoo.

The mother obviously wishes to speak, but is too shy to do so, and holds out towards me the branch of a fig tree upon which repose some delicious-looking figs, and one of the children has a bunch of grapes.

With smiles and sign language I accept her offering, trying to convey my pleasure, then an inspiration comes, and uttering the word 'cioccolato', I tell her to wait and fly indoors to raid our chocolate ration, which we draw each week from the NAAFI. I rush back, hoping the little family is still there, but I need not have worried – the magic word has been understood and the expression in the eyes of the children is good to see. Smiling and saying, 'Cioccolato, bambinos', I offer it, and the beaming mother accepts with a quiet dignity. The last I see of them is the children following their mother up the drive, turning back to smile at me, their little faces already furnished with brown moustaches and beards.

Tuesday, 6 August 1946

I am getting to know the German SEPs who come down to work in the villa. At first I just saw them as members of a hated race with whom we had waged a deadly war to preserve our liberty, but now, as day after day I am perforce thrown into their company as they clean the villa [unhappy with Maria's efforts, Evelyn has over-come her reservations and engaged them to clean upstairs as well as downstairs] and tend the garden, they are emerging as fellow human beings. One of the indoor gang, a tall, serious-looking man with glasses, was obviously in pain one day and I enquired through the interpreter what was wrong and was told it was earache. Having suffered from an abscess on the eardrum myself I know what earache can be and got him some aspirin. He was so grateful it made me ashamed. Later I discovered he could speak a little English and he showed me snapshots of his wife and three children in Germany. Then the others, tentatively and very respectfully, proffered 'snaps' – pathetically crumpled – of their wives and families, which they all carried in their pockets. One had lost both parents in one of our raids on Hamburg, another had a brother taken prisoner by the Russians, another's brother was 'missing'. As I listened to these stories, so common to us all, I realised how stultifying and harmful hate can be and yet, remembering, I cannot but wonder – were the positions reversed – if these very men, being Teutons, would not obey orders and, very correctly, of course, pop me into a gas chamber if told to do so. However, there it is, they are now individuals to me.

Sunday, 11 August 1946

A month since I landed in Naples! I still feel rather like Cinderella must have felt after her fairy godmother waved her wand. There is a parallel, of course, for one knows this is just an interlude, and that soon twelve o'clock will strike and all will vanish. Very soon the Occupation Forces will be leaving southern Italy, and all this beauty and way of life will be only a memory – this exquisite villa; the moonlight evenings on the patio; the view from the belvedere at night with Naples and the harbour lying lighted up below and a huge moon rising across the bay. Vesuvius, sometimes clearly seen – so that one can discern the streams of dried lava that in their deadly course have flowed down its scarred sides – sometimes veiled in heat mists, or loveliest of all, bathed in the roseate rays of the setting sun.

How shall I look back upon this life here, the *dolce far niente*, which can only be expressed in Italian and to which I have so willingly fallen (perhaps best expressed in English as 'sweet idleness')! The cool early mornings, the long hours I spend on the shady patio, where I also lunch, before retiring to my darkened room for siesta. Then tea on the patio again, where I remain until (what I most look forward to!) Rex returns in the evening from Caserta.

It is a disgracefully lazy life, but it is really too hot to do anything, and indeed there is little I can do here.

These halcyon days, which pass like a dream, are weaving memories which I shall always cherish, golden hours which I shall relive in all the years to come and will lighten the black austerities of peace to which I shall have to return all too soon.

Evelyn and Rex learn that their new washerwoman is a notorious prostitute, and that Rouse is also mixed up with some undesirable characters. Rex appoints a new batman, Hopwood, and Signor Cenzato finds them a washerwoman 'of impeccable character'.

A brighter piece of news is that Evelyn is to be allowed to accompany Rex on his tour of duty in Austria. Torchlight, *a train used by Mussolini and his entourage, will take them, their car and new driver, Wooley, who has replaced Lewis, to Udine in north-eastern Italy. From there they will go by road to Klagenfurt, Graz, Vienna and Venice before returning to Udine and the train.*

Sunday, 8 September 1946

Packing, which I put off each day hoping the hot spell would break, has had to be done today, although the bedroom is like an oven and closely shuttered against the Khamsin, the hot wind of the Sahara. Rex and I tackle our cases, he with the help of Hopwood, between long drinks of lime and soda, while Maria rushes around doing last-minute ironing and Oscar cooks us pastries which he insists we should take on our journey. We find time to go out to the patio (it is like opening an oven door) to give Leslie, the lizard we have been feeding, the last meal of fat flies he will get for ten days. He is growing quite stout and is far the biggest lizard on the patio. He is now so tame that he comes running up the colonnade when he hears my or Rex's whistle and has even taken to coming onto the patio, where he waits hopefully till we go out to him.

Villa staff Oscar, Maria and Leo. The man in spectacles
beside Oscar is probably the interpreter

Today is his red-letter day as I give him five newly swatted flies and after lunch Rex gives him another five, so it is hardly surprising that he does not turn up for his usual evening meal and we conclude he is sleeping it off!

Go upstairs to my bedroom and find that Maria – in a most unaccustomed excess of industry – has seen fit to empty the entire contents of Rex's two pillows onto the balcony, as according to her the cases were *sporco* and must be washed. View with dismay the two large heaps of feathers and kapok. Tell her she must return the fillings to the pillowcases at once (in dumb show). What a time to do this!

Loud exclamations from Rex's dressing room reveal the fact that the tin of sugar packed in his air travel bag with his night kit was insecurely fastened and the sugar is now deposited all over the contents of the bag. Hopwood and Leo rush to succour him, while Major Lee-Wood (who is staying here in our absence) and I, unable to resist it, tell him he will probably now have ants in his pants! This is not well received!

Later they board Torchlight, *which Evelyn describes as 'luxurious in the extreme'. Evelyn and Rex have a private suite and a comfortable lounge next door. The train is full of men in uniform – officers of the Army, Navy and Air Force – with only a few females on board.*

At 9 p.m. precisely, just as we are being served an excellent dinner, *Torchlight* leaves Naples and we are afforded the instant relief of the coolness caused by motion – the first time we have felt cool for days. After dinner we sit in the Pullman lounge and talk until after 11 p.m. when we retire to our comfortable beds. In spite of the blessed coolness I am too excited to sleep. At 1.15 a.m. as I peep out of my window, the train having stopped, I catch sight of the name 'Roma' and get my first glimpse of Rome as we pull out of the station.

Just a fleeting impression of moonlight, fine tree-bordered roads, high and imposing buildings and a cypress-planted cemetery. Even so, it is enough to stir the heart and it is with a thrill that I realise I am within the precincts of the Eternal City, cradle of our European civilisations in which so many stirring centuries of history have been written!

Later we run alongside the broad and lovely Tiber, and at last sleep claims me as we race on towards Florence, our next stop. The adventure has begun.

Monday, 9 September 1946

Morning tea is brought in at seven, and later we enjoy a lovely breakfast in one of the two large dining saloons. It is evident the train is very full.

After breakfast I repair to our Pullman coach to write up my diary. As we approach the Apennines the character of the country is changing, grass begins to appear, trees are more evident and away to the left a mountain range lifts proud crags to a blue sky, flecked with white clouds. Presently villas and farms dot the hills and countryside.

On the outskirts of Florence, villas of white and terracotta appear, with gardens gay with autumn flowers. The lovely city has suffered from the demolitions of the Germans in their retreat with the loss of its most famous bridge, and the railway station and environs from Allied bombing, but otherwise is undamaged. How much I wish we could stay here and sample its many treasures!

As we are having our drinks in the bar I look out of the window and see we are running alongside the Italian Rhine, now reduced to a small stream between wide banks. Here and there pools remain in which women are washing clothes and linen, beating them on the stones of the rocky riverbed.

All the bridges over the rivers have been destroyed either by the Allied bombing or by the Germans in their retreat, and now as our line crosses the river, the train slows down to a cautious crawl as we proceed gingerly over what looks like a very flimsy temporary bridge. Far beneath in the dry riverbed lie twisted girders and huge masses of masonry – all that is left of the original bridge. Rex, deep in conversation and with a pink gin, seems unaware of our hazards. It is with a sense of thankfulness that I at last realise we are resuming our normal speed and are safely over.

The tunnels that we constantly pass through on our way through the hills have also had their share of bombing and demolition and their fissured sides and roofs are shored up and supported by struts and concrete. All along the route lie the twisted remains of bombed trains, rusted and smashed, mute witnesses of the fearful carnage during the bitter days of battle.

Just before 6 p.m. when we are assembled in the cocktail bar, we pass through Usetta, badly bombed, and later Padua. And so another day ends with dinner and conversation in the saloon before bed.

Udine, our destination, is reached at 11.30 p.m. and *Torchlight* is shunted into a siding for the convenience of those, like ourselves, who wish to sleep on the train and make an early start in the morning.

Tuesday, 10 September 1946

A heavenly morning, the sky a deep blue, the air crisp, the sun warm. After an early breakfast we join the car, which has been off-loaded, with Wooley in charge, and set off. This is the beginning of our 'tour'.

We pass through Udine, a railway junction of importance, badly bombed, and we are glad to leave it, taking a broad road running through flat pastureland. Straight ahead in the distance a magnificent range of mountains rise, just catching the early morning sun – the Carnic Alps.

As we pass from Italy into Austria, almost at once there is a remarkable difference. The dark-skinned, dark-haired peasants give place to flaxen-haired, blue-eyed people, the men wearing brief leather shorts over suntanned legs, jackets with gay embroidered lapels and jaunty felt hats, and smoking large curved pipes as they drive their horse-drawn carts, often accompanied by bronzed children who smile and wave to us as we pass.

They are so gay, these charming people, who since Bismarck crushed Austria and in 1882 forced them to become an ally of Germany have been bound to the wheels of the German war chariot and forced to participate in two disastrous world wars.

Rex has arranged that we deviate from our route to visit the lovely Ossiacher See, a lake seven miles long, set in thickly wooded hills. Here on the shores of its deep green waters we picnic in the warmth of the autumn sunshine in perfect peace and isolation.

Before the war this was a favourite holiday resort but now its chalets and hotels are deserted. It is difficult to tear ourselves away from its tranquil beauty.

Klagenfurt, which has been the capital of Carinthia since 1518, has, too, suffered heavy damage by Allied bombing. At GHQ Rex is met by Colonel Davis of our corps and, business transacted, we take the road along the Wörthersee, the ten-mile-long lake, on the opposite shore of which lies Maria Wörth and our destination, the Poste Hotel.

Wednesday, 11 September 1946
Awake to a misty morning, and as Rex has to go off early I decide to be lazy and have my breakfast in bed. By the time I am up and

dressed the sun has broken through and this enchanting place is revealed in all its loveliness. I decide to explore the woods at the back of the hotel and climb up though the pear and apple orchards through meadows knee-deep in clover and buttercups.

Tonight we dined at the Pirker Hotel, very good indeed. We had invited Colonel and Mrs Davis to join us, and afterwards we sat in the bar, which was full of Eighth Army officers, proudly wearing the flash of the famous Desert Rats, emblem of their North African campaign.

Thursday, 12 September 1946

Another perfect morning. An early start on a drive through the most perfect scenery. Deep woods – where the deer lurk – border the road. On the summits of pine-clad hills perch hunting lodges and chalets, and little villages nestle beneath the feudal protection of old grey Schlosses, set high above rushing rivers.

Our next call is St Viet, where there is a large RAOC ammunition depot and vehicle park, which Rex is to inspect. For eight miles along the roadside on either side we pass piles of ammunition in corrugated iron hutments, all of which come under Rex's jurisdiction. Several officers are awaiting his arrival at the depot and he goes off to do his inspection, leaving me with Wooley in the car.

Now occurs one of those incidents that are bound to happen on these sorts of journeys. Wooley having disappeared and the road being quite deserted, this seems a good opportunity to spend a penny, and a thick patch of sunflowers growing along the roadside seems ideal for the purpose. Leaving the car I slip quickly behind them, just as Wooley suddenly appears tiptoeing stealthily round the opposite end. We both retreat in confusion!

After a while Rex returns and we resume our journey. We are now in Styria, a mountainous country with the largest and densest forests in Austria. The first big place is Judenburg, which centuries ago was a Jewish town. An important industrial town and a railway junction of note, this has consequently meant great devastation by bombing. It presents a depressing sight of shattered buildings and derelict trains which we are glad to leave behind.

Our road runs along the banks of the river Mur, and as we pass through the villages we are struck by the marked contrast between Austria and Italy. Here every town and village has the appearance of an early-closing day: streets of shuttered shops, and those few which are open displaying only a few meagre goods. Permits are necessary before anything can be purchased, and the occupying forces are forbidden to buy anything, other than in the NAAFI shops, while in all the transit hotels only three courses are served, all from Army rations. This is right when all go short in Austria, which has suffered far more cruelly than Italy from the war.

Graz, set on its rushing river, is the second largest city in Austria. Here in a large mansion in the main street is GHQ where we find Colonel Ferguson waiting for us. He and his wife are to be our hosts for two days. In their charming house on the outskirts of the town, Mrs Ferguson gives us a warm welcome.

Friday, 13 September 1946

After breakfast Rex departs with Colonel F to GHQ and Mrs F says she and I are to take a tour of Graz, Colonel F having arranged that his interpreter, an Austrian girl named Lili, shall accompany us as a guide.

We drive up to the Schlossberg, a high hill commanding a wonderful view of the city below, laid out in gardens where the citizens of Graz can take their ease. The hill is crowned by a beautiful clock tower.

Here, amongst the lilacs and the blossom, once stood the fabulous Golden Lion of Graz. Now only the plinth on which it once stood remains, for the lion has gone – melted down in the last war to provide the implements of war to defend Graz.

Above us the Liesl, the great bell of the Schlossberg, strikes the hour of noon – a deep, reverberating chime, mellow with the echoes of the centuries, which seems to say, 'Take heart, take heart – tomorrow is another day.'

Lili turns from the sad contemplation of the empty plinth, and glances up. 'We of Graz like to hear Liesl again,' she says. 'You see, she has been silent for six years.'

Later, as we drive through the main street, with its shuttered and depleted shops, she tells me how hard up the citizens of Graz are for everything. This is evident in the shabby and worn clothing of the inhabitants – Lili tells me they have had no clothing coupons for two years.

In the winter the problem is how to keep warm – there is no glass to repair the hundreds of shattered windows.

Lili's father was a banker and they have a large house and garden, but with all amenities swept away in the war this is something of a liability. The food situation is acute. She says that the October ration is to consist of half a kilo of bread (a kilo is two and a half pounds), one pound of meat, no butter, coffee, sugar or tea. Lack of transport makes it difficult to procure vegetables and potatoes from the surrounding country districts, and although not actually starving, everyone is very undernourished.

Because she works as an interpreter for the British Army, Lili gets a light lunch, but she is deeply concerned for her mother, who is very delicate. Lili is engaged to a young doctor and hopes to marry in the spring, but he has been a prisoner of the Russians and has returned consumptive and is now in hospital. How tragic it is – Lili, so young and lovely, yet another one of so many whose lives have been blighted by the war.

When we are having tea, Mrs Ferguson tells me that they help out all they can from their Army rations, and I give Lili the tin of tea we brought with us. She is overjoyed with it, and says it will be a boon to her mother.

Saturday, 14 September 1946

A most beautiful morning for our drive to Vienna. We start off after breakfast. The Fergusons have been most kind and we hope to be able to return their hospitality at a future date.

The road to Vienna runs through superb mountain scenery. All along the route RAOC depots and dumps and vehicle parks are tucked away in the hills. Rex gets out to inspect, and every one of them presents its own particular problems. He copes with these, making notes and decisions, carrying out this onerous business in a way that has won my most profound admiration. I could see how he smoothed the anxieties and solved the problems of the senior and junior officers on his way and how glad they were to see him.

This trip has given me an insight on what a terrific district he is responsible for. He says it will be easier to control when GHQ moves to Padua and the distances are not so great. We shall actually have travelled over 5000 miles from Naples and back on this tour.

We are in the British occupied zone still and there he is, the British 'Tommy', perched on lonely hillsides, camped on the edge of dark forests or upon the banks of rushing rivers, or billeted in requisitioned houses amongst the ruins and the rubble; mute witness to the bitter fighting in which he took part in those last months of the war.

Bronzed and debonair, grappling with every situation as only he can, making friends in his casual, easy way with the local inhabitants, he typifies all that is best in the British character, and is the finest propaganda for Britain in the world.

On we go, through the valleys of the Mur with the timber-pulping stations deep in the forests, through Bruck, climbing higher and higher as we near the Zimmering Pass, where the British zone ends and the Russian zone commences.

We have been warned to watch our step on entering the Russian zone. They are extremely suspicious and see spies everywhere. Rex has been advised to see that all our papers are in order and on no account to deviate from the main road. Their actions are quite unpredictable. The other day, for no obvious reason, they held up three Red Cross sisters for ten hours, and there is no knowing what their mood might be when we arrive on the scene. Rex has most carefully briefed Wooley, telling him to pull up well within the no man's land between the British and Russian zones, and has all our papers to hand.

We reach the last British post, a lovely little chalet, perched high on the thickly wooded mountainside. Before us is the strip of no man's land. The pole is raised by a British sentry, and we move forward. There before us is the Russian check-post, ablaze with red flags. Huge posters of Lenin and Stalin decorate both sides of the road and sentries of the Red Army, bristling with Sten guns, stand in aggressive attitudes under an enormous sign which says 'Welcome to the British Soldiers' – a sentiment which their threatening expressions seem to belie.

Rex leans forward with our papers and passports in his hand and I am just summoning up a rather wavering smile when to our complete surprise and consternation Wooley suddenly accelerates and we flash past the check-post at a brisk pace, expecting at least a shot in our backs. To our utmost amazement, nothing happens!

Whether it is just one of their days to be non-temperamental or whether the sentries were confused by the red pennant with a white star (denoting Rex's rank as brigadier) which flies on the bonnet of the car, we shall never know; but the fact remains that we have actually crashed the Russian zone without a challenge. Even so, Rex is exceedingly annoyed with Wooley, who seems to have no clear idea at all as to why he disobeyed orders, or to realise that his action might easily have led to serious consequences for all of us. As Rex has said, he is an excellent driver but very 'woolly-headed'.

We are now well within the Russian zone, and one is forcibly struck by the marked difference between it and the British zone. The fields are almost empty of labour. Houses – even on this bright morning – are closely shuttered. There are few people in the streets. Red Army soldiers in their bloused tunics and high boots patrol roads and villages, armed to the teeth.

As we leave the pass and cross the great plain that stretches to Vienna, the feeling of depression increases. Wrecked planes and smashed and bullet-riddled tanks, vehicles and guns lie abandoned, rusted and derelict along the wayside. And the town of Wiener Neustadt, where a terrible battle was fought against the Russians, is the most bombed and devastated place we have seen.

We near the environs of Vienna, with the distant hills behind it. Large buildings begin to appear, with more evidence of war-time damage. As we near the heart of the city, placards with huge signs in four languages appear on buildings and at road crossings, reminding us that Vienna is divided into four zones occupied by the British, the Americans, the French and the Russians.

We enter the British zone in time for lunch at the famous Sacher Hotel, now the number one senior officers' transit hotel, where we are booked to stay.

We have been told that as we have only one day in Vienna, we simply must see the Vienna Woods. After lunch Rex has to report for duty, but when he returns we set off. This is a most perfect day for this drive up into the enchanting woods which clothe the hillsides and are of far greater extent than I had imagined. All the way, the strains of Strauss's lovely waltzes echo in my memory until at last we reach the heights on which Leopoldsberg, the ancient castle of the Austrian kings, stands, commanding a magnificent view of Vienna and the Danube far below. From here one can see the terrible devastation wrought by the bombardment of the Russian guns which shelled the city from the far side of the river.

What a difference this Vienna presents from the one of one's imagining! Now she is like a beautiful woman who has been ravished – her lovely buildings gutted and destroyed, her fabled gaiety extinguished. There is an Austrian proverb, '*Biegen, nicht Brechen*' (bending, not breaking), product of the people's turbulent history. They bow to the storm and thus survive disasters which would crush others. Let us pray that this will be true of the present disaster, and that happier times will dawn for these resilient people.

I decide to have a bath in our 'period' bathroom, and I am glad to find the enormous bronze taps yield good hot water. I am feeling nicely relaxed and looking forward to dinner and an early night when Rex returns to say we are expected downstairs to a cocktail party to meet the Ordnance officers and wives, and that Captain Every and his wife will be dining with us. A cocktail party is about the last thing I crave at the moment, but as Rex points out, the officers and wives have laid on the party in honour of the DOS and his wife and I can't possibly say I am too tired. I see his point and rally my flagging spirits, put on my cocktail frock and descend, resolved to put the best face on it I can!

Sunday, 15 September 1946

An early start is scheduled as Rex has to call at Bruck on our way
to Klagenfurt. My passport is only valid till today for entry into
Austria and has to be endorsed before I shall be permitted to leave.
Rex has entrusted Captain Every to do this and after breakfast
waits impatiently for his arrival with passport duly stamped so that
we can leave.

At last Captain Every arrives, very hot and bothered and with
a most extraordinary story. It appears that the Italian authorities
refused to OK my passport, putting Captain Every through a sort
of third degree as to my desirability, and demanded to know what
my surname was before my marriage. Thoroughly flustered and
with visions of his DOS fuming at the delay, poor Captain Every
seems to have completely lost his head! Having of course no idea
what my maiden name was, even so, it is hard to understand why,
instead of saying Brown, Jones or Robinson, he had to reply that
it was <u>Franco</u>!

This fairly puts the cat amongst the pigeons. That the wife of
Brigadier Shillington is of Spanish blood and is possibly connected
to General Franco, the hated Fascist dictator, could lead to all sorts
of very unpleasant political repercussions should the highly suspicious Russian authorities get to know of it. The result of this is that
the Italians absolutely refuse to stamp my visa and demand that Rex
should be sent for immediately.

Rex is furious. He has a very important conference in
Klagenfurt and is already behind schedule. Fixing the unfortunate
Captain Every with an awful look he demands to know why he
was such a 'blankety-blank' fool as to give my name as Franco.
Captain Every can give no better reason than that it happened to
be the first name that came into his head!

Rex and Captain Every now depart in haste to see what can

be done, leaving me prey to the deepest forebodings and anxiety. Here I am, left alone and unprotected! Suppose the Russians have got wind of this? They would think it highly suspicious that the wife of an Army officer should have been a Franco – in their eyes what possible reason could she have had for entering Vienna but to spy for the Fascists? What is to stop them from spiriting me away so that by the time Rex returns poor old Evelyn Franco will be languishing in some Russian zone, never to be heard of again!

These gloomy forebodings are at last interrupted by the arrival of Rex's car (minus the unhappy Captain Every) and out stalks Rex, looking very foreboding indeed but bearing my stamped passport. Wooley puts on steam and we make up for lost time. He has strict orders to pull up at the Russian checkpoint and this time our papers are duly inspected by very foreboding Soviet guards, all armed to the teeth, and I don't breathe freely till we cross no-man's land into the safety of the British zone!

Monday, 16 September 1946

We have a long drive from Maria Wörth (where we spent the night) to Venice before us and have an early breakfast. When we are all assembled to leave, Wooley informs Rex that he took the car into Klagenfurt last night and has lost the starting handle! There is also not enough petrol! He had no right to take the car without permission (what energy, after all that driving!). However, Rex feels Wooley has done a splendid job for the last seven days and lets him off lightly.

The long straight *autostrada* are ideal for quick motoring and the miles are swallowed up as we traverse their poplar-lined lengths. There is little to see and I doze off, glad to be able to relax, until Rex rouses me to see that before us stretches a great causeway – the roadway to Venice, two and a half miles long from the mainland.

And as we travel along with the waters of the lagoon on either side, suddenly the entire heavens seem to erupt into a glory of breath-taking colour, as the sun sinks to rest in a bed of crimson, lemon, orange and scarlet, such as Turner captured for us in his inspired canvas. And then, far away in the distance ahead of us, rises a mother-of-pearl vision, an enchanted city seeming to float between heaven and the sea to which she is wedded – Venice!

Tuesday, 17 September 1946

Rex off early to GHQ Padua, and sends the launch back for me at the Hotel Danieli – the most famous hotel in Venice, now under military control – to go to the Lido. I am anxious to explore this legendary place and I enjoy the trip across the lagoon.

I set off down the long straight road to the sea and come out onto the grand promenade on which stand the luxury hotels, which used each to have its own private bathing beach. They are closely shuttered and badly in need of a coat of paint, but the lovely beach is free to all and I walk to the end of the promenade, passing the shut-up casinos, and come to the famous Excelsior, now closed and deserted.

The pale green waters of the Adriatic still lap these famous sands, but a sad air of desolation broods over all and there is not a soul in sight. With a little shiver, in spite of the bright sunshine, I retrace my steps. How many of those pleasure-loving people have died in the holocaust of war, I wonder, or are the unhappy victims of its aftermath.

The motor-launch awaits me and we are soon speeding back to Venice, getting a marvellous view of St Mark's Basin, the buildings with their delicate colourings and terracotta roofs, the domes and campaniles all set against the blue sky which is reflected in the limpid waters of the lagoon.

Rex has returned after a tiring, hot morning in Padua – it seems I get all the best of this tour! – but of course, as he says, we should not be here at all if he was not on duty. As usual, he doesn't grumble, being one of the most cheerful people possible, and as he has the afternoon off, suggests we have a look at St Mark's. Clutching our guidebook we pass through the bronze Byzantine doors of the magnificent eleventh-century portal and enter the great Basilica. It is filled with a mysterious half-light and at first our eyes are too blinded by the brilliant sunshine outside to be able to distinguish much, though we are aware of its vast size.

Then as our eyes become accustomed to the dim light, certain objects become clear: the pavement on which we stand is composed of thousands of different-coloured mosaics, the high domed ceiling is entirely of gold mosaics and the pillars around us and arches are of marble, alabaster, jasper and porphyry, which send out gleams of light in the darkness.

All around one are priceless treasures of art. Titian, Tintoretto and a host of masters have given of their best to this incomparable shrine; in fact there is so much splendour and grandeur in this vast cathedral that we feel somewhat overwhelmed by it all. However, as GHQ is moving from Caserta to Padua next month, we shall be able to enjoy it all at our leisure, and we decide to treat ourselves to ices at the famous Florian's and emerge once more into the dazzling sunshine of the Piazza.

Saturday, 21 September 1946

We arrived back at the villa at about 8.30 p.m. last night, where Colonel Slingsby and Major Lee-Wood, who have been staying there in our absence, welcome us home and dine with us. The staff seem delighted to see us back.

After Rex goes off to Caserta this morning I go into the kitchen after breakfast. Oscar informs me that my *'reserva* cupboard' has been sadly depleted in my absence. I go with him to inspect it and it most certainly has! From what Oscar says it seems that the Colonel and Major have been entertaining pretty lavishly. Well, well!

Rex returns full of news. He is to go to Rome on duty on Wednesday next, and glory be, I can go with him! As we have to leave the villa for good on 6 October, and we are putting up Brigadier Cansdale here for two nights from 28 September, there will be plenty to get done between our return from Rome and our departure from Naples. Rex says it has been arranged for the officers and wives and families to be accommodated on the Lido until accommodation either in villas around Padua or hotels in Venice are arranged.

As he knows how much I want to visit Pompeii Rex has arranged that an Italian professor, attached to GHQ, shall be my guide. Rex hopes to go later. He says the professor is charming and that he suggests that he should take me first to visit the Naples Museum before seeing Pompeii, as owing to the war the beautiful statues and ornaments have been removed there for safety. So we are off to the museum on Monday.

Monday, 23 September 1946

After lunch Rex's car returns from Caserta, complete with the professor. He is a small, slight, elderly Italian, with lively brown eyes and a charming manner. He speaks perfect English and while the car threads its way through the busy streets of Naples he tells me that the museum was originally a cavalry barracks before being remodelled to receive the antiquities of Pompeii and Herculaneum and the famous Farnese collections. It is now national property.

He explains that, as our time is so limited, he proposes only to show me those objects which bear relation to our visit to Pompeii tomorrow, but as we enter the first vast room of the museum, he pauses to show me some of the most famous works by Phidias, Pericles and of the later golden age of the fourth century BC. Without the professor I would have been lost alone amongst so many treasures.

It is a somewhat overawed me that follows him into the gallery in which are housed the famous bronzes of Pompeii and Herculaneum. Here the professor is the perfect guide, steering me from the Young Satyr, to Apollo, to the Head of a Boy from Herculaneum, wicked old Silenus and the lovely tender Sleeping Faun.

But now we come to the famous Dancing Faun, the Greek figure found in the villa in Pompeii which has been named after him. There he is, dancing for ever down the centuries, and from the crown of his curling hair down to his lightly dancing feet he is the very essence of sheer pagan delight, even to his ecstatic little tail! I fall in love with him on the spot and the professor has some difficulty in dragging me away.

Tuesday, 24 September 1946

A most lovely morning. The professor arrives in Rex's car. Oscar appears, beaming, with an enormous picnic basket, and we set off, taking the road which winds round the bay to the foot of Vesuvius on the opposite shore.

We pass villages and come to modern Pompeii, a somewhat squalid village, and the professor points out the wall of ancient Pompeii which lies higher up the slope.

It is now very hot, being noon, and we find a cool spot to have our lunch. Here Oscar's excellent repast is laid out while Wooley takes his equally generous portion at some little distance.

The professor is obviously a man of intellect and breeding, and as we sit and eat he tells me something about himself. Opposed to Fascism, he lost everything in the war. He says how grateful he is to have found employment at British HQ to help make ends meet for himself and his wife, who is an invalid.

As he talks I notice how shabby and threadbare his suit is (although the linen is most scrupulously clean), how thin he is and how much he is enjoying his meal, and suddenly I realise with a shock that he is hungry! So this is what war can do to a man of his ability and breeding. Once again one is up against its cruel aftermath.

If only there was something one could do to help without hurting his pride. Then my eyes fall on our sumptuous repast, which in Oscar's best tradition is far more than we can eat, and I have an inspiration. Remarking that it does seem as if we have been given far too much, I suggest that perhaps his wife might like to sample some of Oscar's vol-au-vents, the salad and pastries, and that I certainly don't want to take back the grapes and fruit we have been unable to eat. He thanks me with pathetic eagerness and accepts gladly, saying that nowadays, alas, his wife seldom enjoys such delicacies, his pay only allowing for the barest necessities, and I make a mental note to tell Wooley to pack up all that is left and some wine for the professor to take home with him.

As we near the walls of the city the professor points out the trees and vegetation growing some twenty-eight feet above our heads, showing the depth of ash and volcanic dust under which the city was buried.

I soon learn what a matchless guide I have in my little professor! As we advance to the centre of the forum he begins to paint in vivid word-pictures the scene as it would have been before disaster struck the city. And as he speaks, so powerful is the medium of his knowledge and the magic of his enthusiasm that the whole place seems to spring to life. We spend the next three hours walking in the shadows of history as my professor describes and explains every piece of this unique and fascinating place.

Now as our visit nears its close the professor produces a surprise for me. As a privileged person he has a permit to admit us to a part of Pompeii which had only recently begun to be excavated before the war and is still to be explored. We pass through a barrier and find ourselves in a long narrow trench, the walls of which tower above us, with thick vegetation growing along the top. We move down this until the professor stops before a partially uncovered villa. Only the kitchen is exposed; on the hearth lies a cooking pot and cooking utensils and one realises that one is looking at them just as they were left in panic on the morning back in 79 AD. Further on the professor points out in the wall on our right the faint outline of a high arch- way – it is the doorway into a villa as yet unexcavated.

And so we leave Pompeii, crossing the empty forum, leaving the ghosts in peace, and I realise how lucky I have been to have seen this wonderful and ancient city not only in the company of my incomparable professor but also absolutely free from tourists!

Later as I remove my rubber-soled shoes I see that they are thickly coated with a fine grey substance which clings obstinately to their surface and is difficult to brush off. It is the volcanic dust of long-dead Pompeii in which I have been walking – that same sub- stance which once fell so relentlessly to choke out the life of a city.

Across the bay Vesuvius rises, bathed in the blood-red hues of the dying sun. Always before the view has enchanted me, but now I see it in a different light. The vision of the narrow streets of Pompeii, choked with terrified crowds seeking some way of escape, appears before my eyes; I hear the shrieks and crash of falling build- ings as the earthquakes rock the city – the blackness, the horror and confusion – and I turn away with a shudder.

The next day, escorted round some of the main sights of Rome by an Italian contessa, Evelyn is taken to the Vatican.

As we enter the Pope's library we are overwhelmed by the vast size of it, which seems to stretch for ever. This enormous apartment houses over four hundred thousand books and documents of priceless value (amongst the latter, Henry VIII's petition for the dissolution of his marriage to Catherine of Aragon) and superb treasures – gifts to various Popes down the ages. It is all very wonderful but it seems rather out of place – so much grandeur for one who names himself Christ's Vicar on earth, when one remembers the sublime simplicity and poverty of the life of Our Lord.

Thursday, 3 October 1946
Busy packing. We have received a charming letter from Signor Cenzato as follows:-

Dear General,

I have been very sorry not to be able to present my best regards to you and Mrs Shillington – I leave for Roma tomorrow morning at six o'clock.

We hope you will remember 'La Loggetta' with the same feelings with which we will remember your kindliness.

We hope also that you will come back to Napoli, not on duty, but as 'tourists' and that then we shall be able to have you and Mrs Shillington as our guests.

It may be that we meet in Roma, in your hotel!

Believe me.

Yours truly

Cenzato

*

They also receive a beautifully printed photograph of the villa and note from their German POWs, who will return to the 'pool', thanking them for their kindness and wishing them good luck in the future.

In a cold and rainy Venice Evelyn is reunited with Lita and, as there are no villas available, she and Rex take a suite at the Europa, the hotel on the Grand Canal where the Stauntons are staying. This will mean saying good-bye to Oscar and Leo, who had travelled to Padua in expectation of serving them in their new accommodation, but Rex gives them good references and they find a new home with Brigadier and Mrs Bastien.

Evelyn throws herself into her new life, enjoying the company of Lita and other Army wives and making the most of living in a city with so much to see. She often assists Lita with her duties at Venice's Anglican church, St George's. However, with winter on its way, life is not as comfortable as it was at the villa.

Monday, 11 November 1946

Still very cold. The hotel heating is now controlled. We are rationed to hot baths for certain days and there is no central heating until 6 p.m. just before our husbands return from Padua. As it is on for them to have breakfast they certainly have the best of it.

At lunchtime we all sit in the enormous dining room, with its lofty ceiling and mosaic floors, huddled up to the eyes in woollies and fur coats, and wearing fur-lined boots, the children clad as if for mountain climbing! But in the evening – what a transformation! The heating is on, and clad in evening dress we wives float round to the strains of the band which plays during dinner and all is merry as a marriage bell. Such is life in the Army!

Saturday, 16 November 1946

We visit the Doge's Palace with the Fergusons [the couple they stayed with in Graz on Rex's duty tour]. We are almost overwhelmed as we pass from one huge *sala* to another by the wealth of art treasures around us – 'The Rape of Europa' by Veronese, and others by Tintoretto and Tiepolo – and ceilings painted by Veronese. In the *Sala del Maggior Consiglio* (Hall of the Higher Council) we pause before the largest oil painting in the world, 'Paradise' by Tintoretto, which would take hours to study in detail, and on the walls portraits of the Doges.

There is a most interesting collection of arms, about two thousand pieces, which Rex and Colonel Ferguson find fascinating, and the fighting armour of Henry I of France. There is also a chastity belt, at which Mrs Ferguson and I gaze with interest, wondering how on earth the ladies left at home endured such a torment while their spouses were away fighting for years on end, and most certainly none enduring any such restraints themselves!

We cross over that most tragic bridge in the world, the Bridge of Sighs, which leads to the tiny dungeons called *pozzi* (wells), and one thought of all the poor wretches who had passed that way never to return.

Down and down we go, dank, dark and damp, our footsteps echoing in the long corridors. There is one ghastly cell where they used to guillotine the political prisoners they wished to get rid of secretly, which has a grille in the side where they passed the bodies out into the waters of the canal. Mrs Ferguson and I find this and the dreadful atmosphere of this grisly place a bit too much and we are all glad to get out and go to the Danieli for a cup of tea.

I am surprised at the attitude of so many of the young wives here; they seem quite content to lead the same life as they do at home and sit for hours knitting and gossiping, showing no interest in all the treasures of Venice. What a waste it seems! I am so sorry that Rex has so little time for sightseeing – only really the weekend – and after the daily trip by launch and car all the way to Padua and back he needs some time for relaxation. Also he has all these duty trips to fit in as DOS of such a large district.

Wednesday, 4 December 1946

Field Marshal Viscount Montgomery, Chief of the Imperial General Staff, is visiting Venice at the close of his tours of visits to units and formations in Venezia Giulia. He will be the guest of Lt Colonel Sir John Harding and we assemble on the terrace of the hotel to watch his progress down the Grand Canal. It is a real thrill to get this glimpse of this famous wartime general, and as his barge passes and one sees the slight, upright figure of Monty, beloved by his troops, I remember those jaunty Desert Rats of his that we met at Maria Wörth [during Rex's duty tour in September] and how some of the magic of his personality seemed to cling to every one of them.

PART ELEVEN

An Allied observer

December 1946–April 1947

Jack and Mary Heywood are also now in Venice. Jack and Rex have hatched a plan to take their wives with them on their duty tour to Klagenfurt and Graz on 15 December, chartering a diesel train that was used by the US Army.

Thursday, 12 December 1946

This morning the Italian maid who is doing my room suddenly rushes to the window and exclaims excitedly, 'Navy! Navy!' As we do get occasional visits from British warships I also rush to look out, but to my disappointment nothing faintly resembling our glorious Navy is in sight. Instead a very nasty snow storm is sweeping the canal! Later I am informed that what I mistook for 'Navy' was in fact '*neve*', which means 'snow' in Italian and hence the maid's excitement as snow is a most unaccustomed sight in Venice.

I must say the sight of the snow has rather dampened my enthusiasm for the Austrian trip, and when I see Mary she is even more doubtful of the wisdom of this trip in such weather. She has had two serious internal operations and has to be careful, and like

myself she dreads the cold. But our men return from Padua full
of joy; they have arranged for a cook and waiter, and Jack, in his
capacity of 'boss' of the Royal Army Service Corps (RASC), will
provide our food and drinks. They are so like two schoolboys that
Mary and I weaken and just don't have the heart to disappoint
them! I return to the hotel to look out my warmest woollies!

Saturday, 14 December 1946

Awful blow! When our men return from Padua at lunchtime they
reveal that there is <u>no heating</u> on the train! This seems to put the
hat on it, but Rex has been busy and this is where he comes in as
he is able to provide oil stoves and thick blankets. And off they go
to make the final arrangements.

Sunday, 15 December 1946

Fine but very cold. All aboard the diesel at 8 p.m. It certainly looks
an imposing conveyance! The stoves are on full strength and the
saloon is beautifully warm and our berth looks very comfortable
piled up with the blankets Rex has provided. Mary and self, clad as
if for a polar expedition, feel all will be well.

We are served a marvellous dinner (good old RASC) and the
drinks are super. I retire to bed feeling very content, only to find
it is quite impossible to have an oil stove in the sleeping berths,
which are quite icy. So, keeping on our thick stockings, Mary and
I retire under three blankets apiece and I go to sleep with only my
nose showing!

Monday, 16 December 1946

Arrive Klagenfurt Station at 7 a.m. Thick snow outside, and
blankets frozen to the window! Retire underneath, shivering.
Rex – who is up and about to have breakfast with Jack – comes

in to say that the beer bottles resemble candlesticks as the cold has forced the beer out of the bottles! Remarks gloomily that the whisky is frozen also! Later I am served a very nice hot breakfast and Mary and I dress in our warmest tweeds and boots and are picked up and taken to coffee, and afterwards to lunch at the Carinthian Club.

As the men are on duty in the afternoon, Mary and I go to the quarter of Colonel Davis, who is in our corps, where his wife suggests we might like a bath, and it is a joy to soak in lovely hot water before Rex and Jack return to take us to the diesel, where we shall change into evening dress for tonight's party. Or, so we think! Arrive at the station – no train!

There is a frantic search while Mary and I sit in a very cold waiting room. At last the train is traced – someone has pinched it and taken it to Villach! Jack and Rex raise hell and frantic phone messages are sent ordering it to be returned at once! But all hope is abandoned when the answer comes through that it has broken down and is being repaired. Mary and I are livid!

How on earth can we spend the evening at the club without our party clothes? But there is nothing for it but to grin and bear it, which is just what we do as we try our best to look as if we really enjoy dancing in heavy snow-boots and thick tweeds in a centrally heated room, surrounded by a crowd of glamorous wives all dressed up to the eyes for a party in our honour! In the meantime, our men are on tenterhooks as messages fly to and forth between them and Villach as to when the train will arrive as we have to leave tonight for Graz. By 11 p.m. we feel the warmth of our welcome is wearing somewhat thin as no one can leave until we do, and it is with the utmost relief that we hear that the delinquent has returned and we are able to make our farewells and get on board and to bed.

Tuesday, 17 December 1946

Arrive in Graz. Bitterly cold, deep snow. Rex and Jack off early to HQ and Mary and I stay in bed till they come back for us and take us to the Wiesler Hotel where the Fergusons have lunch with us. They go back on duty and Mrs Ferguson, Mary and I go to the NAAFI.

Driving through the streets of Graz, deep in snow, we see people dragging Christmas trees on sledges and are horrified to see that in many cases their feet are bound up in rags or newspaper. It is borne on one once again how dearly these brave, spirited people have paid for their fatal association with Hitler.

The NAAFI here is excellent, selling practically everything, and we buy scarves and some very attractive wooden boxes made in Austria. We feel ashamed of our warm bootees when we see the sufferings of the people of Graz.

Wednesday, 18 December 1946

Horribly cold trip, snowing all the way. We couldn't survive without Rex's oil stoves and the excellent food provided from the kitchen. Have awful congestion in head.

The train breaks down! Here we are stranded in the snow, which is becoming thicker and thicker every moment! After a long delay they manage somehow to get a signal through for a steam engine to come and rescue us. All this is very shame-making, but all Mary and I want is to get back to Venice. By now my throat is very sore indeed and my head is terrible; Mary not too good either. We arrive late, and dead tired I go straight to bed.

Thursday, 19 December 1946

Cold on chest and bronchitis. Spend the next four days in bed. Rex has a cold too.

Monday, 23 December 1946

Up at last. Went with Lita to buy flowers to decorate the church, not feeling too good.

Tuesday, 24 December 1946

Decorating the church. We dine with the Heywoods at the Hotel Danieli – a lovely evening, the hotel prettily decorated, and a splendid dinner and dance afterwards. Mary so gay, and we all so happy.

Wednesday, 25 December 1946

Cold but sunny. Went by launch to church – the decorations looked beautiful and a lovely service. Rex off to Padua to the children's party – and a big special dinner party at night. Dining with the Heywoods again on New Year's Eve.

Next three days spent resting and getting over our colds.

Tuesday, 31 December 1946

Just before dinner Jack rang to say Mary had been taken suddenly ill – her evening things all laid out to come to dine with us. So very sorry! A sad evening without Mary and Jack.

Wednesday, 1 January 1947

Such a perfect day, Rex ordered the launch and we went to the Lido. This is really the only place where you can walk! Venice is always up and down over the side-canals with which the whole city is intersected. We had a good walk along the sands. Hear that Mary is very ill and has gone to hospital.

Thursday, 2 January 1947

Rex has to go to England to the War Office tomorrow. Very short notice indeed. He will be away for two weeks. Very bad news of

Evelyn and Rex on the Grand Canal, Venice

Mary. She has had an operation for stoppage of the bowels – this is serious as she has already had two operations and has been told she must not have another one. I pray that the Austria trip has not been the cause of this illness.

Friday, 3 January 1947

Rex off very early to England via Simplon Orient. Feeling very lonely. At 6 p.m. he returned! Mistake had been made and he is to go tomorrow.

Saturday, 4 January 1947

Rex off early. How I shall miss him! I phoned Jack – Mary's operation was even more serious than we thought. He is very anxious about her.

Sunday, 5 January 1947

Terribly cold spell all over Europe – my poor Rex! Venice is no exception: snow and bitter wind. Telephone Jack – Mary is a little better, thank God.

Monday, 6 January 1947

Temperature below zero. Terrible wind. Didn't go out. There are plenty of people to talk to but I miss Rex so much and wonder how he is.

I have been writing some short stories since I have been in Venice; one is a ghost story inspired by a beautiful pair of gates I saw in an antiques dealer's shop. This is a good time to type them. Tea with Lita and D'Arcy.

Thursday, 9 January 1947

Phoned Jack – he says Mary is much better, sitting up in bed and powdering her nose. Sent her some beautiful red roses. I am so pleased to hear this good news.

Saturday, 11 January 1947

Lita has heard that Mary has had a serious relapse and is not expected to last the night. Oh, poor Jack!

Sunday, 12 January 1947

Dear Mary died last night. How tragic it is. I can hardly believe it. It is less than three weeks since we were with them for Christmas Eve and she was so gay and looking so lovely. What will poor Jack do? I wrote to him. Feeling terribly depressed – do wish Rex was back.

Monday, 13 January 1947

Cold foggy day. I sat at my window looking down on the canal and watched the ferry which plies between the seminary alongside Santa Maria Salute and the landing-stage near the hotel. As it was paddled slowly out of the fog by the gondolier, the picture it made with the shrouded figures of the priests standing in it reminded me of the souls of the dead being ferried across the Styx by Charon in his barge. These gloomy reflections are somewhat dispelled by a cable from Rex to say he spent the weekend with Louis and Ruby Freedman – how I would have loved to have been with them!

Jack Heywood sent his launch for me and we dined in his suite. He wants to take Mary's body to England and has asked me if I will pack up her things for him to take home. It will be a very sad task, but I would do anything for him.

Tuesday, 14 January 1947

I have made friends with Signora Commins, the wife of the Italian manager of this hotel. She is French and speaks good English. She tells me that when the Germans occupied Venice and some of them were billeted in the Europa, her husband had a wireless concealed in the cellar and every night he would go down, under the noses of the Germans, to hear the nine o'clock news from London. She says she was terrified that the Germans would scent a rat when he always made some excuse to be absent at that time, but mercifully they never spotted it.

Saturday, 18 January 1947

Went over with Lita to start packing up poor Mary's things. This is a terribly sad task – she had such lovely clothes and under-things, and many of the dresses bring back memories to me ... Also she has masses of cosmetics – Elizabeth Arden, etc. – and Jack suggests we might like some of them as he doesn't want to take them back to England.

Tuesday, 21 January 1947

Rex back this evening. All is right with the world again! He had a terrible journey on the Simplon as the train broke down and they were held up for hours – no heat, no food and with his usual old-fashioned courtesy he gave up his sleeping berth to an elderly lady and spent a very uncomfortable cold night. He didn't get any food until they changed trains in Milan.

Tuesday, 4 February 1947

Very slowly things are beginning to change here. Various people are being recalled home as the Services leave Italy. The Stauntons are off soon – I shall miss Lita! – and as usual, Rex, being Ordnance, will be the last to go.

We have most lovely shops in the hotel here, selling lingerie of all sorts – the most glamorous being beautiful silk nylon nighties with lace-trimmed negligees to match. We all long to appear in them but restrain ourselves as they are expensive. One little wife, however, confides to me that she has fallen for a shell-pink outfit, and dare not tell her husband, a captain, as she tearfully remarks, 'When shall I ever wear it, with the washing-up to do?'

Sunday, 9 February 1947

Britain under ice! Snow and blizzards. Newcastle and the Lake District completely cut off! The trial of Field Marshal Kesselring commences here at the Court of Assizes, before a British military tribunal. He is charged as a war criminal as having been responsible for the reprisal massacre of three hundred and thirty-five Italians executed in the Ardeatine Caves in Rome. Also of the incitement of his forces to massacre Italian civilians, including women and children, in many villages as reprisal against Partisan activities. Rex can get me VIP tickets to attend this trial and I would very much like to go.

Monday, 24 February 1947

Kesselring trial begins. They are having to smuggle him into the court, so violent is the feeling against him, and there are strict police precautions to see that no one gets into the courtroom with a weapon.

Field Marshal Kesselring and interpreter at his trial
in Venice, February 1947

Thursday, 27 February 1947

I write a long letter to my best friend Jane to tell her all about the trial. I wish so much she was here with me as I know how interested she would be. I can hardly believe that I have sat here for three days now and only half a dozen of all the wives here in Venice have come here, even for an hour, and yet it is one of the most intensely interesting events possible and I feel I am so lucky to be able to attend.

Rex has managed to get me some of the very few VIP seats (he came with me one day but of course he has to go to Padua) and I am now sitting waiting for the court to open. I will try and explain what it is like.

It is a very large grey building on the Grand Canal, very imposing, and I arrive in Rex's launch at the landing stage, which is stiff with Red Caps and the colourful *carabinieri* with their red and blue plumes, armed with Tommy Guns. The whole atmosphere is charged as they await the arrival of the police launch which will bring the prisoner.

I am lucky to be classed as an 'Allied observer' which means I don't have to enter by the public entrance, where everyone has to be searched. Even for the VIP seats one is vetted and one's pass scrutinised three times before one can climb the huge staircase and reach the corridor leading to the courtroom. The corridor is lined with military police and *carabinieri*, all armed to the teeth and standing guard before doors marked 'Defence', 'Prisoner' and 'Witnesses' in both English and German.

The hall, decorated in pseudo-marble, has at the end where I enter a raised semicircular dais on which the judge advocate and the president of the military court sit with the other senior Army officers, flanked on one side by the Italian government observer and on my side by Colonel R. C. Halse, the prosecutor, and with him two interpreters and a colonel of the US Army. I am sitting almost behind Colonel Halse and have a perfect view of Field Marshal Kesselring, who sits opposite across the court with his personal interpreter (and secretary) and his lawyer, Dr Hans Laternser. Both Kesselring and Dr Laternser speak English well, but they display no knowledge in the court and everything has to be said first in English and then in German. Behind the judge's seat there is an enormous Union Jack on the wall.

As the days pass I get to know the people concerned better. The Judge Advocate KC, Mr C. L. Stirling, is a dry, very precise, unemotional character; his job is to interpret the law to the five military members of the court. One of these is Major General Hakewill-Smith, a regular soldier and a CB (Order of the Bath).

Colonel Halse has had experience in prosecuting war criminals and has seen Kesselring's immediate subordinates (von Mackensen and Mälzer) sentenced to death. He is a regular officer and a solicitor, and his knowledge of the law has led him to the legal department of the War Office. He is bulky, impetuous, and at times, I feel, very offensive in his hectoring, and his cross-examinations can be both interesting and painful.

The prisoner, Kesselring, sixty-two years of age, is a Bavarian, a regular soldier of the Wehrmacht, a bulky figure, and uses his right fist clenched to emphasise emotion. He is fighting for his life.

His lawyer, Dr Laternser, is small and very, very alert. He is the one lawyer the accused insisted on conducting his defence. He reminds me of a very alert dachshund as he springs up to query some interpretation he does not agree with, or to the defence of his client when heckled by the prosecutor.

I am very impressed by the rigid justice of the whole proceedings. Again and again these are held up while some knotty point of translation of those long German portmanteau words is spelled out to the consent of Kesselring's lawyer. It is easy to see why Kesselring has so much confidence in him.

As day by day goes by and I attend all, only returning to the hotel for lunch, various witnesses are called. General von Rundstedt witnesses that Kesselring was under the jurisdiction of the SS Chief sent by Hitler; we have eye-witnesses of the shooting of whole villages of Italians in reprisal for Partisan activities. The atmosphere in the court amongst the Italians at these times is one of such hatred that one feels it may explode into violence at any moment.

The trial opens with Colonel Halse accusing Field Marshal Kesselring of offering protection to any German commander 'who exceeded usual restraint' in dealing with Italian Partisans after the bomb explosion in Rome on 23 March 1944 in which thirty-two German policemen were killed. This was in accordance with an order passed down to the army from Hitler's HQ that the ratio of reprisals for German deaths was to be ten to one. 'For every German soldier killed, ten Italian hostages will be shot.'

It was this order which led to the shooting of innocent Italians in the Ardeatine Caves near Rome. Colonel Halse points out that there was no word of a trial. 'Commanders could do what they liked.'

Friday, 28 February 1947

Colonel Scotland is called as a witness for the prosecution. He is the 'mystery man' of the trial and when giving evidence today he causes great surprise by disclosing that he had served with the German Army! He is a slight, unobtrusive sort of man, and he gives evidence as a British intelligence officer on the massacre at the Ardeatine Caves.

Another witness is called, Signor Arleni (whose son and nephew

were victims), who was there after the shootings and who tells us
that the killed came from all walks of life – six generals, four police
officers, priests, doctors, lawyers and shopkeepers – the age of the
youngest being fifteen years old. Three hundred and twenty-three
were identified.

Photographs are produced in court:

1. Victims' bodies in heaps.
2. Victims' bodies disintegrating.
3. Masses of bodies messed up together.
4. Rope used to tie victims.

The Italians in the court sit, looking like Nemesis!

Herbert Kappler is called. Kappler was head of the German
police and security services in Rome, directly under Himmler,
head of the SS. It was under his direct command that the shootings
in the caves took place, and he tells us in impassive tones how he
had to find enough Italian civilians who were 'death worthy', to
use a German expression, in order to comply with Hitler's order.
'There were not enough,' Kappler tells us, 'so he added fifty-seven
Jews.'

Colonel Halse: 'In the list of these names, was any evidence
shown against the names of these Jews?'

Kappler: 'No – only the word Jew.'

Asked by Halse if he had any scruples in carrying out the order,
he replied in frigid tone, 'No – and I would do exactly the same
thing again!'

It is impossible to describe the effect of this man upon the
court – or the feeling of horror with which he inspired me. It
seemed as if there before my eyes was the very embodiment of all
that was most evil in the Hitler regime; he made my blood run

cold. Signor Arleni had previously testified that none of the Jews shot were members of the Resistance groups.

Kesselring is also on trial for the indiscriminate killing of men, women and children in the Fucecchio area, between Leghorn (Livorno) and Florence, by German soldiers. A German, Major Strauch, is called and questioned. He says his orders were to 'comb out' the marshy Fucecchio area for Partisans and that 'every house, shelter, all living persons are to be destroyed'.

Monday, 3 March 1947

Kesselring's defence was carried out by his very able lawyer, Dr Laternser, and also by himself in the witness box.

The defence is that although as Commander-in-Chief of the district Kesselring was responsible for all that went on in the area, he was not fully cognisant of the manner in which Hitler's orders were being carried out. This was because Hitler sent Kappler down to carry them out.

This is verified to a certain extent by Hitler's and HQ's directives, shown in court. There is no doubt that, as Kesselring said himself, 'There was an "iron curtain" between the Wehrmacht and the SS which I was unable to remove.'

He quotes a telephone conversation, witnessed by his Second-in-Command, between Kappler and himself, in which Kappler informed him that he had sufficient number of persons 'who were sentenced to death' for the firing squad, and Kesselring added, 'He felt that he was relieved of a heavy burden.'

I was now getting to know some members of the court. When we had our coffee break we assembled in a small room along the corridor (the judge advocate has his private room) but it was not long before Colonel Halse and Major General Hakewill-Smith spotted me, and I think they were curious to know what sort of an

Allied spectator I was! Anyway, they were very nice to me. When he discovered I returned to the hotel for lunch, Colonel Halse took me for a delicious fish meal at a little restaurant in the Fish Market just behind the Courts of Justice.

He is quite nice to talk to, a very different person to that of the prosecutor in court. The most interesting person I meet is Colonel Scotland. He, of course, speaks German fluently and tells me how he was able to pass undetected as an officer in the German Army. He says that now that his cover is blown through having to appear as a witness in this trial, his usefulness in the Secret Service will be at an end.

I am very intrigued at all this, as in *The Luck of the Navy*, my mother's naval spy play, Mrs Peel put her son into the British Navy in order to spy upon us.

Thursday, 13 March 1947

Tenth day of Kesselring's cross-examination. I have now quite a 'rapport' with Kesselring. I believe that seeing me there day after day taking notes, he thinks I am something to do with the press! Anyway, when he is brought into court, after his usual bows to the members of the court I am favoured with a very courteous bow all to myself. I feel a great sympathy for this man; he is, after all, a fine soldier, and according to his lights [his own conscience] tried his best to conduct the war as an honourable man. As the trial proceeds one sees what a fearful predicament he was in. After the fall of Mussolini, both Prime Minister Badoglio and the King of Italy assured him emphatically they would continue to fight to the end and called upon the Germans to help them. As Kesselring said bitterly, 'We believed them but the facts showed it was not so and we were punished in believing them.'

It was Kesselring who declared Rome an 'open city'. 'Had I removed the order I should have had to send in troops and supplies through Rome and it would have meant air bombardment of Rome as a military objective, which would have included the Vatican City. Mussolini disagreed with me; he said, "Why should the citizens of Rome, who promenade all day, have a better life than my good Italians who are fighting at Cassino?"'

Rome fell on 4 June 1944.

Kesselring was left in a terrible position. In the fighting in the Apennines all his communications were destroyed. He said, 'These were the most difficult defence battles I have experienced' – this from a man who had fought on the Russian front! Month after month they had sacrificed their troops defending Italy on the promise of the King, who broke faith. 'Thirty thousand troops,' he gives as an estimate. His HQ at Frascati was bombed and some of his staff and himself were wounded, and he says, 'The Italians did not send one single Italian to defend the south.'

The Partisans became more numerous and successful because they could draw now on the POWs sent home and British and US POWs who had made escapes. His troops, feeling betrayed by the Italians, changed 'from panic to fury'; anti-tanks were scarce; they had no means of self-defence and 'the clear blue skies of Italy helped the incessant air attacks of the enemy. I had hardly any Air Force at my disposal.'

I can't believe that anyone, least of all a soldier's wife, could hear this and be unmoved.

During these gruelling days of long questioning, I notice that his usually pale face has developed a flush, and that the fingers of his hand are constantly moving; the strain of fighting for his life under the relentless pressure of Colonel Halse's cross-examination is having a very severe effect upon him. I am therefore not surprised when we are told that the general is to be examined by medical experts, and that the court is to be adjourned until he is capable of appearing again.

I am thankful for this humane decision, and as he gives me his courteous little farewell bow I know it will be 'goodbye' as the trial is to be adjourned until after Easter and we are due to leave for England on 15 April.

On 6 May 1947 the court found Kesselring guilty of both charges and sentenced him to death by firing squad. This was commuted to life imprisonment. Evelyn wrote in her diary much later:

I am glad therefore when it is finally concluded that although he does not go free, Field Marshal Kesselring is spared the fate of hanging, which as a brave soldier he certainly did not deserve, and I trust that through all those long years of imprisonment life was not too hard for him. I thank God that it was his fate to be tried by British justice and not that of Hitler and Himmler!

After a cancer diagnosis and transfer to hospital in July 1952, Kesselring was released from his prison sentence on the grounds of ill health. He died in July 1960.

One last note – Kesselring said, 'Germany lost the war because of grave mistakes in organisation in the highest circles and the mistakes of Hitler himself.' When asked why, in view of the magnificent organisation of the Germans, even high-grade officers were not informed of all activities, he replied, 'Hitler always proceeded in two lines so that one could supervise and check on the other.'

Thursday, 27 March 1947

We dine with Brigadier and Mrs Bastien, who have a very nice quarter near Padua. Oscar, knowing we are tonight's guests, has surpassed himself, and after a delicious dinner the Bastiens take us to the servants' quarters to meet our erstwhile staff. There we receive a rapturous welcome from Oscar and Leo, who, assuring us of their undying affection for their 'family Shillington', declare with lamentations that things are not the same here as at La Loggetta, which is all very touching but exceedingly embarrassing, and we tear ourselves away from further displays, hoping most sincerely that our host and hostess were safely out of earshot!

The tempo of departure is quickening and farewells become the order of the day. One regiment is off to North Africa, and as the time of departure of all British troops in Italy approaches, the tempo at Padua also accelerates. Rex, as DOS, will be one of the last to leave and with the problems of so much valuable stores – armaments, vehicles, etc. – either to be sent to England or disposed of here, his time is more and more taken up.

I go over to Padua to lunch with him at the Officers' Club there, where we get an excellent meal washed down with golden Orvieto. The drive out to Padua lies along a dead straight *autostrada*. In the distance rise the Euganean Hills, and along the road are the villas – or the ruins of villas – with their gardens and statues, built by wealthy Venetians between the fifteenth and nineteenth centuries in order to escape the tedium and confines of Venice in the summer months. Here is the Villa Foscari, in which Byron wrote the last canto of 'Childe Harold's Pilgrimage' and parts of 'Don Juan'.

Padua I find fascinating. It is one of the most ancient cities in Italy and in its famous university Englishmen from Tudor days were educated. Here Galileo taught for eighteen years and William Harvey's first thoughts on the circulation of the blood are believed to have occurred. I explore Padua's arcaded streets, her churches and the winding Corso del Popolo, which leads right through the city.

One day, after a night of rain, I am intrigued to see appearing through the coat of whitewash which has covered it, the enormous face of Mussolini with its jutting jaw, depicted upon a wall. How the mighty have fallen!

There is one funny incident before we leave. General Harding, crossing the parking space in front of the hotel, spots Rex's Humber Pullman and enquires who it belongs to. When told Brigadier Shillington, he remarks, 'The deuce it does!' and gives orders to reserve it for himself when Rex leaves Venice! Well, I can vouch for its comfort!

Saturday, 5 April 1947
To St George's Church to do the decorations. I miss dear Lita so much! The flowers are heavenly and the church looks lovely.

Easter Sunday, 6 April 1947
Church – splendid sermon. I wonder where we shall all be this time next year.

The next week is taken up in packing, farewell parties, the pattern of so many occasions in our Army life. But this will be our last station abroad – Rex will be retiring soon and civilian life will not hold out the same opportunities that Army life does. I shall be sorry to leave Venice, this enchanted city. I shall always remember the wonderful lights on the canal and the lagoon; the way the ceilings always have a pattern of reflection of the water; the enchantment of night on the canal, when through lighted windows one gets glimpses of lovely painted or carved ceilings and exquisite Venetian chandeliers.

Rex, Evelyn and a colleague of Rex's at the Europa Hotel, Venice

Eve and Rex on holiday in Cortina, Italy, 1947

And the churches! The number of churches in Venice defies description. I have counted forty-eight in my guidebook! The music of their countless bells drifts continually over the city – a sound I shall always remember, like the whirr of the wings of the hundreds of pigeons in the great piazza when the two Moors beat out the hours from St Mark's clock tower.

Well, all good things come to an end, but none of us wives is looking forward to returning to austerity post-war England, and we don't even know where Rex will be posted. He has written to our good friends, the Glucksteins, to book us a room at the Strand Palace, where Douglas is in charge, until we know our fate.

We shall be two and a half days on the train to Dover.

Monday, 14 April 1947

Left Venice after tea. We have a carriage with two sleeping berths – which close up in the daytime – and washing facilities. The train is crowded with officers, wives and children, many of them our pals.

Wednesday, 16 April 1947

Our second day on the train. We have several dining cars and the food is good. Whenever the train stops we all get out to stretch our legs. One such stop was at Berchtesgaden, and as one gazed up at the mountainside towering above, one thought of Hitler's eerie up there where he entertained his staff and which was the scene of the meeting between him and Mr Chamberlain, when the latter went on his fruitless journey in search of peace.

Later, passing through Munich and seeing the appalling destruction of that city, one realises anew what Hitler's mad dreams of conquest cost the German people. Here we do not get off the train as our stop is short, but as we lean out of the windows crowds of children gather on the platform offering piteous little souvenirs for sale, made out of any bits and pieces, and we give them what we can of chocolate, cigarettes, etc. Such a pathetic sight they are, and when we steam past the dreary camps alongside the railway which are all the homes they know now, we are face to face with the stark misery which the Third Reich brought upon the German people.

We pass through Stuttgart and Strasbourg, both terribly bombed, but are thankful to see Strasbourg Cathedral still standing.

It is difficult to get to sleep with the noises of the train and the frequent stops, when raucous voices shout at one another, and today has been a long journey over the battlefields of France where so many of our bravest and best lie buried.

Thursday, 17 April 1947

Calais! Terribly bombed, great masses of concrete lying in the sea and much evidence of the battles that were waged here. After some delay we board the boat waiting for us and with a stiff cold wind set sail for England. And there as we sight the white cliffs of Dover, this account of Rex's duty tour with the British Army of Occupation in Italy ends, and so after twelve long years does my diary.

Editor's afterword

Details of Evelyn's life in the years following her return from Italy are thin on the ground. The people who might have been able to shed some light on this time have passed away themselves. There are no more diaries that we know of.

We do have some facts. Evelyn's cousin, Elizabeth, was close to her and visited regularly. And we can be sure that Evelyn continued to be a support to her aunts and uncle until their deaths. Indeed, when Uncle Harry died in 1947, Evelyn inherited a share of his estate.

Aunt Alice died in 1950, and Aunt Elsie, the youngest of the siblings, in 1961. Elizabeth's daughter, Jacy, remembers the latter, the only one still living after her own birth, as a bundle of energy and committed to her local church – probably not unlike Evelyn herself!

Harold Clifford died in Southampton in 1946, in his late seventies. Strangely, Evelyn does not mention her father's death in the diaries. Her last reference to him is in an entry written from the ship as she prepares to sail to Italy, when she muses that she might be able to get ashore to see him and Eva while they are docked in Southampton awaiting repairs (although in the end the passengers were not allowed to disembark). He must therefore have died while she was abroad.

A photo taken at the wedding of Jacy Wall's parents, 1946. Aunt Elsie is
front left, Aunt Alice front centre beside Evelyn in the black hat.
The elderly man in the back row is probably Uncle Harry, flanked by
Alexander Clifford (right) and his wife Jenny Nicholson

On their return to the UK in 1947 Evelyn and Rex lived at two
addresses on Richmond Hill in London, first in a hotel and later
an apartment. Rex retired at the end of 1949 and at some point
the couple moved to the flat in Bournemouth that Jacy remembers
visiting.

Although she appears to have given up writing her diary,
Evelyn didn't stop writing altogether after her return from Italy.
We know she adapted her mother's play *The Luck of the Navy* in
1940 while staying with Percy Hutchison, but she also revised
Where the Rainbow Ends in 1972. A more personal passion was
writing short stories for children, though some that she submitted

during the war to the literary agent Mr Albert Curtis Brown were rejected. What a bittersweet irony it is that Shaun, who bought these diaries, should be represented by the Curtis Brown agency today!

She was writing stories while living in the Richmond Hill flat, and the fact that there are two copies of some of them suggests that she continued to submit them, or at least intended to do so.

The ghost story she began in Venice, inspired by a sighting in an antiques shop, is called 'The Gates' and is an accomplished, spooky tale. Whether she submitted it for publication – or if indeed it was published somewhere – we do not know.

It is just one of many questions that I would love an answer to!

Did Jane ever find lasting love? How did the Petersens in Guernsey fare during German occupation of their island? How many of Evelyn's precious wartime friendships survived the post-war years? Did she keep in touch with Eva and her half-siblings after her father's death?

We sometimes hear it said of people that they 'had a good war'. This surely applies to Evelyn and Rex, who must have looked back on that time with pride, satisfaction and many warm memories. Rex's passing in 1963 in his early seventies, with most close family members also departed, must have heralded a lonely time for Evelyn – and we know from Jacy how she adored any sort of company – but one can imagine that she must surely have built up a little world for herself in Bournemouth to sustain her.

Evelyn died in 1981 but the record she has left behind has brought her back to life and given her the audience she deserves. And the story is not over yet. While we were working on this book, Shaun found himself in Blewbury, near Didcot, the village where Evelyn spent several happy months in 1943. Seeing that her old home was still there, he knocked on the door to ask for permission to take a photograph. A conversation ensued, and the result was that the owner of the house produced a scrapbook that Evelyn had kept when she was living there. In it were photographs and ephemera relating to the diaries, some of which are reproduced in this book, and some of which answered outstanding questions we had.

Evelyn continues to surprise and impress us. Who knows what will happen next?

Barbara Fox, 2017

Commonly used abbreviations

ARP Air Raid Precautions

ATS Auxiliary Territorial Service (Women's branch of the British Army)

BEF British Expeditionary Force

BOD Base Ordnance Depot

CAB Citizens' Advice Bureaux

CIGS Chief of the Imperial General Staff

CO Commanding Officer

COO Chief Ordnance Officer

COD Central Ordnance Depot

DADOS Deputy Assistant Director of Ordnance Services

DDOS Deputy Director Ordnance Services

DOS Director of Ordnance Services

GHQ General Headquarters

NAAFI – Navy, Army and Air Forces Institutes (provider of retail and leisure facilities for the Services)

OC Officer Commanding (officer in charge of a sub unit)

RAMC Royal Army Medical Corps

RAOC Royal Army Ordnance Corps

SEP Surrendered Enemy Personnel

WVS Women's Voluntary Services

Acknowledgements

It is becoming increasingly difficult to source such insightful, historic and beautifully written and observed material, so imagine my surprise and delight to find that the *pièce de résistance* in the lot I won at auction was something barely mentioned in the catalogue listing. I knew as soon as I started to read the diaries that I had found something special. However, without Jacy Wall trusting me to take on the mantle of Evelyn's twenty-first-century ambassador, this book would not have been published.

I am also indebted to Rhiannon Smith at the Little, Brown Book Group for believing in the project and enabling us to turn Evelyn's dream of publication into a reality. Rhiannon and her team have done a fantastic job and I could not have wished for a better group of people to work with.

Sometimes the process of transforming dusty old diaries into a best-selling page-turner can be fraught with the stress and pressure of ensuring you do the author proud. Fortunately with Barbara Fox at the helm this has been a total breeze. Barbara's passion and devotion to this project has been outstanding from the beginning.

My most heartfelt appreciation and thanks must also go to

my brilliant and award-winning literary agent, Gordon Wise of Curtis Brown. This year marks our tenth anniversary of being together, not in the matrimonial sense but as agent and client – although with Gordon it always feels far more than that. When I look through Gordon's list of clients I can't help having a chuckle to myself because there amongst all the celebrities and famous folk is a lowly northern lad who is only famous in his own household.

I would like to acknowledge the contribution of Linda Martin for her initial support and guidance; Phil Rogers, who welcomed a total stranger into his beloved Green Bushes in Blewbury and let him walk away with Evelyn's album (see afterword); Ken Fisher in California, who was kind enough to answer my emails and supply me with the delightful photograph of his grandmother, Eugenia; and my wonderful partner, Joan Bower, for giving me the freedom to indulge my passion and for looking after my horse, Reuben, in my absence.

Finally, I need to express my utmost thanks to Evelyn. In these times of political upheaval and unrest perhaps we should all be more like her – with her British pluck and no-nonsense attitude – and keep calm and carry on.

Shaun Sewell, Northumberland 2017

I have loved being part of Evelyn's world and would like to thank Shaun for thinking of me when he was looking for an editor for this project. Thanks also to my agent, Sallyanne Sweeney, for her constant support; copy editor, Richard Collins, for his helpful comments and suggestions, and my husband, Mike Fox, who also read and commented on the text.

Barbara Fox, Crawley 2017

*

My heartfelt thanks to Shaun and Barbara for their complete commitment to presenting Evelyn's extraordinary account of these years. The process has also, for me, provided a poignant reminder and lasting testament to the Clifford family, who had great character and many talents, but sadly not one for producing descendants.

Jacy Wall, Dorset, 2017